BACK ON THE MAINLAND
Creating Pacific Island Food at Home

"Once you have traveled, the voyage never ends, but is played out over and over again in the quiestest chambers. The mind can never break off from the journey." – Pat Conroy

BACK ON THE MAINLAND
Creating Pacific Island Food at Home

Terry Rutkas

Oceanika Press
Santa Fe Springs, California

Copyright © 2012 Terry Rutkas

All rights reserved. No part of this publication may be reproduced, stored in a retrieval system or transmitted in any form or by any means, electronic, photocopy, or otherwise without prior written permission of the copyright owner, except for brief quotations included in a review.

Publisher's Cataloging-in-Publication data

Rutkas, Terry
    Back on the mainland : creating Pacific Island food at home / Terry Rutkas.
    p.cm.
    ISBN 978-0-9856933-0-5
    Includes index and bibliographical references.
1. Cooking, Pacific Island. 2. Cooking, Tropical. 3. Cooking, Micronesian. 4. Cooking, Polynesian. 5. Cooking, Melanesian. I. Title.

TX725.T69 R88 2012
641.599 --dc23   2012910129

We have done our best to make sure the instructions and/or recipes in this book are correct. However, users should apply judgment and experience when preparing recipes. The publisher accepts no responsibility for the outcome of any recipe included in this volume.

Oceanika Press
www.OceanikaPress.com

Printed in the United States

CONTENTS

PREFACE 1

MOLOKA'I 5

SHARING FOOD IN OCEANIA 9
   A Harsh Paradise 11
   Pacific Islanders and Food 13
   Food Preparation and cooking 17
   Islander Tastes and Preferences 20
   The New Arrivals 21
   Back on the Mainland 23

THE ISLAND MARKET 27
   Fruits and Vegetables 29
      Coconut – *Cocos nucifera*, Niu **(HA, FJ, MQ, TO, CK, SA)**, Ha'ari **(TA)**, Niyok **(GU)**. 29
      Taro – *Colocasia esculenta*, Taro **(TA, CK)**, Talo **(SA)**, Kalo **(HA)**, Da lo **(FJ)**. 30
      Giant Swamp Taro – *Cyrtosperma chamissonis*, Babai **(KI)**, Iaratz **(MH)**, Lok **(YP)**. ... 31
      Banana – *Musa sp.*, Fa'i **(SA)**, Mai'a **(HA)**, Mei'a **(TA)**, Siaine **(TO)**, Chotda **(GU)**. 31
      Breadfruit – *Artocarpus altilis*, 'Ulu **(HA, MQ)** Uto **(FJ)**, 'Uru **(TA)**, Kuru **(CK)**,
      Lemai **(GU)** 32
      Cassava – *Manihot esculenta*, Yuca, Manioc, Tapioca, Tavioka **(FJ)**. 33
      Yam – *Dioscorea alata.*, Uhi **(HA)**, Uvi **(FJ)**, 'Ufi **(TA, TO, SA)**. 33
      Sweet Potato – *Ipomoea batatas*, 'Uala **(HA)**, 'Umara **(TA)**, Kumara **(CK)**, Kumala **(FJ)** 34
      Sugar cane – *Saccharum sp.*, Ko **(HA)**, To **(TA)**, Tolo **(SA)**, Dovu **(FJ)**. 34
      Arrowroot - *Tacca leontopetaloides*, Pia **(HA, TA, CK)**, Masoa **(SA)**, Mahoa'a **(TO)**,
      Yabia **(FJ)**, Gapgap **(GU)** 35
      Ti - *Cordyline fruticosa*, Ki **(HA)**, Ti Pore **(NZ)**, Si **(TO)**, Lauti **(SA)**, 'Auti **(TA)** 35
      Chili Peppers – 35
      Tropical Fruits – 36
      Citrus – 37
      Leafy Greens and Other Vegetables – 38
   Meats and Seafood 39
      Pork – *Sus scrofa*, Pua'a **(HA, TA, SA, MQ)**, Vuaka **(FJ)**, Puaka **(TO)**. 39
      Chicken – *Gallus gallus*, Moa **(HA, TA, SA)**. 39
      Beef – Pipi **(HA)**, Bulamakau **(FJ)**, Povi **(SA)**. 40
      Mutton Flaps and Turkey Tails – 40
      Canned Meats and Fish – 41
      Fresh Fish – 42
      Crustaceans – 44
      Mollusks – 45
      Octopus and Squid – 46
      Palolo – 47
   Condiments 48
      Seaweed – Limu **(HA, SA, TO)**, Rimu **(NZ, TA, CK)**, 'Imu **(MQ)**. 48
      Sea Salt – Pa'akai **(HA)** 49
      Sauces – 49
   Spices 51
      Furikake – 51
      Curry – 51
   Nuts and Seeds 52
      Kuku'i Nut – *Aleurites moluccana* 52
      Tahitian Chestnut – *Inocarpus fagiferu*, Mape **(TA)**, Ivi **(FJ)** 52
      Macadamia Nut – *Macadamia integrifolia* and *Macadamia tetraphylla* 52
      Papaya Seeds – *Carica papaya* 53

- *Pumpkin Seeds – Cucurbita sp.* ... 53
- *Peanuts – Arachis hypogaea* ... 53
- KAVA ... 54

ISLAND FOOD PREPARATION ... 57

- COCONUTS ... 58
  - *Buying a Coconut* ... 59
  - *Opening a Green Nut* ... 59
  - *Opening a Mature Nut* ... 60
  - *Grating Coconut Meat* ... 61
  - *Making Coconut Milk* ... 61
  - *Making Coconut Cream* ... 61
  - *Making Coconut Oil and Butter* ... 61
- TARO ... 62
  - *Handling Taro* ... 62
  - *Cleaning Corms* ... 62
  - *Cooking Corms* ... 62
  - *Working with Cooked Corms* ... 63
  - *Cooking Leaves and Stems* ... 63
  - *Making Poi* ... 63
- BREADFRUIT ... 65
  - *Buying Breadfruit* ... 65
  - *Roasting Whole Breadfruit* ... 65
  - *Roasting Frozen Breadfruit* ... 65
  - *Boiled Breadfruit* ... 65
- BANANAS AND PLANTAINS ... 66
  - *Cooking Bananas and Plantains* ... 66
- YAMS AND CASSAVA ... 66
  - *Cooking Yams* ... 66
  - *Cooking Cassava* ... 66
- DRYING FRUIT, MEAT AND FISH ... 67
- CHESTNUTS ... 67
- MANGO AND PAPAYA ... 68
  - *Buying* ... 68
  - *Removing Papaya Seeds* ... 68
  - *Removing the Mango Seed* ... 68
  - *Cutting the Ripe Fruit* ... 69
  - *Grating the Green Fruit* ... 69
- PINEAPPLE ... 70
  - *Buying and Storing* ... 70
  - *Cutting a Pineapple* ... 70
- MAKING COOKING PACKAGES ... 71
  - *Taro Leaves* ... 71
  - *Banana Leaves* ... 72
  - **Ti Leaves** ... 73
  - *Other Cooking Packages* ... 76

PACIFIC ISLAND RECIPES ... 77

- WESTERN POLYNESIA ... 78
  - *Sosi Pe'epe'e – Coconut Sauce (Samoa)* ... 79
  - *Fa'alifu – Boiled Vegetables (Samoa)* ... 79
  - *Fai'ai – Baked Coconut Cream (Samoa)* ... 80
  - *Povi Masima - Beef Brisket (Samoa)* ... 81
  - *Pisupo with Onions - Corned Beef (Samoa)* ... 81
  - *Sapasui - "Chop Suey" (Samoa)* ... 82
  - *Palusami – Taro Leaf & Coconut Cream (Samoa)* ... 83
  - *Palusami - Casserole (Samoa)* ... 84
  - *Lu Pulu - Taro Leaves & Corned Beef (Tonga)* ... 85

- *Lo'i Feke - Octopus in Coconut Cream (Tonga)* 86
- *Kapisi Pulu - Corned Beef & Cabbage (Tonga)* 87
- *Faikakai Topai - Dumplings in Syrup (Tonga)* 88
- *Suafa'i – Banana Soup (Samoa)* 89
- *To'okutu - Dough Balls (Tonga)* 90

EASTERN POLYNESIA 91
- *Po'e - Puddings (Tahiti)* 92
- *Baked Mape - Chestnut (Tahiti)* 93
- *Koele Palau (Hawaii)* 93
- *Poulet Fafa – Taro leaf and Chicken (Tahiti)* 94
- *Ma'a Tinito – Chinese Meal (Tahiti)* 95
- *Pipi Kaula (Hawaii)* 96
- *Kalua Pork (Hawaii)* 97
- *Laulau (Hawaii)* 98
- *Chicken Long Rice (Hawaii)* 99
- *Loco Moco (Hawaii)* 99
- *Shoyu Chicken (Hawaii)* 100
- *Rewena Paraoa - Maori Bread (New Zealand)* 101

MICRONESIA 102
- *Coconut Titiyas (Guam)* 103
- *Chicken Keleguen (Guam)* 104
- *Mannok Kadon Pika (Guam)* 105
- *Golai Appan Aga (Guam)* 105
- *Mango Chicken (Guam)* 106
- *Finadene Birenghenas (Guam)* 106
- *Breadfruit and Fish Curry (Pohnpei)* 107
- *Crab & Breadfruit Cakes (Marshall Islands)* 108

MELANESIA 109
- *Vakalolo, Cassava Pudding (Fiji)* 110
- *Solomon's Supsup (Solomon Islands)* 110
- *Lap Lap (Vanuatu)* 111
- *Saksak, Papuan Dumplings (New Guinea)* 111
- *Bougna (New Caledonia)* 112
- *Pork and Peanuts (Vanuatu)* 114
- *Peanut and Sweet Potato (New Guinea)* 114

SEAFOOD 115
- *Lawalu (Hawaii)* 115
- *Lomi-lomi Salmon (Hawaii)* 116
- *Poisson Cru (Tahiti)* 117
- *Poke (Hawaii)* 118
- *Fafaru (Tahiti)* 120
- *Island Style Paua (New Zealand)* 121
- *Ginger Fish (Fiji)* 121
- *Whole Fried Fish (Samoa)* 122
- *Dried Ahi (Hawaii)* 123
- *Fakai Ika (Niue)* 123
- *Whitebait Fritters (New Zealand)* 124
- *Reef Caviar (Samoa)* 124
- *Qari Vakasoso (Fiji)* 125
- *Fish Heads and Bele (Fiji)* 125

SOUPS 126
- *Green Papaya and Fish Soup (New Caledonia)* 126
- *Sua I'a (Samoa)* 127
- *Ramen and Saimin (Hawaii)* 128
- *Coconut Crab Soup (Marianas Islands)* 130
- *Fish and Coconut Soup (Fiji)* 130
- *Mussels in Broth (New Zealand)* 131

CURRIES AND STEWS 133

    Chapati (Fiji) *133*
    Egg Curry (Fiji) *134*
    Coconut Chutney (Fiji) *134*
    Chicken-Backs and Dalo (Fiji) *135*
    Chicken Curry with Fei and 'Umara (Tahiti) *136*
    Pork Curry with Taro (Tahiti) *137*
    Kale Kapa Ika (Tonga) *138*
  SALADS *139*
    Sesame Cabbage Salad (Hawaii) *139*
    Hawaiian Macaroni Salad (Hawaii) *140*
    Papaya Salad (Cook Islands) *140*
    Mainus - Potato Salad (Cook Islands) *141*
    Ogo Seaweed Salad (Hawaii) *141*
    Raro Tarati (Cook Islands) *142*
    Ho'i'o Fern Salad (Hawaii) *143*
    Daigo Kimchee (Guam) *143*
    Sweet Potato Tops (Pohnpei) *144*
  RICE *145*
    Steamed Rice (Hawaii) *145*
    Fried Rice (Hawaii) *146*
    Red Rice (Marianas Islands) *147*
    Musubi (Hawaii) *148*
    Broiled Sushi (Hawaii) *150*
  CANNED MEATS AND FISH *151*
    Spam *151*
    Corned Beef *151*
    Salmon, Sardine, Tuna and Mackerel *152*
  CONDIMENTS, DRESSINGS, MARINADES *154*
    Finadene (Guam) *154*
    Papaya Dressing/Marinade *155*
    Chili Pepper Water (Hawaii) *155*
    'Inamona (Hawaii) *156*
    Tai Oporo (Cook Islands) *156*
    Miti Hue (Tahiti) *156*
    Miti Viti (Fiji) *157*
    Mitiore (Cook Islands) *157*
  SWEET AND REFRESHING *158*
    'Otai (Tonga) *158*
    Guri Guri (Hawaii) *159*
    Kava Colada *160*
  IMAGINARY SOUTH SEAS RECIPES *161*
    Rumaki *161*
    Crab Rangoon *162*
    Shrimp and Papaya Curry *163*
    Kona Krab Salad *163*
    Korean Barbeque *165*

GLOSSARY **167**

SELECTED BIBLIOGRAPHY **171**

APPENDIX A: THE ETIQUETTE OF SHARING IN OCEANIA **173**

APPENDIX B: SUGGESTED READING **175**

APPENDIX C: THE CANOE PLANTS **177**

APPENDIX D: PACIFIC ISLAND RESOURCES **179**

INDEX **180**

PREFACE

When a new Hawaiian barbeque place opened a short way from here, it bothered me that Kalua Pork was being sold at a fast food franchise. To my mind, Island food should be down-home, back country, a little rough, cooked over glowing embers, served from old pots and banana leaf platters, eaten with bare hands at sunset, while sitting cross-legged on a pandanus mat, surrounded by dark-skinned people, listening to the hiss of a gas lantern and the rumble of the surf breaking on the reef. Let's see them put that in a Styrofoam takeout box with two scoops of white rice!

I love Pacific Island food and I have fond memories of sharing meals with Island friends. The obligations of career and family keep me from visiting as much as I'd like; so, between visits I read, I write and I daydream about the Islands. I've been studying about the Pacific, the Islanders and their cultures for over forty years; nevertheless, I live on the Mainland.

Years ago, we could never find real Island food here, the kind that Islanders grew up eating at home. As time goes on, and more and more Islanders come to live on the Mainland, Island specialties are easier to find. However, long before that, I had to struggle to make Island food myself or do without. This book started as a project to organize my Island recipes, and to fill in some gaps. I've added some notes, stories, essays and a few comments to provide background about food in the islands. This is the result.

❧❧

When I was a young man, in college, my parents sent me to Hawaii for a summer, with the understanding that I would take a class at the University of Hawaii, and not just surf all day. I agreed and planned to take accounting—my major at the time. True to my word, I enrolled in an accounting class, and attended for one whole day before dropping it. If you've ever taken accounting, you know how much homework there is, besides, it was summer, I was in *Hawaii* and I never liked accounting anyway, but I digress.

Still feeling obliged to take a class, I flipped through the course schedule. There was nothing—nothing without homework—then I saw just what I had been looking for, the perfect choice: Geography of the Pacific, M-Th 9:00-11:00. Without a clue about what manner of course that might be, I signed up and walked into class on day 2. I couldn't chosen better. It was amazing, full of interesting stuff about Coconut Trees and Cargo Cults; Typhoons and Trade winds; Explorers and Blackbirders; Volcanic Islands and Coral Atolls; and why the dirt in Hawaii was red. That summer, Hawaii would be my homework. I went exploring with local friends, seeing things I had studied about in class, things I never would have seen nor had time to see, had I not dropped accounting like a hot rock. We went spearfishing and picking opihi, climbing volcanos and visiting ruins.

I also discovered "real" Island food that summer, something I really knew nothing about. I grew up when the popularity of South Seas restaurants, like Trader Vic's and Don the Beachcomber, was at its highest. What they served was Cantonese food with pineapple and Polynesian sounding names. South Seas restaurants are fun (I still like them) but not knowing any better at the time, I thought that was Hawaiian food. I soon learned that adding pineapple to Chinese food doesn't make it Hawaiian and I don't think the Chinese claim it either.

When, my first Adventure in Paradise came to an end I returned to the Mainland and dropped out of college to spend a few years mis-spending my youth. I eventually finished school, had a great career, married and continued to daydream about the Pacific.

A strong American dollar made it possible to travel to French Polynesia, Fiji, Samoa and New Caledonia; New Zealand, Micronesia and even back to Hawaii. Almost without fail, wherever I went Islanders would invite me to eat with them! They shared stories and forgave my social gaffes until I learned better. I've also eaten at food stalls in town markets and strolled among the vendors asking dumb questions about food. Every Islander has been generous and helpful; every Islander shared what they could. When possible, I always tried to bring a few tins of food or packages of something to share with my hosts; they would never accept any other compensation.

Once back home, I missed Island food. Maybe I could make it myself, maybe share it with my friends and family. There were a few little obstacles to overcome first: I didn't know where to get the ingredients and I lacked a place to build an *Imu*, an earth oven of volcanic stones (also lacking). A casual acquaintance from Hawaii mentioned that she made Kalua Pork in her home oven and her auntie in Hawaii would mail her bags of poi. I didn't act on this advice right away and lost track of her before I got her auntie's address, but that started me thinking; what else could I do to make credible Island food at home?

I thought, perhaps I could get an Island cookbook (the internet was still many years in the future). In spite of promising titles, such as *The Polynesian Cookbook*, they were what we shall call, "imaginary island food," Western recipes with pineapple or coconut shavings. Nothing wrong with that if you like it, but it was not like any food I ever had in a native village. *Trader Vic's Pacific Island Cookbook* (Doubleday) only had a couple of recipes that lived up to its name. Time-Life's *Pacific and Southeast Asian Cooking* was a beautiful book for daydreaming and provided some good information about Pacific cooking before veering off into Southeast Asia. Euell Gibbons' *Beachcomber's Handbook* was not really a cookbook; it was about learning to live off the land like an Islander. (Euell Gibbons may be remembered as the '60s icon of the Back-to-Nature/Natural Food movement; you may have heard of his other books, *Stalking the Wild Asparagus* and *Stalking the Blue-Eyed Scallop*.) One of the only books I found that even attempted to deal with traditional Islander food was Jennifer Brennan's *Tradewinds and Coconuts*, although most of the recipes were probably never eaten in Islander homes. I read it 10 years ago and will defer re-reading it until I've finished this work, lest I become discouraged.

So, what is "real" Island food? The simplest definition would be, "It's what Islanders eat." It could be a meal of local ingredients, using traditional techniques. It could be immigrant food adapted to Island tastes. It could be plantation food or a contemporary Island favorite. It's hard to pin down one definition. The rest of this book will attempt to answer that question.

Yes, Islanders do, sometimes, eat Western food at home, but this is not the place for another pasta or meatloaf recipe (with or without pineapple). However, there are some Western recipes that Islanders have made their own (see "Mainus," for example). I've tried to present representative recipes and some variations from other islands. I have also included a few *faux* Island recipes just for fun, but I have labeled them as such (see the section on "Imaginary South Seas Recipes").

The recipes I share come from many sources: watching islanders cook and asking questions, researching regional cookbooks and figuring things out for myself. I have tried to find as many versions of each recipe as I could, trying to distill the essence of the "dish" so it would work for Western cooks. I've tried to adhere to the traditional recipes without trying to improve them, although you are welcome to change what you wish.

This book has two goals: (1) to introduce Non-Islanders to the Islands and their foodways, and (2) to provide recipes Non-Islanders can make at home. This book is for ordinary Mainland cooks who want to learn Pacific Island cooking. It's easy to prepare traditional recipes and contemporary Island Favorites in your own kitchen.

※※

You may have noticed that sometimes I capitalize "Islands" and "Islanders" and other times I don't. "Islands" with a capital "I" refers to all the islands of Oceania (Polynesia, Micronesia and Melanesia). Sometimes it's just easier to say "the Islands" and "Islanders" when making general statements about the region or its people.

The Islands = Oceania.

I'd been trying to think of a generic term that describes the place we come home to, when we return from Oceania—the inverse of Oceania—and not necessarily the United States alone. The word "home" is too generic so I considered "Mainland"; that's what Hawaiians call the continental United States, but no one else in the Pacific does. I considered the words, "West" or "Western," terms referring to the countries of North America; Western, Northern, and Central Europe; Australia and New Zealand. That was more to the point, but "West" also suggests a direction. If you think about it, only Australia is West of Oceania and New Zealand is actually part of Oceania. Of course, if I exclude the Orient, the "East," that leaves the Occident, the "West," which suggests that Oceania is West of "the West" unless we go East... Excuse me a moment—I've just made myself a little dizzy.

After giving it considerable thought, agonizing over it, consulting dictionaries and asking people of several nationalities, I've decided that life is too short to worry about it. I'll just use "Western" or "Mainland" as it suits me and hope this little paragraph explains it to everyone's satisfaction.

Terry Rutkas
Santa Fe Springs, California

Mock coconut crab soup, page 130

Mise en place, Toruw Village, Yap, Micronesia

. . . down-home, back country, a little rough, cooked over glowing embers,
served from old pots and banana leaf platters . . .

MOLOKA'I

They sit cross leggd and having a place spread with [banana] leaves (often under the shade of a Tree in fine Weather) for a Table Cloth and sit at a distance to prevent offending each other by Flapping the Flies away which are often troublesome, ... and having some Clean leaves laid for Plater & dishes the Provisions are set before them & They Cut their Meat or fish with a piece of Bamboo or knife and put it into a Cocoa Nut Shell with Salt water,... eating large quantitys of Bread fruit or Tarrow, drinking Clean water or Cocoa Nut Milk and after their Pork or Fish is done they have a sort of pudding made of Bread fruit Calld Popoe of which each has a shell which when they have eaten finishes this and then they Wash their hands and Mouths, Using a Piece of Husk of the Young Cocoa Nut to clean their teeth, of which they are particularly careful.

James Morrison, Boatswains Mate of the HMS Bounty, 1792

Hawaii, Summer 1966: We were on our way to Moloka'i on a Hawaiian Airlines DC-3 that probably saw service in WWII. Danny, my roommate in Waikiki, had told me his cousin Sonny, on Moloka'i, was having a *lu'au* to celebrate his daughter's first birthday—would I like to go? "Yes, absolutely! That would be great!"

I'd only been living in Hawai'i for a couple of months, taking summer classes at the University of Hawaii. The town was swarming with young *haole* college students, like me, but I mostly hung out with my *local* friends. Being a *local* in Hawaii means that you are related to, at least 25% of the population. Once you get to know a *local* or two you can become part of that network.

In the beginning I'd been sleeping on the floor of a friend's apartment when Danny Kaloi, who lived in the same building, said he was looking for a roommate to share the rent; I volunteered and moved in. Danny and I were friends from the start and his friends and family became my friends too. As a bonus, his girlfriend had girlfriends who needed dates.

My *local* friends found me woefully ignorant and made it their job to educate me. I was tutored in *pidgin*, taught *mauka* from *makai*, and to remove my shoes before I went into someone's home. Everyone knew cheap hole-in-the-wall restaurants and the bars that served free *pupus* (snacks), but not much Hawaiian food; that seemed to be reserved for special events and hotel lu'aus. Now, I was going to Moloka'i for a real Hawaiian lu'au! I don't know what I was expecting, but I was about to learn something about Island life.

Moloka'i was a quiet, rural kind of place. No chic stores, no big hotels, not much in the way of tourist attractions (unless you wanted to see the leper colony). We were picked up from the airport in an open Jeep and taken down a dusty country road. This was the dry side of the island, mostly flat with spiky *kiawe* trees, a kind of mesquite. Sonny's family lived in a simple frame house, raised off the ground on posts, surrounded on three sides by pineapple fields. It was only a couple of steps from Sonny's yard to the first row of pineapple plants and yet no one ate pineapple that entire weekend. I don't think they ever ate pineapple.

By the time we got to Sonny's house, the pig was already cooking in the *Imu* (an underground oven of red-hot stones); all we had to do was open some cold bottles of Primo beer and hang-out for the next few hours. It would probably take that long to meet everyone; after all, it was a Hawaiian family. I reckoned forty-plus Hawaiians and one *haole*—me.

There were white haired *tutus* (grannies) on a bench under a spreading *kiawe* tree, their husbands on another, crying babies, men and women of various ages in small groups, people in cars pulling up to drop off cases of beer and pots of food, conversations, joking and laughter, kids running around and at the center of it all was Sonny. Sonny was a big man in his mid 30s, tough, someone I wouldn't want to cross, but friendly and smiling, a perfect host, completely in charge, holding his little daughter with one hand and holding a beer with the other. Sonny's wife was just a little younger, serious and comfortable, but still pretty. She was imperturbable as she dealt with the cooking and family dramas. There were two older daughters, sturdy Hawaiian country girls maybe 14 and 16, flirtatious, bold and eager to arm-wrestle young men and capable of winning too. Almost everyone could play the guitar and sing. So, except for the distinctly Hawaiian faces (and musical talent), this could have been a picnic with my family, only more fun.

I was starving by the time the *imu* was finally opened. I had a vision (influenced by South Seas movies and tourist brochures) of a perfectly cooked suckling pig—what came out was something quite different. When the dirt was shoveled away and the sacking and banana leaves removed, I saw my first *kalua pua'a*, roast pig. It was 100, maybe 150 pounds of steaming, savory pork, held together in a basket of chicken wire. Sonny and his friends lifted it carefully from the pit and transferred it to a galvanized washtub where the meat fell from the bones. Makeshift wooden tongs picked out a half dozen stones the size of baseballs.

I was the only *haole* among the guests, so I suppose Sonny felt he had to explain things to me. "They put hot stones in the body to help cook from the inside too. Come, see this." The tub was carried to the kitchen where Sonny used his hands to pick out the bones and shred the meat to pieces. It was "Ow, ooo, ow!" as he worked, grinning as if it were all for show. When that was done, he added handfuls of rock salt to the hot, greasy pork.

"Try some," he demanded.

It was good—no, actually, it was fantastic—the best thing I'd ever eaten. Savory and smoky. The grease and the salt and the starving only made it better.

"It's great, better than I expected," I confessed.

"Yeah, it's da bes'. What you expec', maybe da kine peeg wit da apple in da mout?" he joked.

"No, no, of course not," I lied.

Meanwhile outside, tables were being loaded with platters, pots and bowls. I couldn't recognize most of what they put out. There was *kalua pig*, of course, some sort of stewed green vegetables, plates of raw fish, and something with seaweed, a barrel of *poi* and black crabs the size of a baseball glove. This wasn't the buffet at Trader Vic's.

I'd never given much thought to what Islanders ate. *South Seas* restaurants served a type of Chinese food and I took it for granted that Island food would be the same. The lu'au of my imagination had just been hijacked and left me a little uneasy.

I considered myself an adventurous eater; I liked *Sashimi*, but *Aku* (chunks of raw fish with the skin left on) wasn't nearly so refined. Aluminum pots and enameled bowls held quantities of ghastly, gray-green-*something*, purple-gray-*something else*, and something that looked like it was scraped from a tide-pool. It all seemed so—well—*Savage*. I didn't know what to do with it. None of this was made for people like me. This was food from another world. There was no thought of catering to the tastes of outsiders.

I wasn't enthusiastic about some of these dishes, but I was determined to try everything. I was certainly curious and I was definitely hungry. A feeing of exhilaration was taking over, as if I were about to surf a fast breaking wave. I filled my plate and sat down to eat.

Danny and his family may have sensed my apprehensions; they may have even felt a little amused, but they encouraged me to "try this" and to "try that," watching to see how I managed. Not only was the food unfamiliar, I didn't know how to eat it. I watched my neighbors for clues. When I saw the others eating *poi* by swirling large gobs of the sticky stuff on the end of a spoon, I did the same. I quickly felt more at ease, learning from my new island "family."

Each taste of Island food, with its curious textures and unrecognizable ingredients, seemed to say something about life and survival in the middle of the Pacific, what exactly, I couldn't tell. I just knew this was an adventure and I felt lucky to have been included. Would my friends at home have felt the same?

The black crabs were gone before I could get one; they were a special treat for the Hawaiians, who were eating parts I didn't know were edible. I made up for my loss by having more of everything else. My appetite and willingness to try everything seemed to please those around me.

I won't try to describe each dish, however, *poi* was the perfect complement to *kalua pork*—I mentioned how good that was—and the *gray-green stuff* was surprisingly good too; my earlier apprehensions had been for nothing. This was a feast, good food and plenty of it.

I began to realize it wasn't simply the food (or the Primo) that makes a lu'au; it was the *aloha*, the spirit of love, respect and good will; it was sharing and inclusion.

❧

Later that evening, when the sky had turned black and hung with a million stars, a single light hanging in a tree, made a hole in the darkness around us. Three of the "uncles" picked up their guitars took a place under the light. It seemed we were getting ready for a night of old-style Hawaiian music. "We won't be hearing any tourist songs tonight." I told myself. "We've left that back in Waikiki."

It began with a few bars of introduction—an upbeat tune, vaguely familiar—and then they started to sing; strong, clear voices, harmonizing as they probably had their whole lives. The words swept over us, across the pineapple fields and out into the darkness. White haired *tutus* nodded in recognition, as if the words were from an ancient chant.

Deep within my heart lies a mel-o-dy,
A song of old San Antone

San Antone? As in Texas? I felt like I'd just stepped off a cliff. I turned to Danny, "That's not Hawaiian! That's *cowboy* music!"

"Well, that's what they like. They grew up with it. The GIs brought it in the '40s. You know, during the War." Danny tried to calm my apparent distress, "They'll probably do some Hawaiian songs too."

. . . Well, this was what I came to find. It wasn't a tourist lu'au, selling stereotypes, but it wasn't what I expected either. It was simply family and friends having a birthday party. I know they don't eat like this every day; this was a celebration, a time to remember who they were: ordinary people, whose ancestors sailed to these islands 1,500 years ago, and they celebrate that through the food they eat. I liked these people and I liked what they liked, but the cowboy music?

Bro-ken song, empty words I know,
Still live in my heart all alone.

When I looked around, everyone seemed to be enjoying the song; Sonny no longer seemed so intimidating; the grannies and their husbands seemed straighter and younger; and the babies stopped crying. I was sitting there, listening in disbelief when I noticed my feet tapping to the music.

For that moon-lit path by the Alamo,
And Rose, my Rose of San Antone . . .

As the last notes trailed off into the night, an explosion of whoops, laughter and shout-outs filled the void. Everyone was beaming, including me. It no longer mattered what they played; I was ready to take this party late into the night. What could have been better than this: good food, good company, good music and a million stars to watch over us in the warm tropical night.

It's been a long time since then, but sometimes on hot summer nights, when it's clear enough to see the stars, I find myself thinking about that weekend and I start to crave *kalua pig* and *poi*. In my imagination I can hear *Rose of San Antone* playing and smile, because I know it wouldn't be a "real" Hawaiian lu'au without it.

SHARING FOOD IN OCEANIA

Sharing food in Oceania is an expression of solidarity that validates kinship ties
and defines a host of rights, duties and obligations between people.

Countries and their Cultures, 2011

A visit to the Pacific Islands will send you home with more than a set of photographs and souvenirs. In my case, it sent me home with the desire to return and learn more about the islands and the people. One of the best ways to do that is to eat what the Islanders eat. Pacific Island food is the living history of the Islands and all who have come to live there. When Pacific Islanders share a meal, they invite you to be part of their unique Island culture. Who could refuse?

Oceania encompasses the archipelagos of Melanesia, Micronesia and Polynesia. It is an imaginary "continent of islands" with separate geologies, habitats and cultures. Anchored in the vast Pacific, the region is sometimes known as, *the South Seas*. Oceania was first discovered and colonized by prehistoric seafarers from Asia, who sailed in ocean-going canoes, navigating three million square miles of ocean 4,000 years before Christopher Columbus ventured beyond the sight-of-land.

The peoples of Oceania share a common food culture, inherited from their ancestors, transported to each new colony, adapted to local conditions, but varying little. Their food and methods of preparation existed for thousands of years and are as distinct as those of the Chinese or the French.

Food for the early Oceanians was adequate—sometimes abundant—sometimes not. Between what *Nature* could provide and what *Man* had brought, the menu was fixed. Nothing new was added to the Island pantry—although, some things were taken away as human occupation drove species to extinction. Whatever food they had, successfully nourished those robust peoples, whose island civilizations flourished, remote and unknown to the rest of the world.

All That changed once foreigners from halfway around the world arrived. Samoan legends called the first Europeans to arrive *Papalagi*, Sky-Breakers, for they appeared on the horizon one day as if they had burst from the sky. The new arrivals were also called *Haole*, *Popa'a* or *Tauiwi* depending on the Island, Hawaii, Tahiti or Aotearoa (New Zealand)

Eventually, foreigners became commonplace. Peoples from the West and the East began to migrate to Oceania, each bringing their own cultures and cookery, creating new food traditions, blending their cooking styles and ingredients with those of their Island predecessors.

Native Islanders have often regarded foreign foods as novelties or status food, incorporating them into traditional fare. Immigrants have used Island ingredients more out of necessity. Today, it is commonplace to see a *Tahitienne* buying a French *baguette* from a Chinese bakery; Fijian women making Indian *chapatis* and drinking tea; or Hawaiian surfers eating *laulau* with white rice.

One aspect of Oceania stands out in my mind: how sharing food is about more than just eating. Rarely will you find someone eating alone; the act seems to require the presence of others. Islanders who regularly eat together are what anthropologists call, a "commensal unit." Food sharing can identify or affirm kinship or clan allegiance but it can extend beyond clan and family to express friendship or an alliance with outsiders. Sharing food strengthens the bonds that hold Island communities together. The etiquette of sharing assures a place in the hierarchy and acknowledges ones role in the community.

"The sharing of food serves to re-create an order disturbed by an event such as a birth, a marriage, or even more, a death." (Douaire-Marsudon in Tcherkezoff, 2008:210) The arrival of visitors (strangers in particular) also disturbs the order of daily living; sharing food can be a way to restore that order. Visitors who share food become, in some sense, part of the family. For instance, in old Hawaii, family meals were shared from a calabash (a gourd or wooden bowl) thus the term "Calabash Cousin" was bestowed on non-relatives who regularly took meals with the family.

Englishman, Will Mariner, who lived among the Tongans during the years of 1806—1810, tells us:

> Tongans regarded food as everybody's right. If one was hungry and without food, it was only necessary to go to the nearest dwelling where people were dining and sit down with them. In fact, Tongans took a dim view of the European custom that required them to be invited to a house before being able to eat there. (Ferdon, 1987: 107)

Generosity and hospitality are still alive in the Islands; you can experience it for yourselves. When you travel in the Pacific, expect to be invited by the locals to share a meal. As you walk through a village, you may hear people call out "Have you eaten?" Do not pass up the opportunity to join them. When Islanders offer a gift of food, they will give the best they have, however humble. Show that you appreciate their hospitality by partaking in what is offered, if only just a small amount. There is no better way to be accepted into a family or a community. Even in cosmopolitan Hawaii, once you become acquainted with local families, you can expect to be invited to a birthday, a graduation or a club Lu'au.

Island food is home-style food—*if home happens to be in the middle of the Pacific.* From a simple home meal to a feast. It is meant to be shared with friends and family, invoking a sense of place and community.

A HARSH PARADISE

Have you ever been to an Oceanic Eden, a lush green island, an oasis in the Pacific? Have you ever seen coconut palms swaying in the Trade Winds, picked a banana from alongside the road, stretched out your hand for mangos hanging just beyond your reach, watched islanders harvesting pineapples, scooped the black seeds from a papaya and eaten the golden fruit, chewed on sugarcane, seen a breadfruit tree heavy with fruit, or been intoxicated by the fragrances of gardenia and plumeria? These islands really can seem like a paradise, but was it always like this?

The ancient navigators who discovered these islands arrived hungry and exhausted after long voyages at sea. Unfortunately, they did not find any of the freely available food you or I may have found on our visits—not even coconuts. They found sprawling vines, curling ferns, swaying grasses, towering trees, but little or nothing to eat on the land. It was amazing they found anything growing at all, considering the origin of the islands and their locations.

Sixty-five million years ago, far from the nearest continent, plumes of incandescent magma rising from deep within the earth, burned through the earth's crust and erupted from the bottom of the sea. An undersea mountain began to grow. It would take hundreds of thousands of years for the volcano to breach the surface, spewing its fiery lava and clouds of dazzling white vapor. It would take that long again to exhaust the volcanic pressures, leaving an island of barren rock standing alone in the sea. Still, much later, molten magma would find another crack in the bottom of the sea and another island would grow, then another and another until island archipelagos had spread across the Pacific like handfuls of stars flung across an empty night sky. The islands of Oceania stood alone, isolated from each other and the rest of the world. By the time the ancestors of Man walked the plains of Africa, the islands of Oceania were in place—waiting. They would continue to wait for another million years.

The seas around these new islands gave passage to tiny marine organisms. Coral polyps, carried by the currents, attached themselves to the flanks of the volcanoes, each secreting a hard calcium nest. Billions upon billions of polyps would eventually build forests of living coral beneath the surface. A multitude of other sea creatures would join them to create thriving reefs, teeming with life.

Over time, most of the islands would subside under their own weight, leaving a ring of living coral growing in their place. Tropical storms raged over these reefs smashing the coral, heaping up coral boulders and sand into low mounds, just dry enough to be called islands.

If any tree, bush or flower; if any lizard, snail or insect were going to inhabit these *High* or *Low* islands, it would have to cross at least a thousand miles of open ocean to get there. Many small events—over great spans of time—did what they could to cause that to happen.

Tropical sun, wind and rain eroded the hardened lava. Hurricane winds swept seeds, spores and insects high into the sky, sometimes dropping them on volcanic soil. A migrating bird, landing to rest on a barren island, preened its feathers dislodging a burr. Seeds and nuts that could tolerate seawater, occasionally, survived to wash up on remote shores and take root. Slowly, in the course of millions of years—more or less—terrestrial life started to take hold on each island. Species adapted and evolved new forms until every niche was filled—still, it was only a tiny fraction of the flora and fauna found on the far-off continents.

Finally, one more migrant crossed the sea, (this time on purpose) the ancestors of today's native Pacific Islanders.

The islands of Oceania were the last places on Earth to be inhabited by humans. How humankind discovered and settled Oceania is an obscure epic; the exact origins of the people are still a matter of on-going research. What archeologists can tell us, however, is that about 4000 years ago sea-going peoples from Asia entered the Pacific. During the next three thousand years their descendants had discovered and populated the most remote and challenging environments on Earth. These Stone Age (Neolithic) peoples sailed wooden canoes made with stone tools and sewn together with handmade twine. Without instruments or maps, they found every remote scrap of land that could support them. The sea was not a barrier, it was a highway, and the Neolithic navigators were prepared to survive wherever it took them.

Whereas the land was poor in food resources, the reefs and surrounding oceans were troves of treasure. These people—so well adapted to the sea—knew how to make use of everything that grew, swam, or crawled in the ocean. As rich as that might be, they still needed more to make uninhabited islands into sustainable homes.

Plants and animals, from their former homes, sailed with them on their voyages of discovery. These prehistoric migrants were experienced growing and transporting the plants their ancestors had cultivated in Asia and New Guinea, namely: coconuts, breadfruit and taro; bananas, yams and more; together with flowers, medicinal other useful plants*.

Pigs, dogs and chickens were brought as livestock; lizards, rats, and snails came as stowaways.

The first Islanders transformed the landscape and so has every new arrival—for better or worse.

* Appendix C: The Canoe Plants

PACIFIC ISLANDERS AND FOOD

Native Pacific Islanders are gourmets with sophisticated palates. Surprised? There are 300 varieties of *taro* and 70 varieties of breadfruit and Islanders can spend hours debating their relative merits and the best methods of preparation. Many *popa'a* think all fish taste more-or-less the same; Islanders can probably tell you what fish they are eating by taste or smell alone. We hear a lot these days about how cooks should use simple methods that allow the natural flavors of the food to come through. If that's gourmet cooking, then Islanders are certainly gourmets. Unlike Western or Asian cuisines, Islanders did not use spices or sauces; rather they have acquired a taste for the subtle natural flavors and textures produced by Islander cooking and food preservation techniques.

Pacific Islanders categorized food into two types, *kai*, staples and *kinaki*, relish (maori terms). *Kai* was the main part of the meal, cooked, starchy vegetables (e.g. taro, breadfruit, and yam). The protein foods (e.g. fish, pork, chicken) were *kinaki*, along with fruits and vegetables. Fijians make a further distinction between protein food (pork, chicken and fish) and non-staple vegetables (taro leaves, seaweeds, fruit.) which they consider "supplementary food."

A meal would never be considered a proper meal without *kai*, a staple of some sort, no matter how much meat or fish there was, but usually there was no meat or fish at all. Captain William Bligh spent many months observing life in Tahiti and wrote the following:

> ... Animal Food is rarely made use of by the general run of the People here, that it may be said it is not eat[en] by them at all, and I firmly believe that the greatest Chiefs do not touch it one day out of ten through out the Year. Fish however falls generally to the lot of the Chiefs every day, but it is here in very Small quantities, and among the inferiour order very small indeed... (Bligh 1789:II, 31)

Cooked starchy vegetables, Taro, Breadfruit, Yam, Sweet Potato or Green Bananas were eaten at every meal and in large quantity. These were simply roasted or boiled and eaten as we might eat a boiled potato (except with their hands). Each culture had its favorites; Tahitians and Marquesans favored Breadfruit; Hawaiians preferred Taro, particularly when pounded into Poi; the Maori were obliged to eat Sweet Potato because other tropical plants did not grow in New Zealand's climate. Farther west, Melanesians preferred Yam, cultivating giant specimens.

The signature dish of Polynesian cookery was *Po'e*, a pudding-like combination of cooked starchy vegetables or fruit (e.g. banana, native vi), pounded and softened with water or coconut cream, to be re-cooked into a "pudding" (Kirch and Green, 2001: 157). Melanesians and Micronesians: each had their own versions of *Po'e*.

Coconut, particularly coconut cream, plays a major role in the cuisines of Oceania. Te Rangi Hiroa (1930: 136), who studied and wrote about the material culture of Samoa observed:

> The outstanding value of the coconut is evident. In some form or other it enters into combination with every vegetable food and most marine flesh food except the larger fish ... But it is the expressed coconut cream that is invaluable in so many preparations ... it is indispensable to the most important made up dish, *fa'ausi* (various baked puddings with coconut cream). It provides the only sauce for meat, vegetables and puddings. Without the coconut, Samoan cooking would be resolved into its primary elements.

Many Island cultures had their principal meal at the end of the day. Snacks of fresh fruit or leftovers were eaten in the mornings, later, perhaps a slice of raw fish while fishing or a banana picked along the trail on the way to some task. Hiroa goes on to say:

> The Samoans are very early risers. When busy with their cultivations they go off at daybreak without having any set meal. If there are any cooked *talo* or breadfruit left over from the previous day, these may be eaten. They return about 10:30 or 11 a.m. with a load of *talo*, breadfruit, or bananas. The oven for the morning meal is then prepared. This is a hearty meal and combines the morning and midday meal of three-meal races. Enough is usually cooked to provide for the evening meal. Thus, besides the vegetables, extra packages of fish and *palu sami* are cooked. These remain unopened ... [until] the evening meal [which] usually takes place after sunset (Hiroa, 1930: 137,138).

One of the most cherished misconceptions about the Pacific Islands is they are Oceanic Edens where no one toils to survive, all one has to do is reach out a hand and pluck food from the trees! The truth is that within Island societies a considerable part of the day was devoted to the acquisition and preparation of food. Anthropologist Raymond Firth (Firth, 1966: 53) describes working and eating on the Polynesian outlier of Tikopia:

> As the sun declined from zenith, the place begins to waken. People came in singly or in little groups, nearly everyone bearing some contribution to the forthcoming meal. This preparation and consumption of food is the chief point of the day's activities, the focus of the energies of each member of the community ...
>
> In a civilized environment one is apt to look upon a meal as an interval in the real business of life ... In a primitive society, it may be, as it is in Tikopia, the main daily business in itself ... People in this island community do not arrive home to snatch a meal and return to work; the attainment of the meal is the fulfillment of that work.

Sharing food with visitors is a reciprocal obligation in which the host takes pride in providing sustenance to his guests and the guests respond by showing expressions of enjoyment, but there is more to the etiquette than just that.

Willowdean Handy, the wife of eminent Pacific ethnologist E. S. C. Handy, wrote about their lives, working in the Marquesas. In her memoir, *Forever the Land of Men* (Handy, 1965: 133), she tells how they tried to repay the kindness of their Marquesan hosts with a "European" meal. Realizing that one guest—a particularly large man—could hardly be filled by his share of the meal, she asks:

> "Are you satisfied?" I asked Haa-pu-ane, in a customary Marquesan phrase.
>
> "No," he answered slowly, "not heavy."
>
> "What would you like?" I asked feebly.
>
> "Popoi," [fermented breadfruit paste] was his prompt answer, and he gestured a big round stomach.
>
> What he meant was so interesting that I forgot to be embarrassed. It was a tight, full feeling in the stomach he craved, the weight of food [that gives a] comfortable feeling.
>
> "I have no popoi," I said without apology, since we were speaking frankly and objectively.

"No matter." His casual dismissal of the lack told me that he was placing the emphasis of [this evenings] entertainment where it belonged—on kaloha.

Clearly, Haa-pu-ane preferred more familiar food, but he was certainly a gracious guest, exhibiting another Islander quality, *Kaloha:* love, respect and good will. The Handys should have known that a host must provide abundant food for the guests and the guests must eat hardily to show appreciation.

Islanders love food and enjoy the act of eating, particularly the ancient Tahitians, who would fast for several days so they could consume large quantities of food later (Oliver, 1974:I, 222). Joseph Banks, naturalist with Captain Cook on the first expedition to Tahiti, gives an elaborate account of one man's meal, wherein he describes the enormous quantity of food this privileged person is served and finishes by assuring the reader it was not an exaggeration:

> It may be thought that I have given rather too large a quantity of provision to my eater when I say he has eat[en] 3 bread fruits each bigger than two fists, 2 or 3 fish and 14 or 15 plantains or Bananas, each as large as 6 or 7 inches long and 4 or 5 round, and conclude his dinner with about a quart of a food as substantial as the thickest unbaked custard; but this I do affirm that it is but few of the many of them I was acquainted with that eat less and many a great deal more. (Beaglehole 1962:I, 346-347)

The sea was the source of most animal protein. Coral reefs are the most productive marine habitats in the world. Hundreds of species of reef fish, crustaceans and mollusks flourish on and around a coral reef. Pacific islands that have coral reefs—and not all of them do—have almost limitless seafood for the taking. Offshore, beyond the reef, is the realm of large and small schooling fish, lone predators, porpoise, whales, and sea turtles.

Islands disrupt the slow moving currents at the bottom of the sea, causing the upwelling of tiny creatures from the depths. These feed small schooling fish like chub, sardines and anchovies, they in turn, feed the larger pelagic species (e.g. bonito mahi-mahi, and billfish) and, of course, the sharks that haunt the reefs, inside and out.

Islanders had a vast knowledge of local fish, their habits and the techniques to catch them. The repertoire of fishing techniques included netting and angling (fishing with hook-and-line). They trolled the open ocean with lures made from pearl shell, to catch the large pelagic species. They built stone weirs to capture fish and stone fishponds to collect and fatten them.

Margaret Titcomb, Librarian Emeritus at the Bernice P. Bishop Museum, wrote a series of monographs on the food customs of the old Hawaiians. Among her works are *Dog and Man in the Ancient Pacific*, *The Native Use of Fish in Hawaii* and *The Native Use of Invertebrates in Old Hawaii.* In the latter, she points out, not only the importance of marine food resources, but also the *kai/kinaki* duality in Hawaii:

> In Hawaiian food economy, there was great dependence on marine resources to supplement *poi*, the starch mainstay among land foods. The figurative expression for food was *i'a a me poi* (fish and *poi*). The term *i'a* signified not only fish but all animal foods from sea and land. (Titcomb, 1978: 326)

Fishing was traditionally men's responsibility and their sport; anglers took great pride in their prowess and knowledge of fishing. Women usually gleaned the reefs for mollusks, crustaceans, urchins or anything edible. Islanders ate nearly every invertebrate found on the reefs: octopus and squid; shrimp, lobster and crab; marine snails, clams and more.

The peoples of Samoa, Vanuatu and Fiji wade into the lagoons, under the waning moon, to scoop up the wiggling tails of *palolo* worms. These are delicacies to be eaten on the spot.

Hawaiians risk life and limb to pick limpets *(opihi)* from the rocks, amid crashing surf. Hawaiians also gather *wana*, sea urchins, when available. They prepare them by knocking off the spines and cracking them open with a rock. The choice parts were the "five orange-colored 'tongues' of gonad *(elelo)* . . . but the fluid, *(kai wana)* was also [collected for flavoring] . . . The combination of *kai wana* and *elelo* made a relish that was eaten with *poi* or sweet potatoes." (Titcomb, 1979: 371)

In New Zealand (*Aotearoa*), the first Polynesian immigrants (ancestors of the Maori) soon realized that the tropical plants they had depended upon for food, medicine and clothing would not grow in the temperate climate. Fortunately, New Zealand had its own resources. The newcomers had only to discover them, and re-invent their culture. Sweet potato *(kumara)*, one of the few plants that did survive, sustained them while they hunted for local foods. Local greens, thistles (puha) and fern tips took the place of taro leaves. Bulrush (raupo) pollen was steamed to make a sort of bread. Native birds were exploited; some, such as the giant (12 ft) Moa, were hunted to extinction. They gathered mussels (kaku), oysters, scallops and abalone (paua) from the rocky shores and fished for eel and freshwater species in the rivers and streams.

New Zealand provided the Maori more kinds of animal protein than they had in the tropics, but they had a serious shortage of *kai*, carbohydrates, the starchy staples that were once the bulk of their diet. It wasn't until the introduction of European cereal crops (corn, wheat) and potatoes that the Maori finally had a reliable supply of carbohydrates for their needs (Leach, 2010, 24)

Famine and food shortages were always a possibility for Islanders. For example, breadfruit trees, being seasonal, produce large quantities of fruit for a short time and then nothing for another year. The Marquesas Islanders fermented and stored huge quantities of breadfruit when there was a surplus. Uncooked breadfruit was placed in storage pits. As the fruit softened, they were taken from the pit, peeled, cored and set aside again to continue ripening. After a few days, the ripe pulp was placed in leaf-lined pits to ferment. Fermentation pits could be 6-10 feet deep and contain as many as 20,000 breadfruit. The fermentation process preserved the fruit so that it could be stored for months—even years. The fermented pulp was pounded into a "pudding" called *popoi* or wrapped in leaves and roasted. As you might suspect this product has a pungent aroma. The Marquesans thought the smell improved the taste.

Food has been the center of Island life, the major occupation and preoccupation. To gather, to cultivate, to prepare, to cook, to eat and to share food was the point of living. When food was plentiful, they took great pleasure in methodical over-indulgence.

You could say the peoples of Oceania lived well. They did what they could to adapt the environment to their needs and then adapted themselves to what they could not change. By doing so, there was usually enough to sustain them and often an abundance. In spite of the limitations imposed by life in the Pacific, they were able to make the most of what they had.

It wasn't an Oceanic Eden, but it was the Pacific Islanders' ideal of happiness and fulfillment.

FOOD PREPARATION AND COOKING

As important as what Islanders ate, is how they prepared it. These methods date back to the time prehistoric navigators sailed from Asia. Not only were they constrained by what foods the islands could provide, the tropical climate made it necessary to gather and cook fresh food almost every day.

To start, many foods are not cooked before eating. Fruit is usually eaten fresh, as are pandanus keys and sugarcane, which are chewed for the sweet juice. Some fish and mollusks are eaten raw as soon as they are caught.

Fermentation and dehydration were the most common techniques for preserving food for times of famine or voyaging. The people of the islands came to prefer the taste and aroma of certain preserved foods (although we may wonder why). Fresh fruits such as banana and mango can be dried (dehydrated) to preserve them and concentrate the flavors. Fish and octopus are also preserved by salting and drying.

Roasting over a fire of hot embers (or hot stones) is the easiest way to cook simple meals. Fish can be skewered and held over the fire or set directly on the embers if the skin is tough. Breadfruit is often roasted, unpeeled and whole, by piercing the end opposite the stem and placing it directly in a wood fire for an hour; the scorched skin is peeled off afterwards.

There were no fireproof containers, so liquids were boiled or steamed in gourds or wooden bowls. Several small volcanic stones were heated until red-hot and dropped into the liquid, using a split piece of a palm frond, as tongs. When one stone lost its heat, it was replaced by another, straight from the fire, until the food was thoroughly cooked.

The Earth Oven

The earth oven has been used in Oceania for thousands of years. In Hawai'i, it is called *Imu*; in Tahiti, *Ahima'a*; in Fiji, *Lovo*; in Samoa, *Umu*; and in New Zealand it is called *Hangi*. Preparation requires a considerable amount of work and time; therefore, it is reserved for special occasions where many types of food (and a lot of it) can be cooked at once. There are two types: above ground (Samoa) and below ground, but the principal is the same.

Cooking with an earth oven is a communal affair; everyone participates: digging, gathering fire wood and stones, dressing the pig, cleaning the fish, chopping vegetables, making coconut milk, gathering banana leaves and ferns, assembling the food into packages and of course standing around, commenting and giving advice

Start with a hole in the ground. The size depends on the number of people to be fed and the size of the largest item (e.g. pig) but it's usually about 4 feet long, 3 feet across and about 1 foot deep. The bottom of the hole is filled with layer of kindling and layer of dry firewood, followed by a layer of volcanic stones. Set the wood on fire and leave it to burn until the volcanic stones are red-hot (perhaps 3 or 4 hours).

While the oven is heating, dress and season the pig, fish, or chicken. Prepare the vegetables, coconut cream and the special foods to be wrapped in leaf packages.

When the stones are red hot, remove any unburned pieces of wood. Cover the hot stones and embers with green sticks or banana stalks and a bed of banana leaves to keep the food from resting directly on hot stones and embers. Reserve a few fist-sized stones for the cavity of the pig.

Because flesh foods will cook long and slow, the meat tends to fall apart. Place the pig in a coconut leaf or chicken wire basket that will survive the cooking, and place the pig on the bed of leaves, along with chicken, taro and breadfruit. Prepared foods such as *laulau*, fish, and vegetables are individually wrapped in banana or *ti* leaf packages and placed among the larger items. All the food is covered with more layers of banana leaves and damp ferns then old pandanus mats or wet burlap sacking. Shovel the dirt that was dug from the hole back over the mats to seal in the heat. Finally, the oven is left to "cook" for several hours before it is opened.

Opening the oven always draws a crowd. The first sight of the cooked food and the aromas in the air stimulate the appetite, but patience is necessary. The packages, chicken and breadfruit must be removed and set aside. Finally, the pig is removed and prepared for serving.

After the long, slow cooking, the meat literally falls apart. The pieces are placed in large wooden bowls or platters where men remove the bones and pull the chunks of pork apart into smaller pieces. Handfuls of sea salt are added to the tender, juicy pork and it's ready to eat.

Mats and banana leaves are spread on the ground. Platters of pork and fish are arranged on the mats along with the packages of cooked food, coconut milk, sea salt, seaweed and other islander condiments and fresh green coconuts for drinking.

Raw Fish

Islanders have a special fondness for fish and uncooked fish in particular just as Western cultures have for pickled herring and lox (cured salmon). Islanders have several traditional methods to prepare and eat uncooked fish:

- The first method is simply to eat the uncooked flesh on the spot while fishing, or cut-up and served at mealtimes. Raw fish was usually eaten seasoned with salt.

- The second method is to cut raw fish into small pieces and mix it with chopped seaweed and salt. This is known as *poke* in Hawaii. Today there are hundreds of *poke* recipes, which may include soy sauce, or sesame oil, and various chopped vegetables or sauces.

- The third method is called *lomi-lomi* (massaged) in Hawaiian. With this method, the preparer lightly mashes the raw (or salt preserved) fish with his fingers to soften the texture (not reduce it to pulp); today onion, tomato and chili pepper are mixed with the fish.

- The fourth method is "cold cooking" where raw fish is marinated in either salt water, lemon or limejuice until the flesh turns opaque, then mixed with chopped vegetables and coconut milk.

- The fifth method is to preserve the flesh by drying. Later, the dried fish can be softened in water, and roasted on a fire. Drying changes the taste and texture.

- A sixth (but probably not the last) method was practiced in New Zealand. The Maori would bury the large meaty foot (i.e. muscle) of an abalone (*paua*) in the earth until the quality of the meat changed into "a compact mass that might be cut as a cheese is" (Best, 1929: 78).

Cooked Food

The following are brief descriptions of traditional Hawaiian cooking methods (Titcomb; 1972: 23-25):

- *Kalua* – Baked in an earth oven (i.e. *imu*) – Whole pigs could be cooked along with other foods. Fish would be wrapped in leaves to protect them from direct heat, and ashes. Long, slow, moist cooking in the *imu* imparts a smoky flavor.

- *Ko'ala* – Broiling on hot stones or embers, turning occasionally to cook all sides, No wrapping is used. Raw fish with tough skin can be cooked this way.

- *'Olani* – Toast by holding pieces of fish over hot coals and turning to cook all sides, figuratively *to wilt hau leaves over a fire*. Requires tough fingers to withstand the heat!

- *Hakui* – Steamed in a closed container - fresh fish placed in a calabash and *pohaku 'eho* (red hot stones an inch wide) are placed on top, another piece of fish is laid on top and a tight fitting lid to keep the steam in. The fish was occasionally wrapped in leaves. Also called *Puholo*

- *Lawalu* – Filleted or dressed fish wrapped in *ti*, banana or wild ginger leaves, baked in an *imu* or broiled over heated stones.

- *Pulehu* – Cook by shoving food into a heap of ash and hot embers, for instance, sweet potato or *kuku'i* nuts. These vegetables were roasted in their skins to protect the flesh from burning.

Cooking utensils

Utensils, if they can be called that, were fashioned from the simplest of materials found at hand.

- Volcanic stones were ideal for cooking; they hold the heat and will not shatter in the fire. Because there is no stone on coral atolls, and because coral blocks crumble with repeated heating, volcanic stones were an important trade commodity.

- Makeshift tongs for handling hot stones were made from coconut stalk, bent in half. Tough coconut palm baskets could withstand the heat if not placed directly on hot stones.

- A sharpened stick was used to husk coconuts, but some Islanders could just as easily strip the husk from the nut with their teeth, however the latter was not an everyday practice.

- Scrapers to grate coconut meat and peelers to remove the rind from breadfruit were fashioned from seashells (the remnants of earlier meals). Pounders or pestles to make poi and po'e were made from stone, dense wood or sometimes coral.

- The leaves of the Banana, Ti and Breadfruit were used to make cooking packages to hold "loose" and fragile foods such as "puddings" or fish for cooking. They are strong enough to survive the cooking over embers or in the *Imu* and they add subtle flavors.

- Bamboo, when split, acquires an edge sharp enough to cut meat as easily as a steel blade. Several such knives could be made in seconds.

ISLANDER TASTES AND PREFERENCES

Not only do the methods above cook the food, they impart a smoky taste—even the stone boiling method. Coconut milk that has been thickened by stone boiling takes on a different flavor than just heating it on a stove. Anyone who has eaten food cooked over a wood fire will know the flavor I am talking about—and who doesn't like a wood barbecue? However, some Islander's tastes may surprise Westerners.

- As I mentioned earlier, Islanders are connoisseurs of the subtle flavors of natural food, but sometimes they liked to "adjust" the flavors. The simplest method is to dip a morsel of food in a bowl of seawater to moisten and salt it. Cooked breadfruit, taro or yams were dipped in coconut milk for the taste and for the oily lusciousness—the way one would use butter on potatoes or oils on salads.

- Hawaiians always had salt with fish and salted surplus fish to preserve it. Sea salt was collected directly from the rocks where surf spray dried; salt drying ponds were built to harvest larger quantities. Hawaiians added small amounts of the native red clay to color and flavor it. They also combined it with finely chopped *kuku'i* nut for additional flavor.

- Tahitians who craved a "big taste" made a marinade for raw fish called *Fafaru*. It took a very brave or a very desperate person to invent this potion. Several fish were placed in a deep bowl and covered with seawater. It would be set aside for a few days to let the tropical heat do its work (need I explain?). Strain the liquid and throw away the fish. Use the strong smelling liquid to marinate chunks of raw fish for about 6 hours and enjoy.

- Unlike Westerners, most Islanders enjoy eating the whole fish: the head, tail and bones. Fish, such as *'O'io* (bonefish), can be eaten raw, when the small bones are soft. Certain smaller fish are eaten in one bite without cleaning first. The head and oily parts along the backbone were considered the most flavorful. Fish bone is an excellent source of calcium. Of course, chewing bones requires strong teeth, which islanders had before the introduction of Western foods*.

- Perhaps eating to survive has obliged Islanders to eat things we, in the West, would find unappetizing. There are a couple of delicacies you may wish to decline, if offered: *Palolo*, the sexual reproductive organs of a marine worm, detached from the body to float freely in the lagoons, scooped from the water and eaten on the spot, and *Sea* (say-uh), the raw innards (guts) of a sea slug, a Samoan delicacy; it is sold in island markets in reused soda bottles and eaten without further preparation.

- Eating is an important part of Island life, particularly Samoan life. It is an enjoyable but a serious business, therefore, talking stops. I have even experienced it at restaurants in Apia where dinnertime conversation was met with polite head nods and facial expressions, no talk.

- Some islanders prefer their cooked food to cool before eating; after all, it is too hot to handle with bare hands. While waiting, they might nap in some comfortable spot so that, upon awakening, they would be rested and refreshed for the serious job of eating.

---

* Specifically refined sugar, which has spawned an epidemic of tooth decay and loss.

THE NEW ARRIVALS

Customs, material culture and languages have been evolving ever since the first people sailed to Oceania, but food culture probably did not. Islanders fished from the same ocean, transported the same gardens from one island to the next and they cooked in the same manner for thousands of years. Life could have continued like this if it were not for the *new arrivals*.

In 1521, Ferdinand Magellan, a Portuguese explorer sailing for the Spanish Crown, was the first European to traverse Oceania—missing hundreds of Polynesian and Micronesian islands—to, eventually, blunder into Guam and the Marianas, before sailing off to the Philippines. Spanish, Dutch and English explorers came and went. Englishman Samuel Wallis discovered Tahiti in 1767; French explorer Louis Antoine de Bougainville followed in 1768. Capt. James Cook led three expeditions into Oceania (1769-1780) to systematically explore the region. Afterwards, Russians, Germans and Americans sent expeditions to explore this vast, new world of islands.

Written accounts of the Pacific islands ignited a passion for the *South Seas*. Adventurers and opportunists sought passage to make their fortunes. Sailors jumped ship to exchange their lives of toil for an idyllic life of pleasure. Missionaries embarked to save souls. Nations sent navies to acquire colonies. Whalers searched for new hunting grounds and Merchants sought whatever made a profit. Eventually visitors became residents. The new arrivals had come to stay.

- By 1741, The Marianas Islands had been Spanish colonies for 176 years. Violence and disease had reduced the native population from 80,000 to less than 5,000. The survivors, mostly women, eventually intermarried with the Spanish, Mexican and Filipino troops, adopting their cultures, becoming the Chamorro of today. (Levy, 2003, 176, 177).

- By the 1850s, American settlers in Hawai'i had acquired lands for large-scale plantations; a profit could be made if field hands and laborers toiled long hours for low wages. This was not a proposition that appealed to the native Hawaiians*. The only recourse for plantation owners was to transport workers from countries that were overburdened with people willing to trade labor for survival, i.e. China, Japan and the Philippines. The Portuguese followed in 1899, the Puerto Ricans in 1901.

- In 1865, William Stewart, a Scotch planter in Tahiti, petitioned the French Government to allow him to import 1000 Chinese laborers to work on his cotton plantation. After the enterprise ran its course, some Chinese stayed-on to build new lives for themselves in the islands. They soon realized that they had more in common with the Tahitians than with the French colonial bourgeoisie. The result was Chinese-Tahitian families.

- From 1879 to 1916 over 60,000 indentured workers arrived from India and South Asia to labor in the sugarcane fields of Fiji. At the end of their contracts, the Indians who could not afford passage home remained in Fiji. Some rented parcels of land from native Fijians to farm, others moved to the towns and opened shops and restaurants.

- During WWI, the Japanese Navy seized German possessions in Micronesia (i.e. Palau, the Marianas, the Caroline and Marshall Islands). Although the occupation was brief (officially ending with their defeat in WWII), the influence of Japan is still felt. Micronesia is now a Japanese tourist destination.

---

*As long as they were able to be self-sufficient and not dependant on wages for their livelihood.

No matter what their origin, every immigrant group finds comfort in their own food. Each starts by adapting their own familiar dishes, using what is available locally. Layers of history and necessity eventually create new food cultures.

Hawaii is the most cosmopolitan archipelago in Oceania. Practically every cuisine from Europe, Latin America and Asia is represented; fast-food franchises and chain restaurants dot the landscape; high-end hotels and resorts from Kauai to the Big Island take pride in having World-Class Pan-Asian, Pacific Rim or Fusion restaurants featuring Celebrity Chefs. But, where is the Hawaiian food? Over the years, immigrant cultures have blurred the distinctions between Island favorites and actual Polynesian traditions. Layer upon layer of food traditions, cross-cultural borrowing and reinvention have spawned new Islander food traditions, sometimes resulting in improbable combinations, sometimes without a single island ingredient—nevertheless, they could only have come from Hawaii. Consider the following meal from a typical Hawaiian Plate Lunch menu:

Laulau and *Lomi-lomi* Salmon,
Cabbage Salad, Hawaiian Macaroni Salad,
two scoops of White Rice.

- *Laulau*—Authentic Hawaiian food using Island ingredients
- *Lomi-lomi* Salmon—Hawaiian concept using only foreign ingredients
- Cabbage Salad—American Cole Slaw with an Asian style dressing
- Macaroni Salad—A denser version of American Macaroni Salad
- White Rice—The Japanese variety of short grain white rice.

The main dish, above, could have been Portuguese Sausage or Korean barbequed Beef or Japanese Chicken Katsu; all are examples of foreign foods that have been integrated into *authentic* Hawaiian dishes. Rice and potatoes have taken the place of traditional Islander starches. A bag of rice, purchased at the market, costs less than *Poi* and feeds more. Economics may influence everyday meal planning, but special events often include both traditional and introduced foods.

They call it *Local Food* in Hawaii, the food that has evolved from the contributions of immigrant cuisines, adapting what seems positive from the host culture, keeping what is important from their own and creating a unique blend. Local Food is important because it is one essential thing the various peoples of Hawaii share in common. To be a Local is to eat Local Food. The same applies across Oceania where immigrants have come to live.

Several hundred years of Spanish occupation has made an indelible mark on the way the Chamorro, the people of Guam and the Northern Marianas, eat. What would be called a *Lu'au* in Hawaii is called a *Fiesta* in Guam. *Titiyas*—Chamorro *Tortillas*, *Tamales*, and *Escabeche* are more examples of Spanish/Mexican influence. However, Spanish is not the only influence; the Chamorro have embraced American, Japanese, Korean and Filipino foods. Chamorro Fiesta cooking is another unique expression of the merging of "foreign" and Islander food cultures.

The almost inexorable Westernization of the Pacific continues to change the Islands. You can expect to hear the usual grumbling and moans of "You should have been here 20 (50, 100) years ago"—with some justification, but if Hawaii (the most Westernized of the Polynesian islands) is any example, the traditional foods will survive, in some form or other.

BACK ON THE MAINLAND

The first time I went to Hawaii, I came home with containers of *kalua pork* and *poi* in my pack. Back then, the only place to get real Island food was *in the Islands*. I have been to many more islands since then and I still crave Island food when I am home, only now, I can have Pacific Island Food whenever I want!

Within a reasonable distance from where I live in Southern California, there are numerous Asian and Islander markets that can provide almost all the ingredients I need to make a proper Island meal. There are scores of places where I can get "Plate Lunch" (Hawaiian style, fast food) and almost every month there is an Islander festival or a fund-raiser where I can get Samoan, Tongan, and Fijian, Chamorro and Hawaiian food.

What do you do if you live in Austin, Boston, Denver or Fort Lauderdale? What about Vancouver, Montreal, Marseilles or Melbourne? Just do the same thing they do in Las Vegas, Salt Lake City or Auckland: find local Islander communities (they are everywhere) and ask where they shop; look in the phone book for Islander/Asian food shops and markets; get on the internet and search, you will find that Island foods are more available than you think.

Supermarkets on the Mainland are offering more exotic food all the time. Expatriate Islanders are opening stores selling familiar island food to their own communities and would love to have you for a customer too.

My first impression of Island cooking was "it's just like camp cooking," and that's true in villages where meals are prepared in *cookhouses*, simple open shelters, with wooden boards to prepare food, a few simple utensils and a wood fire in a hearth of volcanic stones. Island Food on the Mainland is just made in a different kind of *cookhouse*.

Mainlanders, and Islanders living on the Mainland, have the convenience of their modern kitchens. On islands, where food preparation is a family or community affair, cooking chores are another form of socializing. On the Mainland, ovens, stoves and kitchen appliances make the job easier for otherwise busy home cooks.

Some Island food will be new to Westerners but they are sure to become favorites. The traditional cooking techniques are easily adapted to modern kitchens, so there is no reason not to make it at home. The influence of Asian and Western food makes for hearty, enjoyable meals that are both exotic and familiar at the same time. While it may be necessary to make substitutions when Island ingredients are not available, and while it may be necessary to "adjust" the recipes for Western palates, you will be able to enjoy "real" Island food in your own home.

❧❦

Today, Pacific Island food is not what it once was; indeed, the very act of eating has evolved from simple survival to *Fine Dining*. Fine dining in today's Pacific are "island inspired" creations, found in up-scale restaurants and gourmet kitchens. I believe "island inspired" recipes owe more to Asia, Indonesia and France than any place in Oceania. The recipes you will find here are traditional fare, as prepared in the homes of the peoples of the Pacific.

Islanders who live close to their roots love certain foods most Mainlanders would never consider eating, these are definitely acquired tastes: *Sea*, the innards of a sea slug, eaten raw, and *mutton flaps*, fatty cuts of belly meat imported from New Zealand and Australia, just to name a couple. Our recipes will <u>not</u> include any such items, so if you are looking for mutton flap recipes, sorry.

My wife, Kathy grew up eating typical Mainland fare and has some serious opinions about what she likes and dislikes, so I was pleased (and surprised) when she told me she liked *Laulau*, *Lomi-lomi Salmon* and roasted Breadfruit—but she did not like *Poi*. No problem, eating should be enjoyable, not a challenge. Choose what you like, make substitutions when you want. These recipes and techniques are meant for Mainland cooks and kitchens; it won't be hard to find something you like.

Recipes are one thing and menu planning is another. Islanders will eat simple family meals at home (usually boiled vegetables and fish or whatever is on hand); however, special occasions call for a feast. Each Island culture has their own recipes, but you will often find the same or very similar foods across all of Oceania. So, when planning an Island menu at home, don't be too concerned about mixing regional dishes; you're planning a feast, not taking an anthropology exam!

Menu Suggestions

Samoa

Sapsui, *"Chop Suey"* ... 82
Palusami, *Creamed Taro Leaf* ... 83
Pisupo with Onions, *Corned Beef* ... 81
Fa'alifu, *Boiled Island Vegetables* ... 79

Tahiti

Poisson Cru, *Salad of Raw Fish* ... 117
Banana Po'e, *Baked Pudding* ... 92
Poulet Fafa, *Creamed Chicken* ... 94
Pork Curry with Taro ... 137

Hawaii

Lomi-lomi, *Raw Fish Salad* ... 116
Kalua Pork, *Roast Pork* ... 97
Shoyu Chicken, *Chicken in Soy Sauce* ... 100
Hawaiian Macaroni Salad ... 140

Micronesia

Breadfruit and Fish Curry ... 107
Coconut Crab Soup ... 130
Sweet Potato Tops, *Salad* ... 144
Fa'alifu, *Boiled Island Vegetables* ... 79

Melanesia

Lap Lap, Cassava Pudding ... 111
Pork and Peanuts ... 114
Baked Green Papaya ... 35

New Zealand

Mussels in Broth ... 131
Rewa Paraoa, *Maori Bread* ... 101
Povi Masima, *Corned Beef Brisket* ... 81
Sweet Potatos

Marianas Islands

Daigo Kimchee, *Spicy Radish* ... 143
Shrimp Kelaguen, *Marinated Shrimp* ... 104
Mannok Kadon Pika, *Spicy Chicken Stew* ... 105
Red Rice ... 147

Cook Islands

Whole Fried Fish ... 122
Mainus, *Pink Potato Salad* ... 141
Raro Tarati, *Salad with Corned Beef* ... 141
Ripe Bananas and Limes

Fiji

Chapati, Flat Bread ... 133
Egg Curry ... 134
Ginger Fish ... 121
Fish and Coconut Soup ... 130

"Imaginary Island"

Crab Rangoon ... 162
Shrimp and Papaya Curry ... 163
Korean BBQ Beef ... 163

The previous and following menu suggestions omit a few items; use the following rules-of-thumb to complete the menus:

- In Hawaii, *Poi* is always served at lu'aus. On the mainland, a taste is usually enough for *haoles*, but if you have guests from Hawaii, you will need more. Save time; buy it pre-made.

- Cook Islanders put baskets of ripe bananas and limes on the table. In Fiji, my hosts provided small red chilies with meals. These are practices I would recommend for any Island feast.

- Don't forget to place Island condiments and sauces on the table. That also means various hot sauces and Shoyu (soy sauce), *Finadenne*, and small containers of Sea Salt, *'Alaea* or *'Inamona*.

- Barbecued Chicken or *Kalua Pua'a* (Roast Pork) will usually star at the Mainland lu'au, or if you prefer, Grilled Fish, Ribs, Chops or Steaks. However, it is possible to create a vegetarian menu.

Preparing an Island feast can be a lot of work; that's why most of them are potluck. The following menu is rather elaborate but it would make an amazing lu'au. It would certainly feed many people and the work (fun?) could be shared. If you have a large group for a lu'au, consider this suggestion for managing a potluck: (1) Decide on a menu. (2) Copy recipe pages and place them in sealed envelopes. (3) Have a drawing where participants select an envelope. (4) Prepare and bring that dish to the potluck. (5) If anyone is left, they can bring their own Island favorites.

Pan Pacific Lu'au (Potluck)

Poke, *Raw Fish* ... 118
Daigo Kimchee, *Spicy Radish* ... 143
Raro Tarati, *Salad with Corned Beef* ... 141
Hawaiian Macaroni Salad ... 140
Poisson Cru, *Salad of Raw Fish* ... 117
Poulet Fafa, *Creamed Chicken* ... 94

Egg Curry ... 134
Golai Appan Aga, *Baked Banana* ... 105
Shrimp Fried Rice ... 146
Papaya Po'e, *Baked Pudding* ... 92
Otai, *Watermelon Drink* ... 158
Fresh Fruit

In most cases, our lu'aus will be a little more manageable, such as the following menu.

Family and Friends Lu'au

Kava Colada ... 160
Reef Caviar, *Caviar on Toast* ... 124
Sesame Cabbage Salad ... 139
Kona Krab Salad ... 163

Korean BBQ Chicken ... 165
Salmon Lawalu, *Baked Salmon* ... 115
Palusami Casserole, *Creamed Taro Leaf* ... 84
Grilled Pineapple

Simpler parties can feature Island specialities or faux Island foods as snacks.

Party Snacks

Broiled Sushi ... 150
Spam Musubi, *2-inch pieces* ... 148
Corned Beef Manapua ... 151

Crab and Breadfruit Cakes ... 108
Rumaki, *Chicken Livers and Bacon* ... 161
Island Style Paua, *Abalone* ... 121

One afternoon, a while ago, decided to have a last minute Lu'au. Some Chamorro friends had built and launched a 47 foot Sailing Canoe based on a Marianas design that last sailed in 1742, so we put together an after-work party to celebrate, to eat and to *talk story* about canoes, sailing and boatbuilding, a mini-feast on short notice for a dozen or so people.

The Last Minute Lu'au

Diago Kimchee
Spam Musubi
Grilled Salmon
Short Ribs
Sesame Cabbage Salad
Golai Appan Lemai, *Breadfruit in coconut milk*

Chamorro Daigo Kimchee was easy to make from store-bought Pickled Daikon Radish, Cucumbers and hot sauce, all of which we had on hand. Because Spam is a Chamorro favorite, we purchased Spam Musubi, freshly made, from the local Hawaiian take-out shop, and cut them into smaller pieces (1 ½"). These were the appetizers. We made a quick visit to Costco for Salmon fillets, which we cut into individual portions and grilled while we had drinks and appetizers. Also from Costco, a couple racks of pre-cooked Short Ribs that we heated in the oven. Cabbage salad was quick to make and we thawed some frozen *Lemai* (breadfruit) and simmered it in coconut milk. I wanted to add a Mac Salad but there wasn't time; as it was, there was more food than we could eat.

Here are a few more suggestions for serving Island food:

- Practice before inviting your friends over for a lu'au. For instance, struggling to crack open a coconut while people are watching may be entertaining for them but frustrating for you; or if you insist on making *poi*, make sure you know the pitfalls.

- Plan your menus around how comfortable your guests are with new foods. The first time I served Island food to friends they just didn't get it ("where's the pineapple?"). Now I mix it up with barbeque or "island inspired recipes" to put them in an Island (receptive) mood.

- Serve your Island food *Plate Lunch* style. Use plates or divided Styrofoam food trays, already plated with food so that everyone gets a sample of each dish. Then they can go back for "seconds" of their favorites.

- Dress up the presentation on the plate with some sliced fruit (e.g., grilled pineapple, papaya) Place your entrees on a piece of banana leaf. Use flowers (e.g., gardenias or hibiscus), coconuts or bananas to dress the table. Offer guests the choice of eating with chopsticks, utensils or bare hands.

Have some fun with your meal. Play island music, put a little umbrella in your drink, decorate with flowers, wear Hawaiian shirts, Sarongs and Muumuus, and have a good time. Just because we've run aground on the Mainland doesn't mean we can't bring some Island spirit home with us.

This book was written for ordinary Mainland cooks who want to learn Pacific Island cooking. Add a few Island dishes to your backyard Lu'au and give it a real Island flavor (pun intended). It's easy to prepare Traditional Recipes and Contemporary Island Favorites in your own kitchen.

THE ISLAND MARKET

Most of the taro, cassava, breadfruit and even coconuts can be bought only in the market...Very few of those living in the environs of Papeete have access to land on which to gather coconuts for making the coconut cream which is such an important part of Polynesian cooking.

French Polynesia, Nancy J. Pollock, Ron Crocomb, 1988

Welcome to the Island Market. Until the arrival of Europeans, there was no need for markets in Oceania. Every community was self-sufficient. Trading was only practiced between people living near the sea and people living inland, trading fish for inland produce. Once islanders started to trade labor for money and moved into towns, they no longer farmed and fished. Markets were established where rural islanders could sell their excess produce to town dwellers, islander and non-islander alike.

Today, in the Pacific, most food is imported; (subsistence farming and fishing are mainly practiced on the outer islands) consequently costs can be as much as 3 times higher than on the continents. In the larger towns, such as Suva, Noumea or Papeete, western style markets offer imported and processed foods. In smaller towns, weekly farmer's markets sell freshly caught local fish and just picked produce. They usually start early—before the sun rises—and close by 8AM.

Many Islanders, living in rural areas, can still grow their own food, but even they may need to go to the market occasionally; a taste for soy sauce, orange soda or a can of mackerel can only be satisfied by a trip to town. Even today, in Micronesia, islanders make impulsive canoe voyages, across hundreds of miles of ocean, to buy cigarettes and other seemingly trivial store bought goods.

For Western cooks, shopping for Island ingredients can seem a like a voyage—navigating from supermarkets to shops and across the internet. This chapter introduces the Pacific Island ingredients you will be using. If Island ingredients are new to you, and you find yourself asking "What is that?" and "How do you use it?" then this is the place to answer those questions. Consider this your tour of the Island Market.

We on the Mainland will probably have to do some searching for some Island foods, but Mainland markets are becoming remarkably diverse. What you can't find at your local Supermarket can probably be found at Asian or Latin American markets or other ethnic specialty shops.

Ship Arrival Day: Impromptu market on the beach to sell produce and fish - Fiji.

Island Codes:

CK	Cook Islands	NR	Nauru	SI	Solomon Islands
EI	Easter Island	NC	New Caledonia	TA	Tahiti
FJ	Fiji	NM	Northern Mariana Islands	TK	Tokelau
GU	Guam	NZ	Maori, New Zealand	TO	Tonga
HA	Hawaii	NU	Niue	TV	Tuvalu
KI	Kiribati	PW	Palau	VU	Vanuatu
MQ	Marquesas Islands	PG	Papua New Guinea	WF	Wallis and Futuna
MH	Marshall Islands	SA	Samoa	YP	Yap

AT ONE TIME, WESTERN MERCHANTS EXPLOITED the natural resources of Oceania by establishing trading stations in the Islands. Islanders could purchase tobacco and Western goods in exchange for pearl shell, copra (dried coconut meat) and local produce. Robert Dean Frisbie, an American writer who arrived in Polynesia in 1920, had managed just such a trading station; he reported that a 500% return on investment was considered modest. Frisbie made the following sign to establish the prices for his goods (Frisbie, 1929, 47):

```
1 stick tobacco .......... 8 coconuts
1 ships biscuit .......... 2 coconuts or 2 eggs
1 box matches ........... 2 coconuts or 2 eggs
1 fish hook .............. 1 coconut or 1 egg
1 yard brass wire ........ 1 coconut or 1 egg
1 lollie ................. 1 coconut or 1 egg
```

FRUITS AND VEGETABLES

COCONUT – *Cocos nucifera*, *Niu* **(HA, FJ, MQ, TO, CK, SA)**, *Ha'ari* **(TA)**, *Niyok* **(GU)**.

Life in the Pacific would have been very different, indeed, if it were not for the coconut. The coconut has been called *The Tree of Life*, and rightly so. Islanders joke that the coconut tree is their *department store*. Every part of the tree provides something useful: The **trunk**: timber for building; the **leaves**: baskets, mats and thatch; the **roots**: dyes and medicines; the **husk**: twine and rope; the **flower bud**: food, sweetener and alcohol; the **shell**: drinking cups and spoons; the **palm ribs**: firewood and kindling. The **nut**: oils, drinking water, milk, food, animal fodder. The list goes on.

Coconut Water - Young, green coconuts (drinking nuts) contain pure, refreshing water, slightly sweet with a tang like sparkling water (with no bubbles). On many atolls, where fresh water is scarce, coconut water is the main source of drinking water. At this stage, the meat is soft and eaten like custard with a spoon. Coconut water is available in drinking cartons in mainland markets.

Coconut Meat - In a mature brown nut, the meat is hard, slightly sweet, and good to eat straight from the shell. There is less water than in green nuts and it's not quite as refreshing, in my opinion.

Uto - In its final stage, the nut sprouts the first young leaf of a new tree and sends roots into the ground. The cavity of the nut fills with a spongy mass that has absorbed the liquid and the meat. This is called *Uto* on many islands. It can be eaten raw or cooked.

Coconut Milk – The meat of a mature coconut is shredded and the fine white shavings are squeezed (usually with a little water) to produce a creamy liquid that is used in cooking or as a condiment.

Coconut Cream – Place coconut milk in a bowl and refrigerate an hour or two, or place the bowl in a cool place for 8 to 10 hours. A layer of cream will rise to the top. Carefully spoon it into a separate container.

Coconut Oil and Coconut Butter – Coconut butter and Coconut oil are the same thing. When it's stored at a temperature below 78° F, (25° C) it's coconut butter, when it's warmer than that the *butter* melts and becomes coconut oil.

Coconut milk, coconut cream, coconut oils and butters can be purchased at Asian markets, at health food stores or on-line. Oils for cooking or eating should come from fresh coconuts. If you're buying commercial products, check the labels for suitability.

Coconut oil is said to be easily digestible but it's also high in saturated fats. Proponents of Coconut oil/butter contend that it's "good fat," 50% Lauric acid, that will not elevate "bad" cholesterol levels (LDL), and it's slightly lower in calories than most vegetable oils. You are probably already using coconut oils in butter substitutes, chocolates and other commercially produced foods.

Coconut Toddy – Toddy is made by cutting off the flower of the palm; the watery sap that exudes is collected and starts to ferment naturally. In a few hours, it becomes a sweet alcoholic drink called *toddy*, *tuba* or palm wine. (I have been told, by someone who should know, that you could wake up with a real bad hangover.) If, instead of letting it ferment, the sap is boiled down, it becomes a concentrated sweetener, used in place of sugar or syrup.

Heart of Palm – The fibrous pith from the inner core of the growing bud of a palm tree. It has a fresh crunch but not much taste. Also known as "Millionaires Salad" because the whole tree must be killed to harvest it. Heart of Palm is normally harvested from very young trees grown for that purpose or trees that have been knocked down in a storm or felled to clear land. It is sold in mainland markets, in cans and ready to eat.

TARO – *Colocasia esculenta*, *Taro* **(TA, CK)**, *Talo* **(SA)**, *Kalo* **(HA)**, *Da lo* **(FJ)**.

The origin of Colocasia is a little obscure but it is certain that it entered Oceania from Asia/Indonesia long before recorded history, carried by the earliest Neolithic navigators. Taro is considered superior over other starchy vegetables in Oceania because it is high in vitamins and minerals, easy to digest and has properties that reduce dental caries and gum disease. (Photographs on pages 62 and 63)

All parts of the taro can be eaten: the corm, the stems above ground and the young leaves, often in combination with coconut milk or cream.

Caution must be taken when eating taro. Uncooked corms, stems and leaves contain calcium oxalate crystals which cause a burning sensation in the mouth and throat as they pierce the mucous membranes. Cooking will dissolve the crystals making taro safe to eat. Cooking times: Corms boiled or baked, a minimum 45-60 minutes.

Taro Corms – The corm is often mistakenly called the "root"; it's the starchy, bulbous, portion of the stem beneath the ground. Scrub thoroughly before cooking. There are two ways to cook them: 1) Roast in an underground oven for several hours or 2) boil whole for an hour (more or less). Let the corms cool then scrape off the skins and any dark parts beneath. Taro is now ready to eat or process further e.g. pounded into poi, or as an ingredient in recipes.

Taro Leaves – "Polynesian Spinach," is rich in iron and calcium. Taro leaves are called *lu'au* in Hawai'i (a *Lu'au*, the feast, is named for them). *Lu'au* is used in traditional dishes with pork or chicken or as a side dish like mustard or turnip greens. Some consider taro leaves to be similar in taste to spinach. (See Bun-long taro).

Taro Stems – *Haha* (HA). Cut stems into chunks and use as a vegetable in soups, stir-frys and as a side dish.

Bun-long Taro – A Chinese variety. Most taro leaf (*lu'au*) and stems that are sold in Hawaiian markets come from this variety, because of its leaf size and tenderness. Leaves are good for making taro leaf packages. Sold as "taro" in Asian markets, it has a different texture and taste; it may not be suitable for making *poi*, but perfectly fine as a cooked vegetable.

Poi – The traditional method is to pound cooked taro until it is a soft smooth pudding. The poi maker sits on the ground straddling the poi board. He wets his left hand with water and turns the taro while pounding it with a stone pounder in the right. This long, laborious procedure was performed almost daily to provide the staple food of the Hawaiians.

It's possible and preferable to buy *poi* already made. It is available on-line, frozen or dried. It would be best to find a local store that sells it fresh. ***Sour Poi*** is *poi* that has started to ferment after a few days. Some people like to eat it with salty fish.

GIANT SWAMP TARO – *Cyrtosperma chamissonis*, *Babai* **(KI)**, *Iaratz* **(MH)**, *Lok* **(YP)**.

Cyrtosperma chamissonis and *Alocasia macrorrhiza* (*Ape* [HA]) are two other genera that are sometimes called taro but only *Colocasia esculenta* is *true taro*. These species have an edible corm which can grow very large, 10 pounds or larger. The cooked corm has a mealy consistency but does not seem to be as irritating when not thoroughly cooked (Murai, Pen, Miller, 1958, 90).

Cyrtosperma and *Alocasia* species are sold as ornamental garden plants e.g. "Elephant Ear."

BANANA – *Musa sp.*, *Fa'i* **(SA)**, *Mai'a* **(HA)**, *Mei'a* **(TA)**, *Siaine* **(TO)**, *Chotda* **(GU)**.

Several varieties of banana were planted across Oceana by the prehistoric navigators. The banana is another multi-purpose tropical plant. Banana trunks are used to line underground ovens to keep food dirt-free and provide steam for cooking. The ashes from burnt leaves are a salt substitute and leaf fibers are used for cordage and weaving. The leaf buds and male flowers can be cooked and eaten and the "tree" has a starchy corm that can be used as famine food. Banana leaves are used to wrap food parcels for cooking, line fermentation pits and act as plate and tablecloth, but best of all is the familiar fruit that can be cooked, dried or just peeled and eaten.

Sometimes multiple varieties are available in Asian or Latin American markets. In the U.S., bananas are usually imported from Central and South America. The following are the varieties you are most likely to find on the U.S. Mainland.

Cavendish – The most popular banana in North America.

Red – Slightly sweeter than Cavendish. Skin turns black when ripe.

Manzano – AKA Apple banana, short and stubby. Ripe when the skin turns black

Baby/Niño – About three inches long. Eaten ripe, baked, broiled or grilled.

Burro -- The burro banana has a tangy lemon-banana flavor, eaten ripe (yellow) or baked.

Plantains – Seldom eaten raw, even when ripe (when the skin turns black). Plantains are cooked by boiling, roasting or frying and eaten as a starchy vegetable.

BREADFRUIT – *Artocarpus altilis*, ʻUlu **(HA, MQ)** *Uto* **(FJ)**, ʻUru **(TA)**, *Kuru* **(CK)**, *Lemai* **(GU)**

Breadfruit is one of the original staples brought by the first people to settle in Oceania. The tree grows to 50+ feet and has large dark green leaves. The fruit starts as thousands of closely packed flowerets attached to a stem. The flowers fuse together and grow into a composite, globular fruit that is light to medium green, changing to yellow-green or yellow-brown when ripe. The fruit has a tough rind with an irregular "honeycomb" pattern. Because there are 70 varieties, details vary. Seasonal: during the wet, rainy summer months (summer in the southern latitudes is winter in the northern latitudes), with a second flush about 5 months later for some varieties.

Young Breadfruit – Young fruits the size of a baseball can be boiled and cut up for salads, stir-frys or curries. While they are immature, there is no need to core the fruit; it will be soft and edible.

Green Breadfruit – Green breadfruit, fully grown but hard, can be cooked and eaten as one might a boiled potato, although it takes somewhat longer to cook. When cooked it has a firm texture and tastes a little like artichoke, in my opinion. The color is greenish. Substitutes: new potato or parsnips.

Mature Breadfruit - Ripe, yellowish or brown breadfruit is soft, has a custardy texture and is slightly sweet. It, too, can be eaten as a cooked vegetable, but it is often mashed and the pulp used for puddings, soups or curries, color is pale yellow. Substitute: white or yellow yams, as they have a similar taste and texture to mature breadfruit.

Caution: Breadfruit stems and fruit can exude a sticky white sap that should be washed off the fruit and yourself with water ASAP. The sticky sap has been used to caulk canoes!

Roasted Breadfruit – Traditionally the fruit is roasted whole by piercing the end opposite the stem and placing it directly on a fire for 45 minutes, turning occasionally. The scorched skin is peeled and the core removed after it has cooled. Cooked breadfruit can be cut up and eaten or pounded into a "pudding."

Breadfruit is grown in Southern Florida and imported from the West Indies. The season is from January to March. Fresh mature breadfruit does not ship well, but it might be available in your area frozen or canned in brine

CASSAVA – *Manihot esculenta, Yuca, Manioc, Tapioca, Tavioka* **(FJ)**.

A native of South America, cassava has been exported to tropical regions around the world; it is popular as a cooked vegetable (rather than a processed food) among native peoples in Africa, South America, Asia and Oceania. The starchy root is best boiled; it tastes something like potato. The cooked flesh is white or light yellow and has a woody cordon (stem) down the center, which should be removed before eating. (Photographs on page 66)

Cassava was introduced to Oceania only recently, sometime in the 1950s. It has been slowly taking the place of taro, yam and sweet potato, because it is easier to grow and to cook (Haden, 2009: 121).

Caution must be taken with fresh roots: Once harvested, they are best prepared and eaten within a day or they will blacken and become inedible. They must be washed, peeled and thoroughly cooked to remove any dangerous enzymes. Roots sold in markets have an edible wax covering to help them "keep" longer. You can also get whole roots and grated roots, frozen. Observe the same precautions. With ordinary care, it's safe to eat.

Cassava has been used as a substitute for other starchy foods such as *sago*. It's usually grated raw and cooked into puddings or dumplings.

Tapioca – A starch used as a thickening agent. It's available as flakes, meal and "pearls." This is the same tapioca used to make *Tapioca Pudding*.

YAM – *Dioscorea alata.*, *Uhi* **(HA)**, *Uvi* **(FJ)**, *'Ufi* **(TA, TO, SA)**.

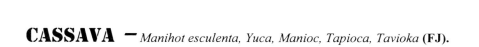

The yam is another "canoe plant," a plant brought by the first discovers of the Islands. *Dioscorea* yams, also known as "purple yams," come in several varieties, from pale white to deep purple. The "Yam" found in Mainland supermarkets is actually a variety of Sweet Potato! You may have to visit Asian, Indian or Filipino markets to find *Dioscorea* yams.

Some Island cultures place a high importance on yams, particularly in Melanesia. The Trobriand Islanders compete with each other to grow the largest yams (up to 7 feet!) and build specially designed structures to store them. In Hawai'i, yams were considered inferior to taro because they couldn't be made into *poi*.

Cooking – Roast or boil yam with the skins on, peel before eating. Boiling without the skin looses vitamins into the water, however if peeled, chopped and cooked in stews or curries, the broth will retain the nutrients. Eat as a cooked vegetable, hot or cooled.

SWEET POTATO – *Ipomoea batatas*, *'Uala* **(HA)**, *'Umara* **(TA)**, *Kumara* **(CK)**, *Kumala* **(FJ)**

How the sweet potato came to Oceania is a mystery. The sweet potato is originally from South America but it has been cultivated in Oceania for at least 1000 years. The word, *kumar*, in one form or another, is used throughout Oceania and by the Quechuan-speaking Indians. (the Incas spoke a Quechuan language). Thor Heyerdahl believed this was one proof that the Polynesians originated in South America. Heyerdahl's theories about the origins of the Polynesians have been convincingly refuted by decades of archeological and anthropological research, but the question remains, "How did the sweet potato get to Oceania?"

Sweet Potatoes come in two varieties, hard and soft. The *hard* variety is marketed as a Sweet Potato and the *soft* variety is routinely sold in Mainland markets as Yams – not the same as true yams at all.

You will probably not be able to judge the color of the interior without slicing through to see. The hard varieties of sweet potato can vary in color from white to yellow and in sweetness—the white being the least sweet. The color of the soft varieties range from yellow to orange.

Cooking – The same methods for cooking yams also apply to sweet potatoes.

Drying – Sweet potato can be sliced and dried to preserve it for storage. Pound the dried slices into a powder to be used with wheat flour in baking.

SUGAR CANE – *Saccharum sp.*, *Ko* **(HA)**, *To* **(TA)**, *Tolo* **(SA)**, *Dovu* **(FJ)**.

A tall perennial grass whose stalks are rich in sugar. *Ko* is a canoe plant, brought by the original navigators. Peeled sections were chewed as a snack for its sweetness and sometimes the juices were added to puddings or cooked foods. Chewing cane was thought to contribute to dental hygiene because of its high fiber and cellulose content.

Caution: Eating sugar cane is relatively harmless, but when it is refined into sugar, moderation is the best policy.

> "...sugar cane was recognized as a local plant, noted for its sweetness... Nevertheless it was the entry of processed refined sugar and other dietary changes introduced through European trading and migration, rather than crude sugar cane, which was responsible for the increasing epidemic of tooth decay in the Region"*

---

* Masi, MB, The pattern of dental disease in the South Pacific area of the Pacific Basin, *International Dental Journal*, 1973; 23: 573-578

ARROWROOT - *Tacca leontopetaloides, Pia* **(HA, TA, CK)**, *Masoa* **(SA)**, *Mahoa'a* **(TO)**, *Yabia* **(FJ)**, *Gapgap* **(GU)**

A flowering plant of the yam family. *Pia* is another canoe plant brought by the original island settlers. A flour made from the starchy roots of the *Pia* was used as a thickener for puddings *(po'e)*.

Arrowroot has no discernable flavor and thickens clear rather than cloudy like cornstarch. Good for clear syrups/glazes on fruits. Arrowroot is not good for thickening dairy-based products but it is good for acidic foods and foods that will be frozen. Where arrowroot is not recommended, we can substitute cornstarch or tapioca flour.

TI - *Cordyline fruticosa*, *Ki* **(HA)**, *Ti Pore* **(NZ)**, *Si* **(TO)**, *Lauti* **(SA)**, *'Auti* **(TA)**

The inedible leaf of the Ti plant has many uses in the Pacific, in this case, as a wrapper in which to cook food. The leaf is sturdy, holds up to cooking, and imparts a subtle flavor to the food. Leaves we are interested in are about 5 – 6 inches across and 20 – 24 inches long.

The starchy root of the Ti is sweet and baked for eating but also to make an alcoholic beverage called *okolehao* in Hawaii. Ti liquor was distilled by the Bounty mutineers who were in hiding on Pitcairn Island. Drunkenness among the crew led to violence and their eventual ruin.

We can find ti leaves at florists shops although we may have to special order them. Be aware that they may have pestisides. It's always a good idea to wash your produce and ti leaves in particular.

CHILI PEPPERS –

Chili Peppers are the fruit of the genus Capsicum that originally came from the Americas. The Spanish and Portuguese brought them to India, Asia and the Philippines in the early 1500s. It is anybody's guess how capsicum got to Oceania after that, although they were planted in Hawaii, in 1815 by a Spanish advisor to Kamehmeha I. Chili peppers are eaten as a spice in recipes or fresh by themselves, particularly in regions where the native food is bland.

The chili of the Pacific is the Capsicum frutescens, varieties of which include Tabasco, Piri-piri and Thai chilies. Red chilies can be added to *'Inamona.* Other chilies like Jalapenos and Serranos can provide a fresh spicy note to salads, soups and marinades.

Caution: Chili peppers contain capsaicin, a chemical that can produce a strong burning sensation to eyes, lips, mouth and other sensitive areas of the body. Whole peppers are safe to handle but cut pieces and seeds can transfer the capsaicin to your hands and remain even after washing; touching sensitive areas with your hands can irritate and burn. It may be a good idea to wear rubber gloves when working with chili peppers. Remember to clean cutting boards, blenders and utensils.

TROPICAL FRUITS –

Native Islanders rarely have fruit with meals; fruit is more for snacking. We, on the other hand, should take full advantage of these delicious fruits—except for one! It's ironic that only one of these is a traditional Island food and, that's the one I don't recommend. The rest were introduced within the last 250 years. I'd say that's long enough to become fully integrated into the Islander diet.

Mango – V*i popa'a* (foreign mango). A beautiful and delicious fruit whose flavor has just a hint of turpentine. The pit is large and flattened making it necessary to cut alongside each side of the pit to get to the fruit. Green mangos can be treated as a vegetable in salads or cut into slices and dried.

Mangos originated in India or Burma and spread to Malaysia and Indonesia before European contact. It appears that the Mango was bought to Oceania only after European contact. There is a fruit called *vi apple*, *Tahitian vi* or *Polynesian plum, which* may have been introduced by Neolithic navigators.

Papaya – *Papaw*. Originally, from Mexico, the papaya has a thin skin and fleshy fruit surrounding a center cavity filled with lots of small, dark, seeds. The fruit is ripe when the peel turns yellow or orange but don't let it get too soft. Eat it ripe by cutting it in half and scooping out the seeds, and then use a spoon to eat the fruit. The Hawaiian varieties are the best tasting, IMO. A variety marketed as *Mexican Papaya* is much larger but less flavorful. *Papaya fruit and seeds are a natural meat tenderizer and also aids digestion.*

Bake ripe papaya like a small squash, cut in half, remove seeds and serve with butter and salt or use the cooked fruit for *jams, chutneys and baked goods.* Use unripe (green) papaya as a vegetable. Shred the green fruit for salads. Green papaya should be soaked in water for at least 30 minutes, rinsed and drained before consuming, to remove any bitterness.

Pineapple – Pineapples are indigenous to South America. It was unknown in Oceania until it was imported to Hawaii in 1813. Later, in the 1890s, they were grown as a cash crop for export and not local consumption. Isn't it ironic that the pineapple has become the fruit most Westerners identify with the "South Seas"!

Caution: Pineapple has enzymes that can tenderize meat. This often results in mouth sores for people who eat too much pineapple. (How much is too much?)

Guava– Indigenous to Mexico and Central America, the guava has been transported to Oceania in post-European times. It is an invasive plant, hard to eradicate. It is good to eat fresh and the juice makes an excellent drink. A favorite contemporary Hawaiian beverage is called POG, Passion Fruit, Orange and Guava.

Passion Fruit – *Lilikoi* (HA). Originally, from South America, it was imported to Australia and taken from there to Hawai'i in 1923. Passion fruit is a climbing vine with distinctive white and purple flowers. There are two varieties of edible fruit, dark purple and yellow; the mature fruit contains a succulent flesh, which can be eaten fresh or pulped for its tart juice. The juice can be reduced to make syrups and jams.

Star Fruit – Star Fruit or *Carambola* is an import from Southeast Asia / Philippines. The fruit has waxy skin and looks like a five pointed star when cut in cross-section. The flavor can be sweet but slightly tart. The fruit is ready to eat when the skin is yellow. Slice and eat or use it in salads or deserts, chutneys and jams.

Watermelon – A vine plant that should be familiar to almost everyone. Originally from Africa, it can be found everywhere in the U.S. and is cultivated on many Pacific Islands where it makes a sweet, thirst-quenching drink (e.g., *Otai*, page 158). The rind can be used for chutneys and pickles.

Noni – A bitter fruit from a small tree in the coffee family. A canoe plant brought to Hawaii by Polynesian voyagers. Some claim therapeutic properties for the juice, but no scientific evidence backs that up. It only contains half the vitamin C as an equal amount of orange juice. Did I mention that it smells bad? I can see no culinary use for this fruit. I list it here because someone always asks. If it must be used, copious amounts of sugar and other fruit juices can mask the flavor.

CITRUS –

Citrus is native to India and Southern China, Northern Australia and New Caledonia. Most types have been introduced into Oceania in post-European times. Citrus can be eaten fresh but it is best enjoyed for its juice. Citrus is also important for marinades and flavorings.

Limes – *Taporo* (TA), the native lime, was most likely brought by Neolithic settlers. It has been used for centuries to marinade raw fish. In the absence of *taporo*, the larger *taporo popa'a* (foreign lime) is used. Limes are suited for growing on atolls. Used for juice or as a flavoring in salads and "cold cooking" seafood.

Kaffir Limes – A native of Southeast Asia and Indonesia. The fruit of the Kaffir lime is considered too acidic for eating but the leaves have a citrus aroma that gives a fresh citrus flavor to soups and curries. Available in Asian markets, fresh, frozen or dried.

Lemons – Islanders prefer limes for marinade; in the absence of limes, they will use lemons. Lemons can be used for pickles and chutneys (peels and all). Lemon makes a tangy dressing for seafood and vegetables. Fresh lemon juice drizzled on food can be used in place of salt. Of course, water and lemon juice, sweetened with sugar makes a refreshing drink.

Sweet Orange – These are the varieties we are most familiar with (e.g. Valencia, Naval and Blood Oranges). In hot tropical climates, citrus, particularly oranges remain green even when fully mature.

Wild Orange – Wild orange is a native of Melanesia. It is a different species than Sweet Oranges. The Wild orange is often mistaken for the Kaffir lime, but the fruits are different. Sweet orange can be substituted if necessary.

Sour Orange – The juice and pulp of the Sour Orange is not eaten, but orange flavored oil can be extracted from the rind. The flowers and leaves can be used as a flavoring.

Tahitian Grapefruit – AKA Pomelo, Larger than a grapefruit but similar in taste. The tart, pulpy sections can be eaten or the fruit can be juiced. Use Grapefruit if Pomelo is not available.

Calamondin – A hybrid of Sour Mandarin and Kumquat, about 1 ½ inch in diameter. Remains deep green in tropical climates even when fully mature (although I have seen some orange ones). A sour but refreshing citrus, it has been used in drinks and marinades. In Hawaii, it is combined with Papaya to make marmalade. Popular in the Philippines and introduced across Oceania.

LEAFY GREENS AND OTHER VEGETABLES –

Islanders have always eaten certain leafy greens, particularly taro leaves. The leaves of foreign vegetables, vines, trees and bushes, imported for other purposes, have been incorporated into local recipes. The following is a partial list of foreign and domestic leaves and vegetables:

Amaranth Leaves – *Amaranthus*, Tropical Spinach.

Chili leaves – *Capsicum frutescens*. Leaves and sprouts. Peppery.

Fern – *Diplazium esculentum*. *Ho'i'o* (HA) the young tops of so-called edible ferns. In the U.S., "fiddlehead" or Ostrich ferns may be used. Asparagus or green beans could substitute. Avoid *Warabi*, *Pteridium aquilinum*, or fernbracken, which may be sold packaged in Asian markets (possibly carcinogenic).

Sweet Potato Leaves – *Ipomoea batatas*. Boil or steam young leaves and the tips of the tendrils. Substitute young spinach leaves.

Kangkung – *Ipomoea aquatica*. A member of the Morning Glory family. Kangkung is an Indonesian name but it is called that, or something similar, across Micronesia. Boil or steam young leaves and stems. I find the stems a little tough. AKA *Swamp Cabbage* and *Ong Choy*. Substitute Bok Choy.

Potato Leaves - *Solanum tuberosum*. *Rewa* (NZ). Potato was introduced to Maori cookery by the English. Eaten as a vegetable, it is also used to leaven bread. Boil or steam young leaves.

Pumpkin Leaves – *Curcurbita moschata*. "Pumpkin tips" are the tender young leaves and tendrils. Pacific Islanders have adopted the Australian definition of *Pumpkin* as a hard rind squash eaten in the mature stage when seeds are fully formed, i.e., winter squash in North America.

European Cabbage – *Brassica oleracea*. Eaten raw as "cole slaw" or as a cooked vegetable.

Chinese Cabbage – *Brassica chinesis*, Bok Choy. Cooked in stir frys or boiled.

Onion – *Allium cepa*. Raw or cooked in coconut cream. The white and brown varieties are used most. Maui and Vidalia onions are "sweet" or "mild.." (Also scallions or green onions.)

Long Beans – *Vigna unguiculata subsp. sesquipedalis*, Snake Beans, Cowpea. Very long green beans! A different species than ordinary green beans. Boil for 4 mins for salads, 7 mins for side dish.

Ginger Root – *Zingiber officinale*, *Rea* (TA), *Avapui* (SA) is used to flavor various recipes. Young roots are fleshy and tender, mature roots are fibrous and best juiced. Turmeric *(Curcuma longa)*, is a member of the Ginger family, its roots are cooked and ground into the familiar yellow-orange powder that is used as a spice in curries and to provide color.

Bele – *Abelmoschus manihot* (formerly *Hibiscus manihot*) – slippery cabbage, sunset hibiscus – a native hibiscus of India whose leaves are often used in cooking or medicinally in the South Pacific. Related to okra *Abelmoschus esculentus*. Substitute okra or spinach.

MEATS AND SEAFOOD

PORK – *Sus scrofa*, *Pua'a* **(HA, TA, SA, MQ)**, *Vuaka* **(FJ)**, *Puaka* **(TO)**.

Pigs were brought by the original settlers of Oceania. The original pigs were an Asian variety, much smaller than European pigs of today, only 40 to 50 pounds according to Captain Cook. The large pigs we find in Oceania today are the descendents of pigs brought by European explorers and others that followed (150-300 pounds).

Pork was typically roasted (*kalua*) in an underground oven. Moist heat and slow cooking produces tender meat that does not need to be sliced—it just falls apart. Today, Mainland cooks have other cooking options:

Conventional Home Oven – Heat oven to a moderate heat (350° F). Season pork butt (shoulder) with Liquid Smoke, rock salt and whatever else you wish (see page 97). Completely wrap the meat in aluminum foil and place it in a pan. Cook for 5 hours. Remove and cool. Shred the meat and season with rock salt to taste.

Slow Cooker - Season pork butt (shoulder) with Liquid Smoke and rock salt and refrigerate overnight. Place the pork butt in the crock-pot. Add liquid, preferably apple cider, not juice. Set the heat to low and let it cook for at least 9 – 10 hours. Remove and cool. Shred the meat and season with more rock salt to taste. Add some cooking liquid to the meat if it seems too dry.

The first time I had kalua pork, the pig did not have any fat trimmed. The pork that came out of the *imu* was very rich with pork fat. As professional chefs know, much of the flavor of the meat is in the fat or as one TV chef says, "Pork fat rules!" The fat carries the smoky flavor and the saltiness. This isn't a low calorie dish but it's a delicious treat that we don't have every day.

In New Guinea and Island Melanesia, pork may be undercooked or nearly raw. This is not a safe practice; Westerners should not eat it in this state, even to be polite.

CHICKEN – *Gallus gallus*, *Moa* **(HA, TA, SA)**.

Moa, the Red Jungle Fowl, was brought to the Islands by the original Neolithic discoverers. The "Red" has been domesticated and hybridized into *Gallus gallus domesticus*, the domestic chicken. It can be prepared by boiling, roasting or barbecued. If you have ever roasted or barbecued chicken, what you have done is not much different from what goes on in the middle of the Pacific. So, there is not much more to say that you don't already know.

In Samoa, chicken is served undercooked, in my experience. It may be the custom to undercook chicken because guests take home leftovers to re-cook later.

BEEF – *Pipi* (HA), *Bulamakau* (FJ), *Povi* (SA).

Unlike pig or chicken, cattle were never part of the Islander tradition until Captain Cook brought them to Hawaii, and those were apparently eaten before they could breed. Around 1794, George Vancouver (who previously sailed with Captain Cook) brought cattle from California as a gift to Kamehmeha I and encouraged him to declare a 10-year *kapu (taboo)* which allowed them time to breed and multiply. Cattle flourished so well they became a dangerous nuisance by running free in villages and gardens until efforts were made to completely domesticate and control them. In 1830, Spanish *Paniolos* (cowboys) from Mexico came to teach cattle ranching and horsemanship. Today the Hawaiian *Paniolo* is every bit as skilled in wrangling cattle as his Texas or Mexican counterpart.

Beef finds its way into Island cooking through the cuisine of immigrants, e.g. the Chinese, Filipinos and Portuguese. *Paniolo* influence is probably responsible for Hawaiian *Pipi Kaula*. "Pipi" means cow, and "Kaula" means "rope" *(beef that looks like rope)* in Hawaiian. *Pipi Kaula* is Flank steak, cut into strips and dried. Unlike beef jerky, *Pipi Kaula* is semi-dried and is usually barbequed later.

Corned-beef—beef cured in brine and spices—is a Western method of preserving beef and an Island favorite. Its use in the Pacific is widespread but usually in the form of canned corn beef. Beef brisket, salted and stored in barrels, is referred to as *Salt Beef* outside of the U.S.

MUTTON FLAPS AND TURKEY TAILS –

Fat carries the flavor of food and adds to the palatability. The right kind of fat in moderate quantities can be healthy, particularly the Omega-3 fatty acids in fish and lauric acid in coconut.

The traditional diet of the Pacific Islanders contained very little fat. Consequently, Islanders never developed any cultural imperatives against the high intake of fats; and they consider a more corpulent body a sign of good health and well-being. Traditional food and active lives maintained a healthy balance—before the introduction of Western processed food*.

Today, easy access to fatty imported food has lead to an epidemic of obesity and diabetes in the Pacific. Meat and poultry processors in Australia and New Zealand have found a market in the Pacific for the off-cuts, the waste that cannot be sold at home. The fatty pieces that would have otherwise been discarded are being eagerly bought up in the Pacific.

In an attempt to control the growing health crisis, Fiji and Tonga have banned the import of Mutton Flaps. Other Pacific nations continue to import them.

---

* For example, the traditional Hawaiian diet may have been "one of the best in the world." It was a simple, high [unrefined] starch, high fiber, low saturated fat, low sodium and low cholesterol diet. It had 12 percent protein, 18 percent fat and 70 percent carbohydrates. By comparison, the typical American diet today has 15 percent protein, 40 percent fat and 45 percent [refined/processed] carbohydrates. Source: Noted Hawaiian Scholar, Dr. George Kanahele, Pookela Hawaiian Culture Course.

CANNED MEATS AND FISH –

Since WWII, Pacific Islanders have acquired a taste for canned (tinned) food. It seems simpler to open a can of mackerel than to go fishing. Spam is popular from Guam to Hawaii and the Samoans and Tahitians love New Zealand tinned corned-beef. Canned meat or fish is ideal for hash or baked into casseroles or manapua (meat-filled buns). Just in case you were wondering, canned meats and fish are cooked before or during the canning process.

Spam – Spam is a cooked meat product made of chopped pork shoulder and ham with salt and a binder to hold it together. It is used in soups and rice dishes. It can be sliced, fried and served for breakfast with eggs. It pairs well with bland foods like rice, potatoes and cassava.

Spam was introduced by Hormel in 1937, just in time for the War in the Pacific. It was a low cost meat product and easy to ship and store. Tons were shipped to the Pacific and much of it found its way into the Islanders' diet. Since then, its popularity in Asia and the Pacific has only increased. Spam and Corned-beef can be found in Mainland supermarkets, in the familiar squared cans.

Corned-beef – *Bully Beef.* In the Pacific, corned-beef: beef brisket cooked in brine and spices, shredded and packed tightly in cans. Like Spam, Corned-beef is easy to ship and store. It can be found on almost every island in the Pacific. The first canned food that came to Samoa was Pea Soup and the Samoans just assumed that's what *palangi* (foreigners) called "food-in-a-can." When corned-beef arrived they just called it *Pisupo*, and that is what it has been called ever since – so the story goes.

The corned-beef sold in American supermarkets comes from South America and has the texture of dog food. Corned beef sold in Oceania comes from Australia and New Zealand; it looks and tastes more like beef brisket, although some brands are rather fatty. Islanders prefer the latter. So do I, once the fat is rendered out. There is no reason we cannot use home cooked beef brisket in recipes that call for canned corned beef.

Mackerel / Sardines – These are cooked fish packed in oil or a sauce. Again, like other canned foods, it stores and ships easily. Because Islanders' everyday meals can be bland, this is a flavorful accompaniment to starchy foods.

Salmon – Used where fresh salmon is not available, or is too expensive, e.g. *lomi-lomi* salmon.

Tuna – Tuna is available everywhere. Large-scale tuna fisheries produce canned tuna relatively cheaply. Many of us have grown up eating tuna sandwiches or tuna casserole. Some of us have only the vaguest idea of what is in those cans.

There are several members of the tuna family: Bonito, Skipjack, Yellowtail, Bluefin and Albacore. Albacore is the only species that can be called "white" while other species must be labeled "light" (refers to the color not the calories). Albacore is high in fat (omega-3) with a mild flavor; it is also the most expensive. Canned tunas can vary greatly in quality from mush to solid meat. It comes in three grades: the best being Solid or Fancy (large pieces), followed by Chunk (smaller pieces) and Flaked or grated (bits and pieces). Canned tuna is steamed in the can to cook and sterilize it.

FRESH FISH –

The principal source of protein in the Islands comes from fresh fish. Pork and chicken were reserved for special occasions. An Islander could usually get all the protein he needed from the sea.

When Islanders go fishing, they don't just drop a line in the water and take whatever bites; they have specific techniques to catch specific fish. Fishing is more than catching food; it's a skill and a point of pride. In the old days, handmade fish hooks of bone or shell that were felt to be especially effective would be given names and passed from father to son. Fishing was survival made into sport, never work.

Here are some of the Island fish we may encounter in recipes or in restaurants. We can probably find these throughout the tropical Pacific by their local names but for our purposes, they are listed by their Hawaiian names, which are being used in U.S. restaurants and markets these days.

'Ahi – Albacore or Yellow Fin Tuna: Typically 75-200 pounds. Fatty flesh, eaten raw as *sashimi*, *sushi* or *poke*, grilled, baked whole in an *imu* or pan-seared. Avoid purchasing Ahi tuna or albacore loins that have too many distinct white lines in the flesh. This is a soft sinew and has a slight stringy texture, not ideal for *Poke* or *E'ia Ota* (see page 117, 118), but fine when cooked, When chopped, the sinew will easily pull away from the flesh. Substitute any fatty, firm-textured fish, swordfish, marlin, mackerel or salmon.

Aku – Ocean Bonito: 2-2 ½ feet. Eaten raw, dried, or baked. Substitutes: mackerel or tuna.

Akule – Big-eyed Scad: 7-12 inches. Eaten raw, broiled or cooked in an *imu* wrapped in *ti* leaves.

A'u – Generic name for large Billfish (Swordfish, Marlin etc.): Traditionally roasted in an imu, Mainland cooks favor grilled "swordfish" steaks.

Awa – The Milk Fish. Silvery/white, 12-14 inches. Chiefly favorite in old Hawaii. Reserved for their own use and kept in stone ponds to fatten.

Butterfish – Black Cod or Sable Fish. There is no Hawaiian name because this is a cold-water fish from the Northern Pacific, however the term *butterfish* is used in Hawaiian recipes. Butterfish is called "butter" because of the fat content. This should not be confused with the small silvery fish of the same name from the American East Coast.

Kamano – Salmon. Another imported fish that has been incorporated into Hawaiian cuisine. Eaten raw i.e. *sushi* and *lomi-lomi* salmon. It can be used in *laulau* in place of butterfish or in *musubi* in place of spam.

Mahi-mahi – Dolphin Fish (not Porpoise!): Grows to 5 feet. Not eaten raw, usually broiled. A very popular dish in Hawaii and the Mainland. Substitutes: monkfish, shark, swordfish or tuna.

Moi – Thread Fish: 1½+ feet. Once reserved for Hawaiian royalty, now, this fish is being raised in giant ocean fish cages for local use and export. Raw, broiled, dried, and cooked in an *imu*.

'O'io – Bone Fish: 2-3 feet. White flesh, mostly eaten raw. There are many fine bones that are eaten with the meat without problems. Cooking hardens the bones. If the flesh is scrapped off the bones, the mash can be fried as "cakes" or boiled in soup as "dumplings."

'Ono – A type of Mackerel commonly known as Wahoo. Grows from 8 – 30 pounds but sometimes more than 100 pounds. Lean and flaky. Always cooked: broiled, dried or baked in an *imu*. Be careful to not let the flesh dry-out in cooking

'Opakapaka – Pink Snapper (?): 18-34 inches. White meat, cooked in any manner. Hawaiians consider this tasteless but foreigners like it.

Opelu – Mackerel Scad: 12 inches. Highly prized food. Eaten raw, dried, broiled and sometimes broiled after it has been dried.

Ula'ula – Onaga, Red Snapper, a flakey textured fish. Raw eaten as sashimi, broiled or grilled. Subsitutes: sea bass, grouper, halibut, pompano, sole, flounder or cod.

Ulua – various species of Crevally (Jack): Species range from 18-200 pounds. Eaten raw or broiled if small and baked if large. Also known as Pompano or, when under 12 pounds, as Papio.

Fish is best if bought and used fresh. That means the flesh should be firm, the eyes clear and the gills bright red, and, of course, it should smell fresh. Frozen fish are fine but cannot be refrozen once thawed. Fish are a good source of protein, rich in vitamins and minerals: calcium, iodine, fluoride and vitamins: A and D. Fish oils are a good source for Omega-3 fatty acids which can help to reduce the risk of heart disease and cancer.

Reef Fish, Yap, Micronesia

CRUSTACEANS –

Shellfish from Oceania will be difficult to obtain on the Mainland; fortunately, what's available in local stores and fish markets is fine for Island recipes. All these are available fresh or frozen, with or without shells in most markets.

Shrimp – Shrimp and Prawns are different, but not by much from a taste and texture standpoint. Both can be boiled and eaten whole or used in salads, curries and stir-fry. They can be butterflied, that is, cut down the back but not all the way through, so they will open up when cooked. The larger varieties (e.g. Tiger Prawns) can be grilled.

Lobster – True lobster, the Maine Lobster, has large meaty pinchers. Unless you see the pinchers, you probably have, what is commonly called a *Spiny Lobster*, *Rock Lobster* or *Langouste*. Happily, both are delicious. Prepare by boiling or steaming. These larger crustaceans can also be partially steamed and finished on the grill by splitting down the middle of the back and placing the flesh side down on the grill. Use a medium or low heat to avoid charring the flesh. Crayfish are fresh water crustaceans with pinchers, related to the Maine Lobster.

Crab – Mangrove crab and Coconut crab are not likely to be available at your local supermarket so feel free to use any crab that is. Alaskan fisheries crab: King crab, Snow crab and Dungeness crab are great, so are crabs from Chesapeake Bay and the Gulf of Mexico. Other species of crab may be available in Larger Asian markets, live in tanks.

Crabs are boiled or steamed. Eat hot or cold; twist off the legs and pinchers and crack them open to get to the meat. Eat the meat straight away or collect the "pickings" for salads and other recipes. Whole live crab can be purchased at fish markets and Asian markets. Crabmeat is sold refrigerated and packaged in the seafood section of some markets. It's also packed in cans. Picked crab should be checked for pieces of broken shell before using.

Imitation Crab Meat is a type of fish cake made from pureed white fish. This is a Japanese process and a product known as *Surimi*. Imitation crab only superficially resembles crabmeat and doesn't taste anything like it; however, it is an interesting food in its own right, which can be used for sushi, salads and stuffing. The surimi process is used to make imitation shrimp and lobster, but it's really all the same. Traditional *surimi* cake, known as *kamaboko*, is sliced and used in Saimin, Hawaiian style noodle soup.

MOLLUSKS –

Mollusks are soft bodied animals that have developed hard calcium shells. If you've been to Hawaii, you may have gone out for drinks and been offered *pupu*, a snack at the bar, usually free. *Pupu* is a Hawaiian word for seashell. Native Islanders ate almost every type of mollusk from giant clams to tiny marine snails. Giant clams, *Tridacna gigas*, the largest mollusk in the world, can grow 4 ½ feet across and weigh several hundred pounds.

There are two kinds of mollusk we'd be interested in, gastropods and bivalves. Gastropods have a single shell (e.g. trochus, abalone, and conch); bivalves have two shells (e.g. clams, scallops, oysters). The part of the mollusk we eat is the "foot," the muscle. You probably have eaten mollusk many times already if you have eaten clam chowder, oysters, fried clams, scallops or *cioppino*, Italian soup with clams and mussels.

Mussels – We have a couple of choices when buying farmed mussels in the U.S.: Mediterranean mussels and Blue or Edible mussels. Farmed mussels come already cleaned but they should be rinsed several times. Wild or self-collected mussels can only be collected in "safe" months. Check local authorities before taking. Thoroughly rinse and scrub them to remove any barnacles or grit. The *byssus* or beard should be removed before cooking. Once the mussels have been thoroughly cleaned, remove and discard any shells that are broken or that do not close when tapped.

Steaming is the best way to cook mussels (and mollusks in general). Use a large pot with a lid. Add an inch of water or stock, bring to a boil and add the mussels. Cook for 6-8 minutes. Discard any that do not open once they have been cooked. Reserve the cooking liquid for broth or a sauce. If you plan to use mussel as an ingredient in other dishes, they should always be cooked first. If you plan to refrigerate or freeze mussels, it should be done as soon after cooking as possible.

Clams – I am using this as a catch-all word for Cockles and Clams. Clean thoroughly and discard any shells that are open or broken or do not close when tapped. Use a large pot with a lid. Add an inch of water or stock; bring to a boil. Add the cockles or clams and cook for 3-4 minutes. Cockles and clams open when cooked all the way through but be careful not to overcook. Discard any that do not open. Tahitian name: *Pahua*.

Scallops - For culinary purposes, there are two types of scallop: Sea Scallops (big ones) and Bay Scallops (little ones). If you have fresh scallops discard the dark "innards" while keeping the white muscle; sauté, grill or poach. You might want to keep the shells as little *pupu* plates.

Opihi – A gastropod that clings to the rocks. Opihi is the Hawaiian name for several edible species of limpet. These are usually eaten raw, as soon as they are plucked from the rocks. It used to be possible to buy them refrigerated by the quart. Can't get opihi? Use oysters.

Oysters – are "shucked" and eaten raw or poached. Oysters can substitute for *opihi*.

Pipipi – Nerites (about ½—1 inch), the most common marine snail in Hawaii are eaten steamed or boiled and picked from the shell with a pin. If you have an aquarium, these are related to the snails you bought to clean algae off the glass. It takes a good handful to make a meal of these.

Paua – Abalone. A gastropod that fastens itself to rocks with its large "foot." The meat is tender and requires a minimal sauté on each side. Abalones are endangered in California and collecting is not allowed south of San Francisco. Commercial abalone farms produce most of what is sold to restaurants in the U.S. and Japan. *Paua* (Haliotis iris), the New Zealand abalone is also being farmed. Farming abalone is sustainable, disease free and environmentally friendly.

California abalone is incredibly expensive, but there is an imitation abalone product (i.e. surimi) that is made from squid that might be worth a try.

Turban Snails –Turbo. Various species of marine gastropods of the family *Turbinidae*. Sometimes eaten raw, but often steamed and pried out of the shell with a pin. Tahitian name: *Ma'oa*.

Top Snails – Trochus. Various species of marine gastropods of the family *Trochoidae*. I've eaten this at the Noumea Yacht Club in New Caledonia, where it was served as *Salade de Trochus*. This is similar to Scungili, an Italian recipe using Conch. The "foot" is boiled and sliced thinly, served with salad greens and dressed with vinaigrette. I've found canned Trochus at an Asian market. Substitute Conch or Whelk.

Escargot – That's right snails. Use them as a cooked replacement for Turbo. These are usually available canned, at the market or gourmet shops.

OCTOPUS AND SQUID –

Hawaiian locals call octopus "squid" and sometimes use the Japanese word, *tako*. The native Hawaiian word for octopus is *He'e*, in Samoa it's *Fe'e* and in Tonga it's *Feke*, and the Maori word is *Wheke* (pronounced nearly like *Feke*).

Pacific Islanders have a unique way to catch octopus. A special octopus lure of a cowry shell and a stone sinker are tied to a thin stick. The lure is lowered on a line to the bottom of the lagoon and dragged along to attract an octopus. The octopus extends a tentacle to investigate and then darts from its hole to envelop the lure. The fisherman, in the canoe above, quickly pulls in the greedy octopus who won't release its "prey."

A most unusual technique was used to catch large octopus in the Gilbert Islands (Kiribati). Sir Arthur Grimble, the Resident Commissioner in the 1930s and 40s, tells of two teenage boys who would swim out to where an octopus was suspected of hiding. One would swim near the octopus' lair until the beast rushed out, trapping him in its tentacles, whereupon second boy would rush in to bite the octopus between the eyes, killing it. The boys coaxed Grimble into joining them in their "game." He was to be the bait! Grimble had an irrational fear of "devil fish," as he called them, but his authority in the islands would be undermined if anyone thought he was afraid to play this "children's game." As Grimble approached the lair, tentacles shot out and in seconds wrapped around his head and shoulders; his worst nightmare was actually happening. An eternity passed (in reality, just a few seconds) before his companion swam in to kill the beast, and both rose to the surface with their prize. The boys were ecstatic with praise. Grimble, still feeling horror and revulsion, had risen yet another step in the estimation of the islanders. (Grimble, 1952: 153)

Octopus – The flavor of octopus has been compared to scallop, only chewier. Octopus and squid are, in fact, distant relatives to scallops and abalone—they are all in the mollusk family. If you can get past the thought of *tentacles* you will find that octopus has a mild, slightly sweet taste, and as for the texture, that depends on how it's cooked.

When working with raw octopus, it's best to wear rubber gloves; some people can develop a rash. If you're buying octopus fresh, you can have your fishmonger clean it for you.

There are many opinions about how to prepare octopus: rub it vigorously with rock salt, pound it on a rock or put it in the washing machine for a cycle or two. The goal is to tenderize the meat, so if you have a method that works for you, use it.

The simplest and most sensible advice I've found to prepare octopus is as follows: Clean it by cutting off the head and remove the viscera. All we want are the tentacles—all useable meat. Remove the beak by cutting around it (at the base of the legs) with a sharp knife and pull it out. Wash the octopus in water and place it in a large pot of boiling water, enough to cover the whole octopus. If the octopus is too big for your pot cut it into smaller pieces. For a small octopus, less than one-pound boil for ½ hour or until the point of a knife can go into the thickest part with little resistance. For larger octopus, it may take several hours—keep testing. Do not overcook the octopus or it will start to toughen. It may be necessary to skin larger octopus after cooking, as the skin can turn gelatinous; rub the skin off under running water. On the other hand, some people like it.

It's ready to eat at this point. You can slice it thin and serve with dipping sauce, cut it into pieces and grill it, or use it in whatever recipes you wish.

Squid – Suppliers and restaurateurs realize that people can be squeamish about the word, *squid*, so they have taken to using the Italian word, *Calamari*, hoping you will think this is some delicious, new, Italian delicacy. A squid by any other name will still taste just as sweet.

Feel beneath the mantle for the stiff "quill" along the back and carefully pull to remove it. Grasp the mantle with one hand and the tentacles with the other and pull to remove the viscera. Cut off the tentacles just before the eyes and squeeze out the beak. Remove the skin and the fins: using a knife cut the skin along a fin, insert a finger under the skin, and start to peel, make sure the fins come off with the skin. Slice the body, lengthwise down the middle and rinse with water to clean. The squid is ready to cook: fried, boiled or braised

Both octopus and squid are sold frozen as well as fresh. Octopus can sometimes be found pre-cooked and refrigerated.

PALOLO –

Palolo worms detach their tails during the waning of the moon in the (Southern hemisphere) spring or early summer. Millions of wiggling tails rise to the surface; in the morning light they burst and release eggs and sperm in a mass spawning. Over the course of several nights, The islanders of Fiji, Samoa and Vanuatu race to the lagoons to scoop up the tails and eat them on the spot. They do not store well (although they can be frozen) which means they must be eaten as soon as possible. This is the sort of thing that doesn't usually appeal to *palangi* (*Western*) visitors, even though Westerners would probably eat caviar, which is essentially the same thing.

Substitute black caviar or flying fish caviar for *palolo*. Imitation caviars or anchovies may work too.

CONDIMENTS

Condiments are added at the table to adjust flavors to suit the diner. Several condiments have been covered in other sections such as Chili Water and Chili Peppers, Coconut Cream and Salt Water. The following are some traditional and imported Islander condiments:

SEAWEED – *Limu* (HA, SA, TO), *Rimu* (NZ, TA, CK), *'Imu* (MQ).

Limu refers to the edible seaweeds (algae) found in Polynesia. *Limu* is eaten as a spice and a vegetable; it provides vitamins and minerals (e.g. iodine) that may be lacking in traditional Island diets. It is gathered by individuals for personal and family use and there are commercial "pickers," who gather large quantities to be sold in markets. Some varieties of *limu* are sold dried, refrigerated or frozen: pickled or mixed with fish.

There are about a dozen types of *limu* that are most frequently eaten in Hawaii. The most popular *limu* sold commercially are:

Limu kohu – Peppery flavor used as a spice. Traditionally reserved for royalty because of its red color. The deeper the red color the stronger the taste.

Limu 'ele'ele – Black seaweed. Sold salted and ripened (fermented). Used as a relish for *Saimin* or raw fish. Substitute shredded *nori* for dried *limu ele'ele*.

Limu manauea – Mild tasting *limu* used as a thickener, but also as a vegetable for salads, soups, tempura, and *poke*. Also known by its Japanese name, *Ogo*.

Limu wawae'iole – Dark green; spongy texture. Used as a vegetable in salads or as a pickle.

Japanese Seaweeds:

Nori is made from shredded seaweed formed into flat sheets. It's mainly used is to wrap *Sushi* and *Musubi*.

Kombu is a type of kelp that, when dried naturally, develops a thin layer of white powder. The dried form is used to flavor Japanese soup stocks. It may be pickled and eaten as a relish.

Ogo is the same as *Limu manauea*. Ogo is red when fresh and green when cooked. *Limu manauea* or *ogo* can be purchased dried on the Mainland. Dried ogo must be rehydrated by placing in a bowl of water to soak for 10 – 20 minutes. Squeeze out the water and chop into about 1 inch pieces.

Ogo is the generic term for seaweed in Japanese, which caused some confusion when I went to buy it in a Japanese market. Apparently, Ogo is only used in Hawaii to identify the specific species the Hawaiians know as limu manauea. Fortunately, the market also sold Hawaiian specialities. When I said it was used for Hawaiian *Poke*, the clerk finally understood.

SEA SALT – *Pa'akai* (HA)

Salt has flavors!!! The table salt we normally use has been refined to remove "impurities" then iodine is added and usually some form of anti-caking agents. Unrefined salt retains the "impurities," which some would call the flavors

Sea salt is made from brine (seawater) which has evaporated, leaving salt crystals. I have found it myself, drying in pockets in the rocks along the surf in Hawaii and used it for impromptu cookouts.

'Alaea – The red, water-soluble clay of Hawaii is added to sea salt, giving it its name. The clay provides additional minerals, but most importantly, it takes the "edge" off the saltiness.

'Inamona – Chopped, roasted *Kuku'i* nuts are combined with *'alaea* sea salt to make an oily relish, used to season *poke*. **Caution**, *kuku'i* can act as a purgative if we eat too much. If *kuku'i* nuts are not available, use cashews.

I use a gray sea salt imported from France for most cooking because it tastes better, in my opinion, and it contains no anti-caking agents. I use *alaea* for Island cooking when I have it. *Alaea* is available from several on-line vendors. Substitute: Kosher Salt.

SAUCES –

There are sauces we cook with and sauces we use at the table. Sometimes the distinction isn't very clear. None of these are native to Oceania but are now associated with "Polynesian" style food.

Soy Sauce – A salty brown sauce made from fermented soybeans. Light soy sauce has a lighter color but more salt. Soy Sauce is the base for most Asian cooking and Asian inspired Island recipes.

Shoyu – Japanese soy sauce made with fermented soybeans and wheat. This is the "standard" soy sauce.

Tamari – Soy sauce made with fermented soybeans, no wheat.

Mushroom – Soy sauce made with straw mushrooms. Darker and thicker than regular soy with a richer (heavier?) flavor.

Unless you have a specific reason for using another type, Shoyu should be the one you use for Pacific Island food.

Hot Sauces – Here are some scorch-the-mouth hot sauces. The Asian hot sauces are going *Mainstream-on-the-Mainland*; even non-Asian supermarkets carry these on their shelves.

Sriracha - Chili, garlic, sugar and salt, finely ground, about the consistency of ketchup, it comes in a large squeeze bottle. It's Hot. Sometimes called *"Rooster Sauce"* because of the rooster pictured on the bottle, but I think *Rooster Sauce* is a brand name for another hot sauce.

Sambal – There are many types of sambal in Indonesia but the one we are most likely to find in the stores is *Sambal Oelek*. It's made by the same people that make Sriracha. Just a mix of chilies, salt and vinegar they call it a chili paste not a sauce; not finely ground like sriracha. This is Hot too.

Korean Kimchee Base – A mixture of gluttonous rice flour, fermented soybeans and red chili peppers.

Tabasco – This is a venerable brew of vinegar, Tabasco chilies and salt. I didn't realize how much Islanders liked Tabasco until I had eaten in Pohnpei (Ponape) and saw the biggest bottles of Tabasco I'd ever seen. The locals were using it by the spoonful, not the drop.

Chili Water is a popular condiment in Hawaii. This potion of red chilies, salt and water is used to add spice and flavor to any dish. Chili water is easy to make at home. (Page 155)

Tai Oporo is coconut milk infused with hot chilies, from the Cook Islands. (Page 156)

Teriyaki Sauce – A sweet mixture of soy sauce, sake and sugar. Meat, chicken or fish are marinated in the sauce and grilled. Nontraditional use is to pour it on the meat after it has been cooked or as a dipping sauce. Some cooks put a little on the spam in Spam Musubi.

Hoisin Sauce – Another sweet Chinese sauce, characterized by a hint of licorice. Used to flavor cooked meats, glazing and as a dipping sauce. An interesting alternative to Teriyaki sauce.

Fish Sauce – Small fish, such as anchovies, are packed in large earthenware jars; first, a layer of salt goes in, then the fish, then another layer of salt. The fish are kept in the jars for as long as 18 months while the fish ferment and the liquids are drawn out. This liquid is bottled as *fish sauce*. A good fish sauce does not smell fishy or strong. The Thai call it "nam pla." This is called "patis" in the Philippines.

Nam pla is used in Thai cooking, as a marinade for meats, and as a table condiment to be used as one would salt. Chopped Thai chilies and fish sauce makes a spicy condiment to spoon on vegetable or noodle dishes.

Toasted Sesame Oil – A vegetable oil made from sesame seeds. Asian cooks use it for flavoring, to impart a rich savory aroma to soups and stir fried dishes. Toasted sesame oil is not suitable for frying or deep-frying, so it is added after cooking. Used in salad dressings or drizzled over cooked fish.

Liquid Smoke – Smoke from burning wood, condensed into liquid or solid form and added to water. An effective way to add a smoky cookhouse flavor to mainland cooked foods. Used in the kitchen, never at the table. Go easy, too much can be overwhelming.

The next two items are strictly used for cooking.

Oyster Sauce – Bottled oyster-flavored sauce is a concentrated mixture of oyster extracts, soy sauce, brine and assorted seasonings. It is used sparingly to flavor savory dishes

Lobster Base – A commercially bottled product, similar to bouillon cubes, used to make lobster bouillon, although it can be salty. Not normally found in Oceanian cookery but used in some of these recipes as a replacement for fish stock.

SPICES

Like so many other introduced foods, spices have merged easily into Oceanian traditions, albeit recently. I believe, had the original settlers of Oceania any knowledge of spices, they surely would have brought them. Today, formerly unknown herbs and spices grow prolifically, for example, vanilla in Tahiti and and black pepper in Pohnpei.

Western cultures were not much different, Europeans were late to appreciate and use spices until contacts with Asia woke them up to the possibilities, less than a thousand years ago.

FURIKAKE –

Furikake is a Japanese seasoning made from seaweed (nori), sesame seeds, sugar, salt, tuna flakes and other ingredients. It's normally used as a seasoning for boiled rice. There are many variations of Furikake. Try it at a Japanese or Hawaiian restaurant or ask someone for a recommendation, or do what I do: just pick one at random and try it. Furikake is available at Asian markets and on-line.

CURRY –

Strictly speaking there is no spice called "curry." The word curry denotes a method of cooking identified with Indian cuisine; the result is a sauce or a stew. What we think of as curry spice is a mélange of spices and herbs that vary from region to region. An Anglicized version of Indian curry became popular in England in the 19th Century and the English exported their version to the rest of the world.

India: India has so many regional cooking styles it's hard to generalize about Indian curry spices but, if pressed, one could mention turmeric, mustard seeds, pepper, cardamom, coriander, cumin and chilies, and many others in various combinations. "Heat" ranges from mild to spicy but always aromatic. We can buy a spice mix called "curry powder" in the little tins but I would recommend buying it in the cellophane packages hanging in the spice section of the market. It's better and a lot cheaper.

Japan: Curry was introduced to Japan by the English and the Japanese made it uniquely Japanese. Japanese use a prepared spice mix, which is pressed into a block, to flavor stews and to serve over rice. This is definitely distinct from Indian curries.

Thailand: Thai curries have a unique style that is fresher than Japanese or Indian. Thai curries have a slightly sweet, herbal character. Thai curries use prepared curry pastes that can be purchased in Asian markets. The three most popular are:

> **Red**: Red chili peppers, shallots, garlic, lemon grass, kaffir lime, salt and shrimp paste.
> **Green**: Same as red, except it replaces red chili peppers with green chili peppers.
> **Yellow**: Same as Red, except it has a turmeric base instead of chili pepper.

Fiji, Samoa, Tonga: Known generally as *kare* or *kale*, a spice blend that is a popular ingredient in curried lamb, mutton, and chicken stew, often made with coconut milk. Fiji has a large and diverse Indian population. *Kare* (pronounced Kah-ray) is a combination of spices that can be found in the Indian markets or as a packaged blend.

NUTS AND SEEDS

Nuts and seeds are two of the most nutritious foods available in the Islands but they are often overlooked. You and I may consider the fruits of a plant to be the end-product but they are just a means for plants to *lure* us into spreading their seeds. Plants put all their energy into producing seeds and nuts to assure the continuation of the species. Nuts and seeds provide us with oils and fats, proteins, vitamins and minerals.

KUKU'I NUT – *Aleurites moluccana*

The nut of the Kuku'i has been used for many things, food, medicine, dye, tattoo ink but it's famous for another thing, candles; the nut contains 50% oil. Several nuts could be threaded on a thin spindle made from the midrib of a palm leaf; when the top nut was lit and would burn for about 10-15 minutes before lighting the next and so on, thus its common name is the *Candlenut*. The oils could also be extracted and burned in a stone lamp with a *kapa* (*tapa*) cloth wick.

When used for food, the nuts must be roasted. Raw nuts are mildly toxic, even when roasted, they act as a laxative, if you eat too many. The roasted nuts are pounded into small pieces and added to salt (and sometimes chilies) to make the Hawaiian relish, *'inamona*. Packaged Candle Nuts or *kemiri* are imported from Indonesia and may be available at Asian Markets. Cashew or Macadamia are oily nuts that can be substituted for *kuku'i*.

TAHITIAN CHESTNUT – *Inocarpus fagiferu*, Mape **(TA)**, *Ivi* **(FJ)**

Mape is the Tahitian name. The nuts are edible after we peel, boil and mash them. I remember the sweetened paste being cooked in short lengths of bamboo (slight taste of bamboo). In Fiji it's called *Ivi*. Fijians bake the mashed nut with coconut cream and sugar in banana leaf wrappers. (Page 93)

If you can't find anyone who imports Tahitian Chestnuts ordinary chestnuts may be substituted. They can be purchased fresh or peeled and frozen.

MACADAMIA NUT – *Macadamia integrifolia and Macadamia tetraphylla*

Macadamia is native to tropical Queensland, Australia. The nut contains 65% to 75% oil (monounsaturated fats) and 6% to 8% sugars. They are now commercially farmed in Hawaii, Australia, South Africa and the Caribbean.

Because of the high oil content, these could be used as *Candlenuts*, or as a replacement for *kuku'i* in *'inamona*. Eat roasted macadamia nuts in salads, curries and stir-fry. Nut flours can be used for baking and sauces, and let's not forget chocolate covered Macadamia nuts.

PAPAYA SEEDS – *Carica papaya*

The fruit and seeds contain papain, which helps digestion and is used to tenderize meat. Both have anti-inflammatory and anti-oxidant properties and promote digestive health

The edible seeds have a spicy flavor something like black pepper. The seeds are usually crushed to release the papain and make them more palatable. Use the seeds for marinades and salad dressings

PUMPKIN SEEDS – *Cucurbita sp.*

The term pumpkin, in the Pacific, refers to several kinds of hard rind squash (e.g. Hubbard, Buttercup [not butternut], and Banana squash) eaten in the mature stage when seeds are fully formed. These vine plants grow well in the Pacific, even on the flat coral atolls of Micronesia.

The seeds of the squash are normally thrown away but they can be a nutritious addition to your diet, roasted as a snack or roasted and ground into flour.

PEANUTS – *Arachis hypogaea*

Peanuts are grown throughout the tropics: Asia, Africa, Australia, Southern USA, South America, with India and China accounting for over half of the world's production. They come to Pacific Island cuisine via the many immigrant contributions to home cooking. OK, peanuts are not nuts; they are legumes, relatives to beans and peas. We will just call them nuts because they have "nut" in their name.

Peanuts are a cheap, nutritious food that is part of the cuisine of Asia and Indonesia and gaining ground in Oceania; there is a Tahitian word for peanut, *Aratita*, which is also the word used in parts of the Cook Islands. In New Guinea, peanuts are a nutritional supplement to the normal diet of tubers and cereals.

Peanuts must be cooked before eating and there are a couple of ways to do that: roasting and boiling. Roasted peanuts in or out of the shell are the most familiar. Boiling is a method suited for Island cooking and it gives the familiar "nutty" peanut a more "beany" taste and texture.

Peanuts add crunch to stews and stir-frys. They are well paired with hot chilies. Peanut butter is a thickener and flavoring for curries and sauces.

KAVA

Piper methysticum, **Kava** (TO, MQ), **'Awa** (HA), **'Ava** (SA), **Yaqona** (FJ) or **Sakau** (Pohnpei) is a mildly intoxicating plant of the pepper family. Rather than intoxicating, I should say calming or "mellowing." After the first cup, you will notice your lips and tongue turning numb. After another cup, you'll start to feel quite relaxed and at peace; your mental clarity will actually be heightened. Eventually you will fall asleep and when you awake, there will be no hangover or residual effects. Taken to excess and over a long time, it will not result in any serious consequences; the worst thing will be a chalky looking skin condition that clears up when kava drinking is discontinued and it's not addicting, nor are there withdrawal symptoms. In fact, kava is used to treat alcohol and drug withdrawal. People who do physical labor find it eases muscle ache.

That sounds wonderful doesn't it? Here is the bad news—it looks like muddy water and it tastes like it too. *Kava* should be used in moderation; it will produce a numbing sensation to the lips and tongue, and make you drowsy after a while. If you are not used to it, kava can make you weak in the knees and affect your reflexes, so, one should not drive or operate equipment after imbibing.

Kava is another canoe plant brought by the original settlers of Oceania. It is used by all classes of people in Fiji for ceremonial and social occasions. Tongans and the people of Vanuatu use it to relax and socialize. Samoans use it mainly for ceremonial occasions. *Kava* use is almost nil in Tahiti, Marquesas, Cook Islands and Hawai'i due to changes in traditional society but rest assured, it's being revived. Vanuatu, Fiji and Hawaii farm it for export. It's being sold internationally and being packaged and processed into new forms, which are readily available on-line, or at Health Food stores on the Mainland.

Here is what you need to prepare *Yaqona* (*Kava*) in the traditional Fijian manner:

- *Yaqona* **Roots**, of course. These will need to be pulverized with a stone grinder or a *Tabili* (a mortar made from a piece of steel pipe closed at one end, and a steel rod to pound the root to shreds). Or, you could just buy it already pulverized.

- **Tanoa**. For casual use, any large bowl will do, for formal ceremonies; you'll need a proper *Tanoa*. A *Tanoa* is a carved *vesi* wood bowl with four or more legs. A *Tui Tanoa* is a braided coconut fiber cord, tied to the Tanoa and always points to the guest of honor at a Kava ceremony. White cowry shell decorations.

- **Cool Fresh Water**, never hot.

- **Strainer**, an *i loba*, made of strips of hibiscus bark or a cotton bag.

- *Bilo*, a coconut cup to drink the Yaqona.

The etiquette for making and drinking Yaqona:

The person who prepares the "mix" should announce that he is about to make the *Yaqona* and *cobo** (clap with cupped hands) 3 times. The *Tanoa* is filled with cool water and the *kava* pulp or powder is placed in the strainer, dipped in the water and squeezed several times until all the essence of the *Yaqona* is infused in the water. All this should be done with great style and dignity.

When the *yaqona* has been made, the mixer will announce that it's ready to serve and clap his cupped hands 3 times, fill the *bilo* and give it to a cupbearer who presents it to the first person to be served.

The recipient should clap once and accept the cup with both hands. He should drink the *yaqona* in one gulp and pass the cup back. To show his appreciation he should clap his cupped hands 3 times.

The cup is refilled and the last step is repeated for each person to be served.

Informal get-togethers can omit some of the ritual, but the drinker should at least observe the *cobo*, it's the traditional way to say Thank-You.

Kava's affects are best appreciated by taking it before or with food.

Kava Clubs

KAVA CLUBS ARE SOCIAL GATHERINGS that are held from Utah to New South Wales (US to Australia). Expatriate Tongans and other Pacific Islanders gather to drink kava, talk and sing. Members claim, with justification, that kava clubs reduce the stress of living in another culture and prevent incidents of violence. Yet there are groups that seek to impose a ban on kava for "moralistic" purposes.

The Sydney Morning Herald reported that before the formation of Kava Clubs in Australia, Tongans had earned a reputation for violence fueled by alcohol. "The [Tongan] churches took the lead in setting up kava clubs, where young and old can drop in any night of the week, the women mostly singing or playing cards on the side while the men sit in circles, drink kava and talk."

The Australian government has imposed tight restrictions on the importation of kava, which worries the Islander communities. "Without kava our young people will return to alcohol" Methodist ministers from Sydney's Tongan community warned.

---

* Pronounced "thombo" see glossary, page 163

Food Preparation, Yap Micronesia

Opening Green Coconuts for Drinking, Yap Micronesia

(My Yapese food and culture informants, Edmund Pasan and John Ranganbay)

ISLAND FOOD PREPARATION

To cut...To tear...To peel...To slice...To scrape...To grate...To pound...To squeeze
...To pinch off...To rub...To wring...To strain...To split...To stir...To wrap up in
leaves ...To cook in the oven...To cook uncovered...To husk coconuts

Samoan Material Culture, Te Rangi Hiroa (Sir Peter Buck). 1930

Te Rangi Hiroa (Sir Peter Buck) describes the manual labor went into preparing meals in Samoa (Hiroa,1930:103,104), using simple pounders, peelers and scrapers of stone and shell, but even more basic tools were employed: bare hands, fingernails and teeth. It even took physical labor to start the cooking fire. Perhaps that is why men did the cooking in Samoa.

In the days before European contact, food was roasted in an earth oven or over an open fire. When an Islander wanted to cook breadfruit, taro or green bananas it was a simple matter to put them unpeeled, directly in an earth oven. However, if he had a delicate piece of fish or a pudding of mashed fruit, he needed to hold the loose ingredients together, protected from ash, dirt and hot embers. The ingenious solution was to wrap such items in large leaves—free and expendable cooking containers.

On the Mainland, and the developed areas in the Pacific, we (and local islanders) have access to modern kitchens and appliances. Delicate food can be baked in a modern oven where the heat can be controlled and the food never need contact direct flame. We can choose to cook our puddings on the stove using a pot, or in a baking dish in the oven. Chopped meats and vegetables can be fried in a pan or boiled in a pot. The Chinese wok can be used to chǎo*, steam and deep fry.

Today, cooking Island food in leaf packages is just a tradition, not a necessity. However, cooking in the traditional way is not totally obsolete. Traditional techniques produce the smoky, homey flavors that can be lost in the modern kitchen. Which brings us to a modern convenience that we haven't discussed yet: the barbeque grill; apparently, the desire to cook over an open fire is a universal urge that cannot be resisted. Instead of hamburgers and hot dogs, grill fish, chicken and lobster.

This section will explain how to work with unfamiliar Island food using Western techniques and a few traditional techniques, if you are interested in learning to cook "Island Style."

---

*See page 134

Food preparation tools of Oceania: Graters and Pounders

Mainland kitchens have most of the tools to make Island meals. Here is a short list of recommended items:

- **CLEAVER** – A sturdy Chinese cleaver will come in handy for cracking open mature coconuts. The back of a heavy cleaver is better than the sharp edge. The sharp edge will be useful for opening green nuts and, of course, cutting meats and chopping vegetables.

- **DEEP COOKING POT** – For boiling large whole Island vegetables and making stock. Use a steamer basket for steaming leaf wrapped foods.

- **NYLON PAINT STRAINER BAGS** – To strain coconut milk, kava or anything—except paint. Also muslin or silk bags to strain kava.

- **BLENDER** – More power the better. Used for poi and purees, cold drinks and condiments.

- **WOK AND WOK UTENSILS** – Ideally, it should be deep and wide with a proper handle. The one I use has a flattened bottom and non-stick coating. Used for Deep-frying, Stir-fries, Curries and Fried Rice. Utensils: Chinese bamboo spatula and a spider (wire basket with a handle).

- **SLOW COOKER** – The next best thing to an *Imu* (earth oven). Cooks low and slow.

- **COCONUT GRATING STOOL** – These are fun and available on-line for less than $20, although not absolutely necessary.

- **TORTILLA PRESS** – If you intend to make many *chapatis* or *titiyas*, this will come in handy.

COCONUTS

Commercial coconut milk producers use highly efficient presses or juice extractors to squeeze the liquid from coconut "meat." This liquid is referred to as *coconut extract*, a much more concentrated liquid than what we can make at home.

When we read the ingredients listed on a can, coconut extract should be listed first, followed by water. On some cans, where the first ingredient is listed as *coconut milk*, it probably means *coconut extract*. When percentages are given, the total for coconut extract and water is 99.99%, however, when no information is given as to the percentage of extract to water, we can assume that ratio is 50/50, which is about what you get by making it yourself. The remaining one tenth of one percent (or less) is a preservative, typically Sodium Metabisulfite and/or Citric Acid. Some producers add small amounts of so-called Stabilizers (Xanthan Gum and Carrageenan) to keep the oil and water from separating, and act as thickeners. Any more additives than that should be viewed with suspicion.

If the percentage of coconut extract is 99.99% with no water added, it may be labeled as coconut cream because it is undiluted and contains a higher percentage of oils per volume. In any case, when you open a can or container (unshaken) you may find a thicker layer floating on top—that is the actual coconut cream.

Of the canned products I have tried, the taste is comparable to homemade and perfectly good to use. You may want to taste test several brands to see if you prefer one over another.

When you make coconut milk for yourself, you can be sure it is fresh and free of preservatives, but consider this: mature coconuts, purchased at the market, cost almost as much as a 14 oz. can of coconut milk. Overall, it may be cheaper and easier to buy rather than make.

Always buy <u>unsweetened</u> coconut milk. If a recipe calls for sweetened, you can always add the sweetener yourself.

BUYING A COCONUT

Mainland markets sell both green and mature coconuts; the mature nuts are completely husked but the green nuts do not have a fully matured shell so they are only partially husked. Of course, you want the freshest coconut you can find but there is no way to tell if they are "good" without opening them. Coconuts keep pretty well, so you probably won't have much to worry about. Both green and mature coconuts should smell clean and fresh when opened. If they don't, discard and move on to the next one.

Although coconuts keep, don't keep them around for weeks or months before using them.

OPENING A GREEN NUT

Green coconuts are young coconuts filled with Coconut Water. The meat inside is still forming and still soft. Green nuts are sold semi-husked, that is, part of the husk has been shaved off with one end sharpened like a very stubby pencil. The following method is the easiest and <u>safest</u> way to open one.

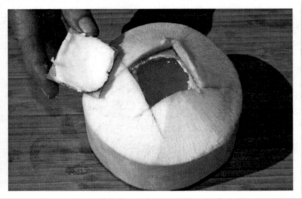

Cut a 2 inch (more or less) square hole in the top of the coconut. The husk of a green coconut is soft, so it will be easy to slice or push a sharp knife or cleaver into the top until it reaches the nut. Give the back of the knife a sharp hit with a piece of wood or a mallet to crack through the thin shell. Make three more cuts like the first. If you've cut deeply enough you can easily pry the square up with the knife or screwdriver. Now you can drink the water directly from the nut or pour it into a container. Once the water has been emptied, bury the cleaver in the top and hammer the husk/nut on a solid surface until it's nearly cut in half, then pry apart. When you have two halves, use a spoon or melon-baller to scrape out the soft meat. Eat it now or save it for later.

OPENING A MATURE NUT

This technique is used everywhere in the Pacific, from the family cookhouse to the fanciest restaurants, from Honolulu to Hong Kong. It requires no special tools and no special skills, but once you've done it you'll feel like a real island cook. I've done it with a dive knife and I've done it with a smooth rock.

Use the back of a heavy cleaver or machete (not the sharp edge), or a tire iron or the edge of a heavy file to deliver a smart whack to an imaginary line running around the middle of the nut. This should start a crack that can be continued all the way around by a few more sharp hits until the nut breaks in two.

GRATING COCONUT MEAT

Coconut "meat" is rasped from the inside of the half-shell. Straddle the coconut scraper. Hold the half-shell with both hands. Scrape the coconut meat against the serrated edge of the grater, while turning and tilting the nut. Try not to cut into the brown shell; all you want are the snowy white coconut shavings.

If you don't have a coconut scraper, pry the meat out of the shell with a stout knife. The meat will not come out easily so it may be necessary to place the open halves in a low oven for 20-30 minutes until the meat starts to come away from the nut. Cut any large chunks into 1-inch pieces. Add the chunks and a little water to a blender (or a food processor); pulse into small shavings.

MAKING COCONUT MILK

Pour 1 cup of hot water (not boiling) per coconut over the grated coconut meat and allow it to stand for 10 minutes; the heat will help "loosen up" the oils. Put grated meat and liquids into a blender and run for a minute or so, until the liquid is white and creamy. Strain the meat and liquid through cheesecloth, a napkin or a paint strainer bag, squeeze out as much liquid as possible into a bowl. The left over coconut meat can re-processed with more water for a second squeezing (but I've never done it), then dried and used as flour for baked goods or as bird food.

MAKING COCONUT CREAM

If left to stand in a cool place, coconut cream will separate out of the milk. Place coconut milk in a bowl and refrigerate for an hour or two. A layer of cream will rise to the top. Carefully spoon it into a separate container. This should work even better with "coconut extract."

MAKING COCONUT OIL AND BUTTER

The traditional process of making coconut oil involves boiling coconut milk until the water evaporates, leaving only the oil. This requires constant stirring and vigilance for an hour. It only takes moment's distraction at the wrong time to create a mess. I don't think this method is worth the trouble when coconut oil and butter are usually available at health food stores, besides there are easier ways. (I leave it to you to research juice extractors. Some make excellent coconut oil/butter.)

Here is a simple technique to make coconut butter. Whip room temperature (below 78° F) coconut cream until lumps start to form. Skim the lumps to a separate refrigerated bowl and mash them together until smooth. If any liquid separates out, discard it. Refrigerate the butter in a closed container. Use it for frying as you would butter or use it as skin softening lotion. Coconut oils and butters should have almost no flavor or smell. As a lotion, it should leave the skin smooth and not oily.

TARO

Colocasia esculenta, Hawaiian taro or "true taro" is the preferred taro for its taste and texture. Asian markets will simply label all varieties as "taro." One way to tell is by the size; Colocasia corms are usually the less than 2 lbs; larger taro corms, up to 10 lbs, may be an unspecified variety of taro grown in Mexico. This taro is softer than Hawaiian and is not as "sticky." If you intend to make poi, use Hawaiian when you can, athough mainlanders may not be able to distinguish between varieties, so ask your supplier.

HANDLING TARO

Taro contains calcium oxalate crystals that cause skin, mouth and throat irritation if not thoroughly cooked. When handling raw taro (i.e. cleaning, peeling or cutting) it is advisable to wear rubber gloves; dishwashing gloves work well.

CLEANING CORMS

Fresh taro corms should be rinsed and scrubbed with a stiff brush to remove as much dirt as possible. I recommend that taro corms be cooked whole and unpeeled for best results. If it is necessary to cut taro to fit your cooking pot, keep the pieces as large as possible.

COOKING CORMS

Corms must be thoroughly cooked (boiled, steamed or roasted) to break down the calcium oxalate crystals; that means about 45 minutes or more depending on the size of the corm. Some people add a pinch of baking soda to the cooking water. Packaged or peeled corms should be cooked until fork tender, smaller pieces cook faster than whole corms. Test for doneness with a fork or the point of a knife.

Fill a pot with water to cover the taro plus a couple of inches — some will boil away during the long cooking. Do not overcrowd the pot. After boiling for the minimum time, use a fork or sharp knife to test for "doneness." Cooked taro should be firm; the fork (or sharp knife) should pierce the taro with a little resistance. I would not advise using a pressure cooker, as you need to be able to test the "doneness" while they are cooking. Packaged or peeled corms cook faster that whole corms and tend to disintegrate into muck if boiled too long.

Remove the cooked taro from the pot and set aside to cool before peeling or cutting.

WORKING WITH COOKED CORMS

Cooked corms can be sticky, so wet your hands, scrapers and knives with water.

When the corm has been cooked, it is relatively easy to scrap the skin off with the edge of a spoon or back of a knife. Scrape or cut out any dark areas and discard.

Caution: Do not toss cooked taro peelings or leftovers down the drain even if there is a kitchen disposal; they will form a thick sticky paste and cause some serious drain clogging.

COOKING LEAVES AND STEMS

Like the corms, leaves and stems must be thoroughly cooked to break down the calcium oxalate crystals. Most leafy greens would perish under such intense cooking but taro leaves and stems hold up remarkably well. Wash the leaves; remove stems and the thick veins. Cut whole leaves, or stems into 2-3 inch pieces. Boil in salty boiling water with a pinch of baking soda. Reduce heat to a simmer and cook for at least 45 minutes. Cooking times can be reduced by cooking in a pressure cooker.

Remove the cooked leaves (or stems), drain and pat dry and allow them to cool before using them in recipes. Discard cooking water.

MAKING POI

Making *poi* at home can be tricky, messy and not always successful; therefore, I do not recommend it, particularly for those who have never had *poi* before. A better option would be to purchase *poi*; it comes frozen, dried (reconstituted with water) and even fresh.

Having said that, here is one method for homemade *poi*:

First, only use *Colocasia esculenta*; other types of taro are not "sticky" enough!

Clean and cook taro corms as described in the previous sections. Cut the corm into ½-inch pieces.

Using a good strong food processor, work in small batches. Add the taro pieces and a little water. How much water is the tricky part: too little water and the food processor will just cut the taro into little chunks; too much water and the *poi* will be too thin. You will have to determine this as you work (start with 1 or 2 Tablespoons). The goal is a silky smooth paste – something like chocolate pudding. If you can twirl a small mouthful on one or two fingers then you have done it right.

Transfer the *poi* to a bowl that has been rinsed with water. Serve from this bowl or smaller individual bowls. Save the leftover by <u>gently</u> covering the *poi* with a layer of water. This is another tricky operation; if the water is poured onto the *poi*, it will make a hole in the surface and dilute the *poi*. This is a definite possibility if your poi is already thin. You will end up with a useless soupy mess.

If you've made it safely to this point, the leftover *poi* can be served again by pouring off as much of the water as you can.

Poi will last for a couple of weeks if refrigerated. If allowed to sit at room temperature for a few days it will begin to ferment. Fermentation has been used to preserve poi but for our purposes, fermented poi acquires a tangy, slightly sour taste that some consider an improvement to otherwise bland poi. That is something you will have to decide for yourselves.

Clean up: use a rubber spatula to get as much *poi* out of the food processor as you can. Dilute <u>small</u> amounts of leftover *poi* with water when washing up so it can be safely sent down the drain. Do not pour *poi* into the sink drain; if you have to dispose of a larger quantity of *poi*, pour it into a plastic shopping bag and tie it up before disposing of it as you would any other food or yard waste, in the trash.

Dry upland taro (Colocasia) growing among sweet potato and cassava

BREADFRUIT

BUYING BREADFRUIT

There will not be many, if any, places to buy fresh breadfruit outside of the islands, where it is grown. I think mature breadfruit tastes the best; unfortunately, the only breadfruit I can find is imported from Fiji and Samoa, frozen and green (immature).

Find stores in Islander communities and let them know you are interested in buying breadfruit. They will tell you if/when they expect to get it and perhaps they can notify you when a shipment arrives; don't wait too long to get it, it can sell out quickly.

Breadfruit is grown in Southern Florida and the Caribbean. That should make it easy if you happen to live in the area. For the rest of us, look for West Indian markets or seach on-line. I've seen it offered on-line, packed in brine and canned! Seasonally available.

** Cooked white or yellow yams can have a similar taste and texture to cooked mature breadfruit.

ROASTING WHOLE BREADFRUIT

Roasting normally means cooking whole mature breadfruit directly in hot coals until the skin is charred and blackened. If you would rather cook it in your home oven, remove the stem and place it in a preheated 350ºF oven for 1 hour. The skin should turn brown. Remove the breadfruit from the oven and cut into slices (like the sections of an orange). Peel or slice away the skin and remove the core and it is ready to serve.

ROASTING FROZEN BREADFRUIT

Thaw frozen breadfruit and cut into 1½-inch pieces. Line a 2-inch deep pan with heavy-duty foil and place the breadfruit pieces in it. Pour 2 cups of coconut milk and an equal amount of water over the breadfruit, enough to come within ¾ inch of the top of the pan. Too much liquid will boil over the top of the pan. Cover with foil and bake in a 350ºF oven for 1 hour.

BOILED BREADFRUIT

Thaw frozen breadfruit and cut into 2-inch slices. Place in a saucepan of boiling water, or simmering coconut milk for 30-40 minutes or until fork tender.

Vegetables cooked in coconut milk can have a white residue that may look odd to mainlanders. It is only thickened coconut milk. It is almost tasteless, but If it bothers you, wipe it off. I like it.

BANANAS AND PLANTAINS

COOKING BANANAS AND PLANTAINS

There are two ways to cook green bananas, peeled or unpeeled. Unpeeled bananas should be washed with soap and water to remove any chemicals or insecticide residue. Place in a pot of boiling water for 20-30 minutes or until fork tender. The peels should come off easily. There was one problem with this method (for me); it left a hard-to-clean residue in my "non-stick" pot!

If you wish to cook bananas peeled, cut the ends of the banana and slice along one or more of the ridges and peel. Cook in the same manner as unpeeled. Do not cook peeled and unpeeled bananas together in the same water, as the residue from cooked peels stains the peeled bananas.

Eat hot or cool as a vegetable dish, in coconut cream or cut up in stews

YAMS AND CASSAVA

COOKING YAMS

Cooking Yam (*Dioscorea alata*, purple yam) is easy: boil with the peel on until *fork tender*. Remove from the cooking water and set aside to cool. Dispose of the cooking water. Remove and cut off any parts that were exposed to the boiling water. Peeling isn't much more work than peeling a sweet potato; use the edge of a paring knife to scrape any stubborn peel off. Cut off any hard or undercooked parts then slice into pieces for serving or mashing.

Purple yams can be used in baked goods and confections, adding a striking purple color.

COOKING CASSAVA

Cassava should never be eaten raw. It should be washed thoroughly and cooked until fork tender. Cassava must be boiled to rid it of a harmful enzyme. If thoroughly boiled cassava is safe to eat. The concern is with *bitter* cassava and that variety is not likely to be sold in markets. Risk is slight, however these simple precautions should be observed nonetheless.

Peel and wash the roots, cut them into pieces, and boil them in water. Cassava skin is particularly tough, so rather than peel with a vegetable peeler, it will be easier to make a cut lengthwise through the skin then peel the skin off like a banana or plantain. OK, that may work fine if the roots are fresh. I probably keep them too long before using, which is why I always have to slice the skins off with a paring knife.

A large pot of cassava will take 30—40 minutes to cook. Start to test for doneness after 20 minutes. When the cassava is cooked, **the cooking water should be thrown away**.

There is a *cordon* or woody stem down the center of the root, which needs to be removed after cooking; if you can get a grip on one end you can pull it out, if not, cut the cassava lengthwise and remove it.

Cassava roots, the tough skin is cut lengthwise and stripped with the help of a knife.

DRYING FRUIT, MEAT AND FISH

The techniques of drying or dehydrating foods are really beyond the scope of this book, but there are a couple of recipes that call for them. In these recipes, I will suggest oven drying; it is easy and doesn't require any special equipment. If food drying or dehydrating is your thing, use the methods you think best. You may also find it interesting to research how traditional foods were prepared for Polynesian voyages.

Dried foods are available commercially. Tropical fruits such as Pineapple, Coconut, Mango and Banana are favorites that can be found in health food or specialty stores. Smoked fish can be found at fish and other markets by special order. Hawaiian smoked Ahi and Marlin can be found on-line.

Whether or not dried foods are used in these recipes, they have a place at the lu'au. Dried fruits can be offered as *pupus* (snacks); as well as smoked/dried fish or *Pipi kaula*, (Hawaiian beef jerky) – and they make good snacks to take along Surfing, Sailing or Camping.

CHESTNUTS

American or Chinese chestnuts may substitute for the much larger Tahitian chestnut, *Mape*. Start by laying out your chestnuts on a cutting board. Cut the nuts in half with a sharp knife. Parboil the halves by dropping them into a pot of boiling water and allow the water to return to a boil. After 2 minutes, remove the nuts with a slotted spoon.

Allow the nuts to cool enough to handle but do not wait until they are cold. Hold the nut half in one hand and pinch the husk side with a pliers; the nut should squeeze out of the husk easily along with any "brown skin."

Inspect the nuts for any that have gone bad and discard. At this point the nuts are only partially cooked. If you are making a pâté, boil the nuts for 30 minutes or until you can pierce them with a fork (fork tender).

For pâté (*Ivi Yatha* in Fiji), mash the nuts or grate them finely in a food processor.

If you just want roasted chestnuts, bake the parboiled halves on a shallow baking pan in a 475ºF oven for 30 minutes.

All this works for fresh chestnuts, old or dried out nuts will be a waste of time. Like many other of these ingredients, Asian markets sell them in packages, already peeled, roasted and mashed.

MANGO AND PAPAYA

Mango and Papaya are two very different tropical fruits, however once they have been sliced and the seeds removed there are similar ways to slice the fruit.

BUYING

Ripe mangos may be yellow, or red and partially green. To test for ripeness, press the fruit with your thumb; you should feel a little "give." A ripe mango will have a distinctive aroma.

Ripe Papayas are mostly yellow. Use the same thumb test as you do for mangos.

REMOVING PAPAYA SEEDS

Slice the papaya in half lengthwise. Both halves should contain hundreds of small black round seeds. These should be completely scooped out with a spoon. If you wish, you can wash the seeds and save them for other uses.

REMOVING THE MANGO SEED

Mango has a large flat seed that needs to be avoided when cutting, fortunately this is easy.

The seed of the Mango makes the fruit somewhat flattened when looking down on it. Position the mango on a cutting board with the flattened sides facing left and right from you. Use a sharp knife to cut down one side about ¼ inches out from the center. As you slice down you may feel the seed; use it to guide your slice down. Do the same for the other side. Next, pare the fruit from both edges of the seed. You should have two mango "cheeks" and two mango "fingers. Discard the seed, there is not much more fruit you can pare off.

There is a kitchen gadget that slices around the seed (you may have seen a similar gadget that slices apples). The mango slicer is positioned over the end of the mango and pressed down, leaving two cheeks and the seed. The slicer leaves a good portion of fruit on the ends of the seed; frugal cooks will want to pare it off and use it for chutneys or salads or just eat it as-is.

CUTTING THE RIPE FRUIT

At this point, you should have fruit, cut in half. Score the insides of the fruit lengthwise and across (½ - 1 inch squares) but don't cut through the peel.

Papaya: Use a soup spoon to scoop out the fruit pieces.

Mango: Turn the "cheeks" inside out and use a sharp paring knife to cut out the mango pieces.

GRATING THE GREEN FRUIT

Both green mangos and green papayas can used in puddings or salads by grating the flesh with a box grater. Mangos should be peeled with the seed in. Papayas should be peeled, cleaned and the large pieces grated.

Special Instruction for using Green Papaya: Green papaya should be soaked in water for at least 30 minutes, rinsed and drained before consuming or used in recipes, to remove any bitterness.

PINEAPPLE

BUYING AND STORING

Pineapples imported into the US from several places: Hawaii (preferably), Honduras and other Central American countries. The fruit is also grown in tropical Australia, Tahiti, India and South Africa. Once picked they will never get any riper; if left too long before using, they will spoil. The best thing is to buy your pineapple the day you intend to use it, but no more than 2 days before.

Examine the pineapple in the store; some green is fine, but it should be yellow or golden, particularly near the bottom. Smell the base of the fruit, it should smell like pineapple but not vinegary or fermented.

If you need to keep it for a few days, remember it will never get any riper so the best thing to do is keep it in the refrigerator; if too cold (below 45°F) it will get watery, if stored too warm it will start to ferment.

Pineapple can be found canned in several forms, sliced, diced or crushed. The fruit is picked and packed, usually the same day, so freshness is assured. Pineapple is very sweet and should not need any additional sweetener. The contents label on the can should say "Pineapple, Pineapple Juice" only. If it doesn't, look for another brand. The biggest advantage to canned pineapple, besides not having to prepare it yourself, is storability. You can always keep some on the shelf for whenever you need it.

CUTTING A PINEAPPLE

Start by slicing off the crown of leaves and about ½ inch of the pineapple off the top and bottom.

Continued next page ...

Stand the pineapple on its base. Looking down, notice there are dark spots or "eyes" along the top edges. Use a sharp knife, placed behind the eye and slice down the side following the curve of the pineapple

Look along cut edge for a line of *eyes* running down the side. This is where you want to make your next slice. Keep slicing off the next line of *eyes* until you have completely peeled the pineapple. Be careful not to slice so deeply as to cut away too much good fruit. If you miss any *eyes*, use a paring knife to cut them out individually.

Quarter the pineapple lengthwise and cut out the hard core. At this point, it's ready to eat or cut into slices, spears, chunks.

MAKING COOKING PACKAGES

TARO LEAVES

There are a few recipes, such as *Lu pulu*, *Palusami* and *Laulau* that call for wrapping ingredients in taro leaves before cooking. These leaves are an edible ingredient in the recipe, but they hold loose or wet ingredients while they cook. Because the uncooked taro leaf packages soften during cooking, they must be wrapped in *Ti* leaves or aluminum foil.

Wash leaves and remove the outer part of the heavy veins to make them more flexible. Select 4 or 5 whole, relatively young leaves, without holes or tears, one large and 3 or 4 smaller ones.

Place the largest leaf in the upturned palm of your hand and layer the remaining leaves, arranging them to make a surface with no holes. Cup your hand and press the leaves down to make a small hollow to hold coconut cream or chunks of meat, depending on the recipe.

For packages that hold liquid ingredients, carefully bring the outer edges up into a pouch to enclose the ingredients, wrap the leaf package in something more durable, such a large square of foil (12"X12"), and seal the pouch closed.

For packages that hold solid ingredients (Laulau), fold the sides in to cover the contents then fold the ends inwards, or fold the sides in and roll it up like a burrito. You should have a small bundle that will need to be wrapped in ti leaves or foil before cooking. Some cooks may wrap a few more leaves around the bundle for more taro leaf flavor. Of course, you should do that before you put on the outer *ti*, banana or foil wrapper!

BANANA LEAVES

Banana leaves can be purchased at Asian or Hispanic markets and are not too expensive. They are sold folded in bundles ready to use. Remove the bundle from the package and carefully unfold; there are usually two or more full leaves, folded. Lay one out on a table or a counter top. Each open leaf should be about 2 feet wide.

Remove the stem by cutting down each side of the stem with a scissors. Be careful not to tear the leaf. Depending on the size of the food you will be wrapping, you will need pieces approximately 12"x12" to 12"x18." The width of half a leaf should be close to 12" so there will be no need to cut that dimension.

Inspect the leaf for holes and tears; you will have to work around them. Measure off the width you want and make a small cut to start a tear; the leaf should tear straight across the leaf. Set the pieces aside until you have enough for whatever you will be cooking.

Banana leaf is "stiff" and has a tendency to break or split when folded, so you will have to soften them before using. Hold the leaf pieces (dark green side up) over a barbecue grill or a stovetop burner until they become shiny; this should take only a few moments. Make sure you soften the whole leaf, but do let it stay on the heat long enough to burn. Notice that there is a direction, perpendicular to the stem, where the leaf folds (and tears) easily.

Wrapping is simple. Each package starts with a piece of leaf, laid flat on your work surface, dark side up. The uncooked food (fish, meat or "pudding") is placed in the center. Fold one side of the leaf over the food, then fold the other side over food. Fold one end of the package over and then fold the other end. You should have a neat package, folded, approximately, into thirds. Use kitchen string to tie the package closed.

Banana leaf wrapping is simpler than wrapping with ti leaves, in most cases. Banana leaves are easier to obtain and cost less too. Banana leaf packages are usually steamed, but can be oven baked or roasted in an earth oven.

TI LEAVES

Ti (ki) leaves are tough wrappers to protect delicate food. The leaves impart a subtle fragrance that Islanders like. You may find ti growing as houseplants at your friends or neighbors, but the leaves are usually too small for wrapping food.

The smallest size ti leaves for cooking are about 20-inches by 6-inches. Larger items (e.g. fish) will need larger ti leaves.

You are most likely to find ti leaves for sale at florist shops and sometimes on-line. Be careful of chemical treatments, such as pesticides and preservatives; check with your florist. Although you willnot eat ti leaves, they will be in contact with food. Wash leaves thoroughly with dishwashing soap and rinse well before using.

Small food items are wrapped *laulau pi'ao* style and larger items were wrapped in *laulau lawalu* style (Titcomb, 1972: 25).

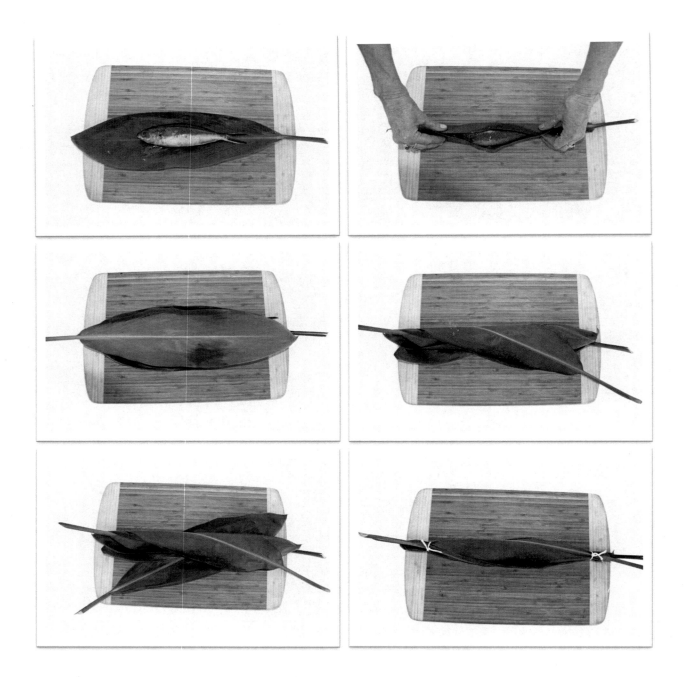

Making *Laulau Lawalu*: Place a fish on top of a ti leaf, shiny side up (the ti leaf not the fish!). The leaf should be wide enough to almost wrap around the fish and long enough to tie off the ends. Cover the fish with another ti leaf (shiny side down), with the tip of this leaf pointing in the alternate direction. Fold the bottom leaf up and tuck the top leaf under the bottom leaf. (You may need a helper to hold it together while you do the next steps) Wrap a third leaf (alternating direction again) diagonally around the other two. Wrap a fourth leaf diagonally in the other direction. Make the package snug and tie the gathered stems and ends tightly with kitchen string.

Making *Laulau Pi'ao:* Fold a ti leaf in half but twist the leaf so that the shiny halves face the same way. This will make an open pouch. Put pieces of fish (or whatever you want) in the pouch. Fold another leaf in the same manner. Put the filled pouch inside the other, face-to-face so that the food is enclosed. Place the combined pouch on one or more ti leaves and bring the stems and ends up to hold the pouches together. Make the package snug and tie the gathered stems and ends tightly with kitchen string.

OTHER COOKING PACKAGES

- Aluminum foil. Anything you can do with a leaf wrapper can be done with foil. I have used foil to cook a whole skipjack tuna (bonito, aku) in a campfire and have seen Yap islanders do the same with reef fish over a makeshift grill. Foil is available everywhere on the mainland and comes in various convenient sizes. Wrap leaf packages in foil to keep them from leaking. Remember that cleanup is easier when you line your baking pans with foil and a layer of foil under your wrapped packages will catch any leaks.

- Cooking Parchment. Fish and some other foods can be wrapped in parchment, Use only for oven cooking, not to be used in contact with flames, direct heat or embers.

- Corn husks. This and banana leaves are used to cook food in Latin America. Works best for steaming food. Soak well before using to make them pliable.

- Ramekins and baking dishes. The only reason the Islanders of old used leaf packages was because they did not have fireproof cooking containers. Many recipes could eliminate wrappings entirely by cooking in a casserole, roasting pan, or in a cooking pot.

- Aluminum "pot-pie" and other disposable foil baking dishes work well for Island foods. Seal contents with foil. I've used pot-pie dishes to make individual servings of *palusami* (page 84) and *lu pulu* (page 85).

"Puddings" are what the early English explorers called the mashed combination of cooked starchy vegetables and fruit. The Tahitians called it Po'e. Po'e can be sweet or savory. There are two kinds of po'e, one that is the consistancy of a thick porridge and one that is re-cooked, into something like a bread pudding.

Re-cooked po'e is wrapped in banana leaves and steamed, baked or roasted. (The po'e pictured has been roasted over a fire) These small loaves are cut into pieces and eaten with sweetened coconut cream.

Pudding recipes that use banana leaves: Vakalolo (page 110), Lap Lap (page 111), Faikakai (page 88) and Mape (page 93)

Po'e can also be cooked in baking dishes in an oven, e.g. Po'e Mai'a (page 92)

PACIFIC ISLAND RECIPES

I opened a laulau, the bulgy bundle enclosed in ti leaves tied with a fiber string, that we saw prepared in the afternoon. It had a strange flavor that combined the richness of pork, the saline taste of salt salmon and the oily sweetness of butterfish. There was a grab-bag delight and suspense in opening those leaf-wrapped items; one could never tell what amazing thing might be inside.

Hula Moons, Don Blanding 1945

Every island has a word for a feast, *Lu'au, Hakari, Fiafia, Tama'ara'a, Katoanga, Umukai, Magiti*, but they all mean the same thing: a celebration with the traditional foods of their islands.

The recipes here are family style recipes. Ideally, they should be made with the ingredients and techniques that are used in the Islands; unfortunately, that is not always possible or practical when you don't live in the Islands. Substitute ingredients where you must.

My goal is to present recipes that are as authentic as possible for Mainland cooks working in their own kitchens. The cooking techniques have been things I've seen or discovered for myself or have learned from Islanders who cook in Western kitchens.

Anyone who has been to a lu'au will recognize some of these island recipes and some will be new. Some may surprise you, for instance, *pink potato salad*. There are recipes for "tortillas" (*Chapatis* and *Titiyas*) and, I just had to add a few "Imaginary South Seas Recipes" because some people expect it. I will explain why later.

This would be a good place to mention that Mainland food can have a place on the Island menu too. barbequed ribs and chops, steak and chicken are good choices. Certainly, any fish or shellfish (e.g., lobster, crab or shrimp) are things Islanders would make for themselves. Fresh raw tuna (sashimi) or any grilled fish transform into Island dishes when served with *Finadene* or *Miti Viti*.

Finally, before we begin, these recipes are only a cross section of the foods you will find in Oceania. Furthermore, every family has their own way of doing things. Some Islanders may say "Oh yes, that's good, but we do such and such." I encourage the reader to use this as a starting point and listen to what Islanders have to say. Hopefully they will invite you to eat as well, and in that case,

Kana Vakavinaka! – Eat Well!

WESTERN POLYNESIA

The first Polynesian cultures, Tonga and Samoa were founded some 3,000 years ago. Their descendants went on to settle in Tuvalu, Tokelau, Niue and the islands of Rotuma, Wallis and Futuna; some continued as far West as Micronesia (e.g. Nukuoro, Kapingamarangi) and Melanesia (e.g. Tikopia, Ontong Java). Each colony then developed independently.

The Kingdom of Tonga is an archipelago of 176 islands (52 of which are inhabited) and the only monarchy in the Pacific. Tongans have had extensive interaction with the Fijians and both cultures and peoples show the influences in both directions.

Samoa is divided into two political entities. but both are a single culture with a common language.

- American Samoa is an unincorporated territory of the United States, bestowing American citizenship and substantial aide. The islands are Tutuila, the largest and most populous, along with the Manu'a Islands and Swains Island.

- The Independent State of Samoa, formerly known as Western Samoa and now simply referred to as Samoa. The two major islands are Upolu, the most populous and Savai'i, the largest.

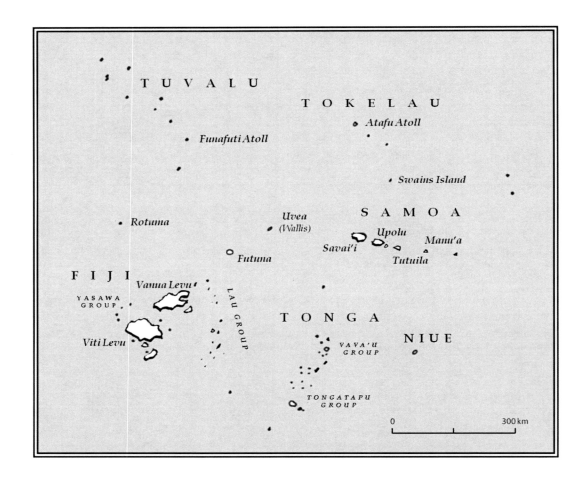

SOSI PE'EPE'E – COCONUT SAUCE (SAMOA)

This savory sauce (*sosi*) is used in various recipes across Oceania. Pre-European condiments for food were simply salt water and coconut milk; morsels of food were dipped in bowls of each to soften and flavor the food. *Miti Ha'ari* from Tahiti is a dipping sauce that combines equal parts seawater and coconut milk; *Sosi Pe'epe'e* is the next step. Onion adds the savory component to the coconut cream.

- 1 medium **onion**
- 1 can **coconut cream** (14 oz) or coconut milk
- ½-1 teaspoon **salt** (to taste)
- 1 tablespoon **all purpose flour** (optional if using coconut milk)

Chop the onion into ¼ - ½ inch dice. Pour the coconut milk into a saucepan; add the onions and salt. Bring the sauce to a simmer (not quite boiling). Continue to simmer and stir until the onions are soft, about 5 minutes.

For a thicker sauce, add 1 Tbsp of flour, mixed well in ½-cup cool water, to the simmering sauce. Continue to simmer and stir until the sauce thickens.

FA'ALIFU – BOILED VEGETABLES (SAMOA)

Fa'alifu is a dish of boiled vegetables *(saka)* in a savory coconut sauce. Taro (talo, kalo) is normally prepared this way but any starchy Island vegetable can be used. Westerners may find boiled taro, yams and green bananas bland when eaten alone but Islanders prefer the subtle flavors (and they are filling). When served with *Sosi Pe'epe'e*, Island Vegetables are a savory treat for Westerners and Islanders alike.

To prepare and boil Starchy Island Vegetables:

Taro see page 62
Breadfruit see page 65
Bananas and Plantains see page 66
Yams and Cassava see page 66
Sweet Potatoes, same as Yams, page 66

Cut the boiled vegetables into serving sized pieces (1 ½ inch chunks), but leave the bananas whole. Prepare *Sosi Pe'epe'e*, thin or thick, to your taste. Pour over cooked vegetables while they are still hot. Allow diners to serve themselves from the pot or the calabash.

FAI'AI – BAKED COCONUT CREAM (SAMOA)

When pe'epe'e (coconut cream) is cooked and thickens into curds, it is called fai'ai. Here are a few *fai'ai* dishes adapted for the home kitchen that are cooked in baking dishes.

FAI'AI VATIA – This dish is very similar to Hawaiian *Haupia*, a sweet coconut cream custard when sugar is added.

- 2 (14 oz) cans **coconut milk**
- 1 cup **sugar**
- 1 cup **water**
- 6 oz **cornstarch** (or Arrowroot starch)

Mix the water, sugar, and cornstarch in a heavy sauce pan, stirring constantly, slowly bringing the temperature to a simmer. Slowly add the coconut milk, stirring constantly.

When the mixture is smooth and thick, pour the mixture into a clean 8 inch square pan. Cool to room temperature, and then chill to firm. Cut the fai'ai into 1—2 inch squares. Serve on banana leaf squares.

FAI'AI LIMU – *Coconut cream and seaweed*

- 4 cups **limu** (any variety except the green grape-like seaweed)
- 1 can **coconut cream** (14 oz)
- ½ chopped **onion**
- ¼ teaspoon **salt**

The limu should be washed of sand and other foreign matter before starting. It does not need to be chopped since it will dissolve in the cooking process. (See limu, page 48)

Mix all ingredients in a bowl and transfer to a baking dish. Cover with aluminum foil. Bake in a 350°F oven for 1 hour. Serve with taro, breadfruit, cooked green banana

FAI'AI VALUVALU – *Coconut cream and Yam*

- 4 cups of grated **ufi** (yam)
- 1 can **coconut cream** (14 oz) or coconut milk

Mix ingredients in a bowl and transfer to a baking dish. Cover with aluminum foil. Bake in a 350°F oven for 1 hour. Serve with taro, breadfruit, cooked green banana

FAI'AI ESI – *Coconut cream and Papaya.*

- 4 cups **esi** (papaya) peeled, seeded, ½ inch slices
- 1 can **coconut cream** (14 oz)

Mix ingredients in a baking dish. Cover with aluminum foil. Bake in a 350°F for 1 hour

POVI MASIMA - BEEF BRISKET (SAMOA)

Sometimes it's hard to believe Samoans existed without "Corned Beef" or "Salt Beef" as the English call it. They would eat it every day if they had it; they sometimes buy it by the barrel. Here are two methods to make *Povi Masima* at home.

- 3-4 pounds **beef brisket**
- 1 **spice package** if included with the brisket
- 1 large **onion**, chopped (optional)
- 1 teaspoon **liquid smoke** flavoring

If the brisket comes with cooking instructions, you may follow those or one of the methods that follow:

Method 1, Stove Top:

Put all the ingredients in a pot with a lid. Add water to cover the brisket. Bring to a boil and then reduce to a simmer. Cook covered for 3-5 hours. Expect the brisket to shrink some in the cooking.

Method 2, Slow Cooker:

Place all the ingredients in the Slow Cooker with 1 cup of water. Cover and cook on low for 10-12 hours.

To serve, cut thin slices across the grain. Leftovers can be used in other recipes in place of canned corned beef (*pisupo*).

PISUPO WITH ONIONS - CORNED BEEF (SAMOA)

"The Samoans are so crazy about pisupo that after grace they often add. "Lord we love you more than pisupo fried in onions." — *More Curious Than Cautious: A Survivor's Adventure through Paradise*, Peter Frasier (2010). You can decide for yourselves.

- 1 large can **pisupo** (canned corned beef)
- 1 cup chopped **onions**

Sauté pisupo and onions in a pan until the onions are soft. Serve hot.

SAPASUI - "CHOP SUEY" (SAMOA)

The last time I was in Apia, Samoa the Chinese restaurants did not serve *sapasui*. *Sapasui* is the Samoan pronunciation of "chop suey" which, I believe means "fake Chinese food" in Cantonese. The basis of the dish is bean thread noodle, also known as Chinese vermicelli or *Saifun*. The Samoan word is *lialia*, meaning, 'to twirl." Samoan "chop suey" tastes particularly good when accompanied by a cold bottle of Vailima beer.

Samoans will make this with fattier cuts of meat. You may wish to use leaner cuts or chicken.

- 1 8.8 oz package (250g) **Saifun, bean thread noodles** (not rice noodles!)
- 2 pounds **beef** (chuck steak) or chicken or corned beef
- 2 tablespoon **vegetable oil**
- 5 cloves **garlic**, chopped
- 1 medium **onion**, chopped
- 1 inch piece **ginger**, grated
- 1 cup **beef or chicken broth** or water with bouillon cube
- 1 cup mixed **carrots and peas** (frozen [thawed] or canned)
- ¼ cup **soy sauce**
- 6 stalks **green onion**, chopped

Bring 3 quarts water to a boil. Add the noodles and turn off heat. Soak the noodles until soft. The Chinese prefer their noodles long and slurpy, Samoans like them shorter. You can snip the noodles into smaller pieces (3"-6") with scissors (push the points of the scissors into the pot of noodles and snip away).

Cut the meat into 1 inch pieces. Heat vegetable oil in a large pot over medium heat and sauté the meat for 3 minutes or until cooked through. Canned corned beef is already cooked so just cook enough to heat through

Add garlic, onions and ginger and continue cooking until the onions soften. Add broth and soy sauce and cook 5 more minutes. Drain noodles and stir into meat mixture along with peas and carrots. (You may have to add more liquid as needed, as the noodles tend to absorb the liquid. Some people like *sapasui* with a lot of liquid, some like it drier. You can add water, stock or soy sauce to get it the way you like it. Garnish with chopped green onions.

Serve Hot with rice, taro, or cooked green bananas. Leftovers are good reheated and served the next day.

PALUSAMI – TARO LEAF & COCONUT CREAM (SAMOA)

I have an acquaintance, who is married to a Samoan woman; they live in American Samoa. We were talking about Samoan food the last time I saw him, when he announced that he "loved" *palusami*. Well, I'm extremely fond of it myself, but there was something in Louie's far off gaze and tone of voice that made it sound like he was confessing to an illicit love affair. He really does *love palusami*... You will too.

Proper Palusami exerts a magic spell on those who have eaten it. The indispensible ingredient is taro leaf (*fafa, lu'au*). I've tried substituting all kinds of greens from Mainland markets and nothing comes closer than Spinach or Chard; they are similar to taro leaf, but not the same. So, if you want the kind of *palusami* that makes men weak with desire, you must get the real thing—taro leaf.

- 40 ounces **coconut cream** or coconut milk
- 1 large **onion** (chopped, small dice)
- 1-2 teaspoons **salt** (to taste)
- 1 tablespoon **all purpose flour** (optional if using coconut milk)
- 40+ young **taro leaves** (no substitution in this recipe)
- 10 squares (12"x12") of **aluminum foil**

Prepare the coconut cream by placing coconut milk, onions, salt and optionally 1 Tbsp of flour, mixed well in ½-cup cool water, into a large bowl or pot. Mix thoroughly.

Pare down the thick stem and veins of the taro leaves and break off the tip of each leaf (Samoans claim it's bitter). Use one big leaf and 3 or 4 (or more if you like) smaller leaves. You can break a bigger leaf to make a smaller leaf if you need too.

Place one large leaf in your left hand, palm up. Place the remaining 3 or 4 leaves on top of each other, rotating each to cover evenly. Cup your left hand slightly, pressing down on the leaves with your right hand to form a bowl to hold the coconut cream.

Pour about ¼ cup of coconut cream mixture into the leaf bowl (more or less, don't overfill) and bring up the leaves to enclose the cream, making the leaves into a pouch. Wrap the taro leaf pouch with a square of aluminum foil (a pouch within a pouch), twisting the top to seal and hold the taro leaf package tight.

Make as many *palusami* as you have taro leaf and coconut cream to make them; you will eat them all.

Boil water in a large steamer pot, Place *palusami* in the steamer basket and steam for 90 minutes, checking occasionally to see if there is enough water.

Alternatly, place the *palusami* in a baking pan. Cover the pan with foil and cook in a pre-heated 350° F oven for 60 - 90 minutes.

Serve with fish, cooked taro, breadfruit or boiled bananas.

PALUSAMI - CASSEROLE (SAMOA)

The classic method of making palusami required making a package from whole young taro leaves, wrapped in ti leaves, because, at one time, that was the only way to cook loose or liquid ingredients. Here on the Mainland, it is hard enough just to get, old torn taro leaves, although, I recently found dried taro leaves at a Filipino market, which could be reconstitued just for dishes like this.

This recipe is made differently but the taste is the same. The casserole version can use the leafy greens that couldn't be used in the traditional method: spinach, chard or older torn taro leaves. Cook Islanders make a similar dish called *Rukau*. The Fijian name is *Rourou*.

- 2 pounds **taro leaf**, fresh spinach or chard
- 14 ounces **coconut cream** or coconut milk
- 1 medium **onion**
- ½-1 teaspoon **salt** (to taste)
- 1 tablespoon of **all purpose flour** (optional if using coconut milk)

If you are using taro leaves, cut the taro leaves into ½ inch strips, boil for 40 minutes, discard the liquid and strain in a collander Empty the collander of a cutting board and chop into bite sized pieces. See page 63 for more information about cooking taro leaves and stems.

If you are using fresh spinach, wash thoroughly to remove dirt and grit. Remove stems. If you are using chard, wash thoroughly and tear into pieces, chop stems into bite size pieces.

Prepare a coconut sauce by combining coconut milk, onions, salt (and optionally 1 Tbsp of flour, mixed well in ½-cup cool water) into a large bowl or pot. Mix thoroughly.

Layer the leaves in the bottom of deep casserole dish (9x13 inch?). Don't worry about how full the dish is because the leaves will wilt as they cook. Pour the coconut milk mixture over the leaves, pressing down with a spoon. Don't fill to the rim, leave about ¾ inch. Cover tightly with a lid or aluminum foil.

Bake in a preheated 350° F oven for 45 to 55 minutes or until the greens have completely wilted and the coconut cream has thickened. Cool for 10 minutes before serving.

Easier Method:

At Pacific Islander festivals on the Mainland, some food vendors find the traditional method of making palusami too time consuming to serve large numbers of people, so they may use the following method. You can use spinach or chard.

Precook chopped taro leaves per instruction on page 63. Spinach or chard per the paragraphs above. Prepare *Sosi Pe'epe'e* (page 79). Add the cooked greens and simmer for at least 20 minutes to incorporate the flavors, Serve.

GOLAI HAGUN SUNI (GUAM):

The Chamorro of the Marianas make something similar to *Palusami*, but use fresh taro leaves, stems, onions and pieces of taro corm stewed in coconut milk, to which they add tumeric and lemon juice.

LU PULU - TARO LEAVES & CORNED BEEF (TONGA)

Lu pulu is a combination of *palusami* and *pisupo*. This version illustrates a simple way to make it at home; alternately, you can use any method of preparing *palusami*, adding corn beef.

- 2 pounds **taro leaf** or chard or fresh, frozen or canned spinach
- 2 15 oz cans **corned beef** (*Pisupo*) or *Povi Masima*, chopped
- 1 medium **onion**
- 1 can **coconut cream** (14 oz)
- ½-1 teaspoon **salt** (to taste)

The exact quantities are determined by the amounts of each ingredient you have on hand and how much you wish to make.

Wash the greens of any dirt or grit. If you are using old or torn taro leaf or spinach, remove the stems and discard them. If you are using chard, remove the stems and chop into small pieces to use. Rough chop all greens. Do not cook the chard or spinach but do parboil taro leaves for 20 minutes, drain and pat dry with a towel.

Casserole Method:

Place the taro/greens in a large bowl and add onions, coconut milk and salt. The mixture should look more green than white. Break up the corned beef and mix it with the other ingredients. Pour into a 9x13 inch baking dish. Leave a little space at to the top of the dish (so it won't bubble over). Make sure the corned beef is evenly distributed in the baking dish. If there is any lu pulu mix left, use ramekins to cook the extra. Cover tightly with a lid or aluminum foil.

Place the dish on a baking tray (you may wish to line it with foil for easy cleanup) and put into a preheated 350° F oven for 45 to 55 minutes.

A More Traditional Method:

Press a 12 inch square of aluminum foil into a small soup bowl. Arrange 4 or 5 young taro leaves or several layers of chopped greens to form a bowl within the bowl of foil and top with about 1 tablespoon of corned beef. Pour ¼ cup (or less, just don't overfill) of uncooked *sosi pe'epe'e* on top of that. Fold up the foil into a tight pouch; twist the top to seal. Make as many pouches as you want, or until you run out of ingredients.

Place the foil pouches on a baking tray (you may wish to line it with foil for easy cleanup) and put into a preheated 350° F oven for 45 to 55 minutes. (or steam the pouches for 55 minutes)

KARA (SOLOMON ISLANDS):

In the Solomon Islands, there is a similar dish, called *Kara*. Peel, wash and grate fresh cassava (available grated in Asian markets). Squeeze out the liquid.

Use either method above, place a layer of grated cassava on top of the greens, coconut milk, onions and salt, then a layer of corned beef.

LO'I FEKE - OCTOPUS IN COCONUT CREAM (TONGA)

When Tongans talk about food there is usually a discussion about what food they like best: *feke* always ranks high. Octopus can be truly delicious or just ok. I've had both, proper cooking is the key. Mainlanders are lucky because it isn't necessary to capture, clean and cook these creatures; they are often available in Asian markets, already cooked and packaged in small portions (one or two tentacles). This is good for two reasons: they are usually cooked properly and you don't have to buy more than you want (or are ready to try).

- 1 medium **onion**
- 1 can (14 oz) **coconut cream** or coconut milk
- ½-1 teaspoon **salt** (to taste)
- 1 pound cooked **octopus**, or squid
- 1 tablespoon of **all purpose flour**

Chop the onion into ¼ - ½-inch dice. Pour the coconut milk into a saucepan; add the onions and salt. Bring the sauce to a simmer (not quite boiling). Continue to simmer and stir until the onions are soft, about 5 minutes.

For a thicker sauce, add 1 Tbsp of flour, mixed well in ½-cup cool water, to the simmering sauce. Continue to simmer and stir until the sauce thickens.

Cut cooked octopus, cut it into bite size pieces (or ½-inch dice). Add the octopus pieces to the hot coconut sauce and simmer for one minute to incorporate the flavors and heat through.

Serve with cooked taro, breadfruit or boiled bananas.

SQUID LU'AU (HAWAII)

In Hawaii, a similar recipe that incorporates young taro leaves (lu'au). It's made wih octopus but called *Squid Lu'au*. Hawaiian locals are in the habit of calling an octopus a squid. You could use cooked squid (calamari); it's easier to find in Western markets. See page 46 for preparing octopus and squid.

There is a Tahitian recipe, *Poulet Fafa* and the Hawaiian version, *Chicken Lu'au* that can be adapted to *Squid Lu'au* by substituting cooked octopus or squid for the chicken (see page 94). It should look more green than white. It will look ghastly, but it's delicious.

If you are using uncooked squid (calamari) clean the squid and slice into rings. Small tentacles may be kept whole. Sauté squid and onions in butter until the onions are soft and translucent

Add the cooked squid or octopus to the *lu'au* sauce and simmer for a few minutes to incorporate the flavors and heat through.

Note: See page 94 for a similar recipe using chicken.

KAPISI PULU - CORNED BEEF & CABBAGE (TONGA)

Instead of taro leaves, cabbage leaves are used to make a pouch to cook the coconut cream and corned beef. This isn't the stuffed cabbage my mother used to make.

- 1 medium **onion**
- 2 cans **coconut milk** (14 oz) or equivalent fresh coconut milk
- 2 teaspoons **salt** (to taste)
- large **cabbage leaves** (4-6 per serving)
- **corned beef** (*Pisupo*) or *Povi Masima*, chopped
- 1 **tomato**, chopped (optional)
- Squares (12"x12") **aluminum foil**

Chop the onion into ¼ - ½ inch dice. Put the onions into a bowl; add the coconut milk and salt.

Select large cabbage leaves with no holes. Trim down any thick ribs. If the leaves are too stiff to form a cup in your hand, blanch in boiling water for a few seconds. Pat dry and allow to cool.

Place a square of foil on a soup bowl and press it down to make a foil bowl. Layer 3 or 4 cabbage leaves on top, pressing down into the bowl to help shape the leaves. Place a portion of corned beef, some chopped cabbage and tomatoes into the cabbage leaf bowl.

Pour about ¼ - ½ cup of coconut milk mixture into the leaf bowl (as much as it will hold without leaking) and start to bring up the outside edges of cabbage and foil the to enclose the contents, forming a tight pouch. Twist or pinch the aluminum foil closed to seal the package.

Place the packages *on* a baking tray and cook in a conventional oven for about 45 to 55 minutes at 350° F. (or steam the pouches for 55 minutes)

This technique also works well with other meats: pork (*lu puaka*), mutton flaps (*lu sipi*) and fish (*lu ika*).

Serve with taro, yam or boiled banana.

PISUPO AND CABBAGE (SAMOA)

- 1 medium **onion**
- 1 medium **cabbage**
- 1 can (12 ounces) **corned beef** (Pisupo)
- 2 **tomatoes**, chopped

Both Tongans and Samoans cook *kapisi* this way; it is simpler to make than the recipe above.

Immerse the unopened can of corned beef in boiling water for 5 minutes to melt the fat. Open the can and drain off most of the fat. Heat a large pot or frying pan. Add the corned beef and chopped onions. Stir-fry for 3-4 minutes.

Chop cabbage into bite-sized pieces (use your own discretion). Add cabbage, tomatoes, and a little water. Lower the heat to a simmer and cook until cabbage is soft (5-10 minutes) stirring often.

FAIKAKAI TOPAI - DUMPLINGS IN SYRUP (TONGA)

Polynesia is known for "puddings," which is what the first Europeans called them. The Tahitians have *po'e*; the Samoans have *fa'ausi*. Faikakai is what you find in Tonga, where the cooked "puddings" are cut up into little dumplings.

If you feel like something sweet these boiled dumplings in warm coconut syrup will fill the bill. Dumplings can be made with other Island ingredients for variety.

TOPAI (FLOUR DUMPLINGS):

- 2 cups **all purpose flour** (*topai*)
- 1 tablespoon **baking powder**
- 1-2 cups of cold **water**
- ½ teaspoon of **salt**

Sift flour, salt and baking powder into a bowl. Pour in just enough cold water to make a stiff batter.

Drop rounded tablespoons of batter into boiling water. If you dip the spoon in the hot water each time before taking a spoonful of batter, it will come off the spoon easier. Boil for about 10 minutes; dumpling should float. Remove from the water and let them cool a bit. Cut the dumplings into ½-1 inch pieces

LOLO (COCONUT SYRUP):

- 1 cup of **sugar**
- ¼ cup of **water**
- 2 cups of **coconut cream**, canned or fresh

Put the sugar and water in a heavy saucepan and melt over gentle heat, stirring until the sugar caramelizes to a golden brown. Add the coconut cream and stir continuously until well mixed and thickened. **Be very careful, the pot may boil up rapidly.** Take it off the fire if that happens. Keep stirring until cream and syrup are mixed well, and turn off the heat.

Place the cut dumplings on a serving dish covered with coconut syrup.

Flour dumplings (topai) are only one type of dumpling; they can be made with more traditional Island ingredients, for example:

FAIKAKAI NGOU'A	Cassava flour and chopped precooked taro leaves
FAIKAKAI MALIMALI	Flour and ripe bananas, mashed
FAIKAKAI MEI	Mature breadfruit, mashed
FAIKAKAI MANIOKE TAMA	Cassava, grated and squeezed dry

SUAFA'I – BANANA SOUP (SAMOA)

Suafa'i is eaten for breakfast or as a dessert. This is one way to use those bananas you've left on the counter too long—the ones starting to turn black. Tapioca pearls give it a chewy texture.

- 8 ripe **bananas** (*fa'i* in Samoa, cavendish on the mainland)
- 4 cups **water**
- ½ cup small **tapioca pearls**
- 1 cup **coconut milk** or equivalent fresh coconut milk
- ¼ cup sugar (optional)

Roughly chop the bananas and add them to a saucepan with the water. Bring to a boil, then reduce to a slow boil and cook for 20 minutes. Smash any large chunks of banana with a fork or a whisk.

Reduce heat to a simmer. Sprinkle in tapioca pearls, a little at a time, stirring to keep them from clumping. Next add the coconut milk and continue to simmer for another 15 minutes. Tapioca pearls are done when they turn from opaque to translucent. Taste for sweetness; if you think it should be sweeter, add sugar.

Allow the "soup" to cool before serving. You can also chill it in the fridge and serve it as a snack.

How Many Does That Serve?

I DON'T KNOW HOW MANY PEOPLE MY RECIPES WILL SERVE and I've given up trying to figure it out.

My breaking point came when I was researching a recipe for Fruit Bat aka Flying Fox. Those strange and beautiful flying mammals may have less meat than a pigeon, but they are cooked and eaten with gusto in Samoa and Guam. I've eaten a small portion of cooked fruit bat and it was ok, but I probably won't be having it again.

Because there is not much meat, the skin is eaten as well. The problem is, the animal is covered in a fine black fur. One recipe from Guam started by instructing the cook to shampoo the fur; you're expected to eat it! This is a showstopper for most non-islanders and the recipe's author knew it, because at the end he wrote:

Serves 2 Chamorros or 15 Haoles

That's when I realized, how can I begin to estimate servings? I'm taking the sensible (lazy) way out and leaving it up to you.

TO'OKUTU - DOUGH BALLS (TONGA)

This is a basic village breakfast, lunch, dinner and rainy day food, to be eaten while drinking cups of hot sugary tea. They are like dumpling, but dense and chewy. Dough balls are not exclusively Tongan; I have had something similar in Fiji and suspect they are made wherever the locals can get cheap imported flour. In Tahiti, a similar recipe, called *'ipo*, adds sugar to the mix. The baking powder was my idea otherwise; non-islanders might find them too dense.

- 3 cups **all purpose flour**
- 2 teaspoons **baking powder**
- 1 cup **coconut**, grated
- ½ teaspoon **salt**
- 3 cups cold-**water**

Sift flour and baking powder into a bowl, add salt and grated coconut and mix well. Add just enough cold water to make stiff dough. Mix until the dough comes away from the bowl. Flour your hands and make small balls of dough (2-3").

Place dough balls on a buttered cookie sheet and cover aluminum foil. Bake for one hour @ 325° F.

Note: You could also steam the dough balls in a steamer. Boil water in a large steamer pot, Place *dough balls* in the steamer basket and steam for one hour, checking occasionally to see if there is enough water.

Allow to cool enough to handle before serving.

Dough Balls for Breakfast – Naviti Island, Fiji

EASTERN POLYNESIA

About 500-1000 years after the founding of Western Polynesia, Samoan explorers ventured far to the east to settle new colonies. Those colonies lost contact with, and were forgotten by their home islands. In isolation, the eastern colonies developed new societies and continued to expand across the Pacific. Hawaii, New Zealand, Easter Island, the Society Islands, the Cook Islands, the Marquesas, the Australs, and the Tuamotus, are classified as Eastern Polynesia, a separate branch of the Polynesian family. "Eastern" in this context is a cultural and linguistic distinction, rather than geographic.

The first colonies were probably founded in the Marquesas, spreading out from there to Tahiti and Easter Island. Tahitians settled in the Cook Islands. Marquesans, followed by Tahitians, settled Hawaii starting 1500 years ago. The ancestors of the Maori migrated from the Cook Islands to New Zealand around 700 years ago.

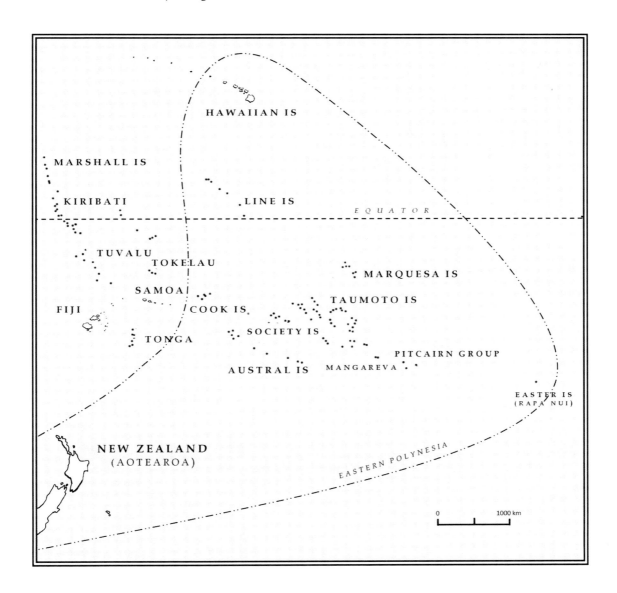

PO'E - PUDDINGS (TAHITI)

Captain Cook described a type of food being prepared in Tahiti that reminded him of the puddings he was familiar with back in England:

> There was also a large pudding which I saw the whole process in making, it was made of Bread fruit, Ripe Plantains, Taro and Palm or Pandanes [pandanus] nuts, each rasped, scraped or beat up fine, and baked by it self, a quant[it]y of Juice express'd from Cocoa nut Kernels was put into a large tr[a]y or wooden Vessel, amongst it the other Articles pipeing hot as they were taken out of the Oven and a few hot stones just to keep the whole semmering; three or four men kept stiring the whole with sticks, till the several articles were incorporated one with a nother and the juice of the Cocoanut was turned to oil; so that the whole was about the consistency of hasty pudding (Beaglehole 1967:206–207).

Po'e was being made before Europeans arrived; however, sugar came much later. Pandanus pulp and bananas (probably not plantains) were the only sweeteners in the original recipes. The starchy components, breadfruit and taro, are now replaced by arrowroot or cornstarch.

Here are two recipes that should give you the basic template for making Tahitian *po'e* at home. You can make other types using other tropical fruit.

PO'E MAI'A - Banana Po'e

- 6-8 ripe **bananas**, peeled and cut into chunks (4 cups)
- ½ cup **sugar**, brown sugar if you prefer it
- 2 **vanilla pods** (the scrapings of) or 2 teaspoons vanilla extract
- 1 cup **arrowroot** or cornstarch
- 1 cup **coconut cream** (see page 61)

PO'E I'ITA – Papaya Po'e

- 4 ripe **papaya**, peeled, seeded and chopped (4 cups)
- ½ cup **sugar**
- 2 **vanilla pods** (the scrapings of) or 2 teaspoons vanilla extract
- 1 cup **arrowroot** or cornstarch
- 1 cup **coconut cream** (see page 61)

Mash the fruit in a blender or food processor. There should be enough mash to make 4 cups. Mix the sugar and starch together and add it the mash along with the vanilla. Mix until smooth.

Butter a 2-quart baking dish and pour in the puree. Bake for 30-45 minutes. Remove from oven and allow it to cool. Cover with plastic wrap and refrigerate until well chilled.

Cut into cubes and serve with coconut cream and, optionally, sprinkled sugar.

BAKED MAPE - CHESTNUT (TAHITI)

I first tasted *po'e mape* on the black sand beach at Matavai Bay, just east of Papeete. (This was where Captain Cook and Captain Bligh anchored their ships when they were here.) Two small Tahitian boys shared their homemade *mape* with me. I had seen pieces of bamboo for sale at roadside stands and had no idea what it was. It turned out to be *Po'e mape* baked in hollow sections of green bamboo.

- 3 cups **mape** (Tahitian, Chinese or American Chestnuts)
- 3 cups **coconut milk**
- ½ cup **sugar**

You may also use packaged and roasted chestnuts, which would be much simpler. See page 67 for more information about preparing chestnuts.

Place roasted chestnuts in a blender or food processor, along with the sugar and coconut milk. Blend until you have a smooth paste. You have a choice of baking in a banana leaf wrapper or in a baking dish. Chose one.

1. "How to make banana leaf cooking packages" can be found on page 72.

2. Butter a 2-quart baking dish and pour in the puree. Bake for 30-45 minutes, or until the pudding is firm and bubbling. Remove from oven and allow to it cool. Cover with plastic wrap and refrigerate until well chilled.

Cut into cubes. Serve hot or cold.

KOELE PALAU (HAWAII)

Here is a simple *po'e* from Hawaii. Its name translates as "dry plough," probably because it is made from *'uala*, sweet potato, which is dug from dry ground—in contrast to taro which is grown in the mud. Also known as *ko'elepalau, poi palau* and *palau*.

- 3 pounds **sweet potatoes**
- 1 cup **coconut milk**
- ¼ cup grated **coconut** (optional)

Place sweet potatoes in a large saucepan; cover with water. Bring to a boil, lower heat, and cook until tender, about 20 to 30 minutes. Peel and mash the sweet potatoes. Stir in coconut milk. Garnish with shredded coconut.

Serve warm or cold.

POULET FAFA – TARO LEAF AND CHICKEN (TAHITI)

This dish can be found at every Tahitian *Tama'ara'a*, party-feast. This is called *Chicken Luau* in Hawaii. Taro leaves, *fafa*, in savory coconut sauce is one of the Pacific's gourmet delicacies. So, unless you are a person who just hates chicken, this dish is going to become one of your favorites.

- 4 cups cooked **fafa**, taro leaves (or spinach or chard)
- 1 pound boneless, skinless **chicken**, in pieces
- 1 medium **onion**, chopped
- 4 cloves **garlic**
- 1 inch piece **ginger**, grated
- 1 ½ cups **chicken broth** or water with one bouillon cube
- ½-1 teaspoon **salt** (to taste)
- 1 can **coconut milk** (14 oz) or equivalent fresh coconut milk
- 1 tablespoon **all-purpose flour** (optional)

Prepare and cook the taro leaves (see page 63). If you are using spinach, wash thoroughly to remove dirt and grit. Remove stems. If you are using chard, wash thoroughly and tear into 2-3 inch pieces, chop stems into bite size pieces. Steam the fresh greens until wilted. Drain excess liquid with a colander.

Heat 2 tablespoons of cooking oil over a medium-high flame. Brown the chicken on all sides, Add the onions, garlic and ginger and sauté until the onion is soft.

Add the broth, salt, cooked taro leaves (or greens), and coconut milk to the pot and simmer and stir for 20—25 minutes or until the chicken is cooked through. For a thicker consistancy, add 1 Tbsp of flour, mixed well in ½-cup cool water; simmer and stir for another couple of minutes

Note: See page 86 for a similar recipe using octopus.

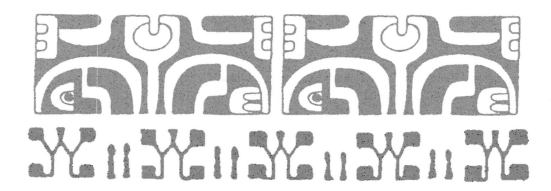

MA'A TINITO – CHINESE MEAL (TAHITI)

As the story goes, *ma'a tinito* was invented by a Chinese cook who worked in a Tahitian prison. The prisoners were tired of eating the same old things and asked the cook for a new dish. The Cook concocted this recipe, pork, beans and vegetables. The story also says that the prisoners were wild about this dish, and when they asked the Cook what it was called, he replied "*ma'a tinito*" (Chinese meal). This has become the favorite Sunday afternoon meal, in Tahiti.

- 1 can of **red beans** (kidney beans)
- 1 8.8 oz package (250g) *Saifun*, **bean thread noodles** (not rice noodles!)
- 1 pound **pork**
- 1 tablespoon **vegetable oil**
- 1 tablespoon **soy sauce**
- 1 inch slice **ginger**, grated
- 2 cloves **garlic**, chopped
- 1 tablespoon **rice wine vinegar**
- 1 tablespoon **oyster sauce**
- 1 **Chinese cabbage**, ½ inch slice
- 1 can **green beans**, drained
- 4 green **onions**, sliced
- 1 tablespoon **cooking oil**

Cook and Drain the red beans.

Bring 3 quarts water to a boil. Add the noodles and turn off heat. Soak the noodles until soft. The Chinese prefer their noodles long but you can snip the noodles into smaller pieces (3"-6") with scissors (after they are soft) if you wish. Drain completely.

Cut the pork into small pieces and marinate in soy sauce, grated ginger, salt, pepper and vegetable oil. Sauté the pork in wok or large pan for 5-10 minutes, medium-low heat. Add the rice wine vinegar and the oyster sauce thinned with a little water.

In a separate pan, sauté green beans with garlic and Chinese cabbage. Do not overcook; vegetables must stay crunchy (al dente).

Layer the ingredients in a large Chinese serving bowl: red kidney beans first, then the noodles, then the vegetables, and meat on top. Garnish with green onion. Serve with white rice.

PIPI KAULA (HAWAII)

Dried beef, Hawaiian style. This is not the leathery beef jerky you find at convenience stores; *Pipi kaula* is a thicker, chewier type of jerky from the early days of cattle ranching in Hawaii. *Pipi kaula*, translated, is "rope beef." This is *paniolo* food, a blending of Hawaiian, Spanish and Mexican influences. Just as Hawaiians loved dried fish (see page 123), they soon discovered the joys of dried beef. Unlike the jerky we find on the Mainland, *pipi kaula* is always grilled before eating.

- 2 pounds of **beef tenderloin** or flank steak
- 1/3 cup of Hawaiian **sea salt** (see page 49 for more information)
- ¼ cup **lemon juice** or water
- ½ cup **soy sauce**
- 2 cloves **garlic**, minced
- 1 teaspoon red **pepper flakes** (optional)
- ¼ teaspoon **liquid smoke** (optional)

Slice the beef across the grain ¼ inch thick; trim all fat and connective tissue. This works best if the beef is partially frozen. Cut into 4 inch lengths.

Make a marinade of all the rest of ingredients by mixing them in a large non-reactive bowl, stir to dissolve and combine wet and dry ingredients.

Add the sliced beef to the marinade. Be sure to coat all the pieces of meat. Cover the bowl with cling film. Keep in the refrigerator 6-8 hours, stirring a few times to keep the meat coated.

Line a shallow roasting pan with aluminum foil (for easy cleanup). Place a wire rack in the pan and place cut meat on top of that, allowing space between pieces for air to flow. Dry the beef in an oven at 100° F to 150° F for 4-6 hours or until flesh is completely dry but soft.

Dried *Pipi kaula* is best if grilled on the barbeque and served hot. Store leftovers in a cool, dry place, preferably in the refrigerator.

There are places in Hawaii where the locals hunt feral pig (escaped domestic pigs gone wild). Life in the wild gives them a gamier flavor. Uncooked pork, particularly wild pig, can be a health risk, however pork sold in the US is raised to minimize the risk, so I think these drying techniques could work with strips of pork, but it is up to you to determine if it is safe.

KALUA PORK (HAWAII)

In old Polynesia, pork was held in reserve for special occasions. Staging a lu'au and cooking a whole pig is extremely labor intensive and requires advance planning and management. See the section on *Traditional Methods of Cooking* for a description of cooking in an Earth Oven. This recipe makes it fairly effortless. At least you won't have to dig a hole in your yard to cook a 200 pound pig!

- 4-5 pounds **pork butt** (shoulder)
- 1 ½ tablespoons Hawaiian **sea salt** (see page 49 for more information)
- 1 ½ tablespoons **liquid smoke flavoring**

Pierce the pork roast all over with the tip of a sharp knife or a fork. Rub the salt and liquid smoke all over the meat. Wrap tightly with aluminum foil and place in a shallow roasting pan. If there is a fat side, place it up. Some people like to keep it in the refrigerator for a few hours before cooking. It's your choice.

Preheat your oven to 350° F and roast the pork for 4 hours.

Remove from the pan, remove the foil and shred the pork with two forks, adding drippings as needed to moisten the meat. Add Hawaiian sea salt to taste.

There is nothing like smoky taste of *kalua* pork. Serve with poi.

Slow Cooker Kalua Pork:

This is an even easier version of kalua pork. I have always used apple cider because it makes a leaner cut of pork juicer and tastier. In the end, there is no apple cider taste or sweetness.

- 3 pounds **pork butt** (shoulder)
- 1 ½ tablespoons Hawaiian **sea salt** (see page 49 for more information)
- 1 tablespoon **liquid smoke flavoring**
- 2 cups **apple cider** (not apple juice!)

Prepare the pork by piercing it with a knife or fork and rubbing salt and liquid smoke over the meat. Wrap tightly in aluminum foil and refrigerate for a few hours, as in the previous method.

Remove foil and place the pork butt in your slow cooker. Add cider and set the cooker to Low and leave it to cook for 9-10 hours.

Remove from the cooker and shred with two forks. Add liquid to the shredded meat as needed to moisten. Add Hawaiian sea salt to taste.

Serve *kalua* pork with *poi* or "plate lunch style," with white rice, and Hawaiian macaroni salad.

LAULAU (HAWAII)

A *laulau* is "a grab bag of delights" to paraphrase author, Don Blanding. *Laulau* is a technique not a recipe but it has come to mean a combination of pork or chicken, and a piece of oily fish wrapped in taro leaves, held together in *ti* leaves. Laulau packages were traditionally cooked in an *imu*, the ingredients roasting in their own juices. In this recipe, the packages are steamed, eliminating the need to dig an *imu*.

- 30+ young **taro leaves** (no substitution in this recipe)
- 10 **taro stems**, chopped and boiled until tender
- 12 large **ti leaves** (or banana leaves)
- 2 pounds **pork butt**, cut into 1 ½ inch pieces (or chicken or beef)
- 1/3 pounds **butterfish** (black cod, sablefish) cut into 1 inch pieces
- 1/3 pounds **salmon**, cut into 1 inch pieces

Wash the *lu'au* and *ti* leaves. Remove any tough stems. Layer one large and four smaller *lu'au* leaves on the palm of your left hand. Lefties can reverse this.

Place 2 or 3 pieces of pork, or chicken, or beef in the middle of the leaves. Place some cooked taro stems, one piece of butterfish and one piece of salmon with the pork, etc. fold the leaves and contents into a tight bundle. See page 71 for instructions about taro leaf packages.

Place 1 to 3 bundles in the middle of a large ti leaf and fold the leaf up. Place the ti leaf on a second ti leaf, lying at right angles to the first. Fold up the leaf and gather at the top with the first leaf. Tie the bundle with a piece of string.

If you cannot get *ti* leaves, wrap individual bundles in banana leaf or aluminum foil.

Boil water in a large steamer pot, Place *laulaus* in the steamer basket and steam for 90 minutes, checking occasionally to see if there is enough water.

If you are using *ti* or banana leaves, serve in the wrapper—leaf wrappers are part of the presentation not for eating.

Serve *laulau* with *poi*, or "plate lunch style" with steamed rice, and Hawaiian macaroni salad.

SEAFOOD LAULAU:

Instead of pork, combine fresh mahi-mahi (snapper, halibut, or even tilapia will also work) with scallops and/or shrimp. Instead of butterfish, use a mix of 1 cup of mayonnaise, 1 teaspoon soy sauce.

Arrange a bed of fresh spinach leaves or chard on a banana leaf (see page 72 for banana leaf wrappers) Place a piece of fish fillet on the greens and top with a spoonful of mayonnaise mix. Put scallops and shrimp on top. Close the package and steam for 15-20 minutes.

Note: A simpler method of preparation is *Lawalu* using banana leaf, see page 72 or page 115

CHICKEN LONG RICE (HAWAII)

The "long rice" in this recipe is the Hawaiian term for bean thread noodles; it has nothing to do with rice. Compare this recipe with *Sapasui*, Samoan Chop Suey—two different ways Pacific Islanders use Chinese bean thread noodles. This is a light, fragrant, soup—some would say stew.

- 8 oz *Saifun*, **bean thread noodles** (not rice noodles!)
- 2 ½ pounds skinless **chicken thighs**
- 1 inch piece fresh **ginger**, minced
- 1 can of sliced **mushrooms**
- 1 **chicken bouillon** cube (optional)
- 6 stalks **green onion**, chopped

Soak the noodles in hot water 30 minutes. Drain well and snip into smaller pieces (3"-6") with scissors or leave it as is. Drain completely and set aside. This should be more than enough for the recipe. When you add this to the broth, you can determine how much to use.

Place chicken thighs in a pot and cover with 3 quarts of water, bring to a boil. Reduce the heat and simmer for 40 minutes. Taste the broth; if it seems "thin," you can add a bouillon cube.

Remove the chicken, debone and shred the meat or cut into one inch pieces. Reserve the broth; there should be at least 2 quarts.

Add one quart of stock, ginger and mushrooms to a two-quart saucepan. Bring to a boil and reduce heat. Add the chicken and long rice and simmer for 10 minutes. You should have enough stock to be slightly soupy. Add more or less long rice, or broth as necessary. Season to taste with salt and/or soy sauce. Garnish with chopped green onion.

Eat with chopsticks and a spoon.

LOCO MOCO (HAWAII)

I believe Islanders think *outside the box*, because they don't realize there is a *box*. This is most apparent in the quirky, home style meals they invent. Loco moco is a breakfast favorite created in Hilo in 1949, as a cheap filling meal for the locals. Now, it's on menus from California to Guam. Just assemble the ingredients on a plate in the following order.

- 2 scoops **steamed rice** (or enough to make a bed for the hamburger)
- 1 fried **hamburger** patty (optionally, with a slice of cheese)
- 2 fried **eggs**
- 1 ladle of **brown gravy** (canned is ok)

SHOYU CHICKEN (HAWAII)

Shoyu is Japanese soy sauce, but this recipe comes from the Chinese tradition of chicken simmered in soy sauce. A close relative of *teriyaki* and Korean barbeque sauce; like those, this recipe uses sugar to glaze the chicken. This is an all time favorite in Hawaii and easy to make.

- 5 pounds skinless **chicken thighs** (20 pieces?)
- 1 cup **soy sauce**
- 1 cup **brown sugar**
- 1 cup **water**
- 4 cloves **garlic**, minced
- 1 **onion**, chopped
- 1 inch of fresh **ginger**, grated
- 1 tablespoon **Hoisin Sauce**
- 6 stalks **green onion**, chopped

Debone and cut chicken into chunks. Remove the skin if you wish. Place chicken pieces in a pot. cover with water and bring to a boil and reduce heat, simmer for 30 minutes. Set the chicken aside. Discard the cooking water.

Place all the remaining ingredients (except green onions) in the pot, mix well, Bring to a simmer, and add the cooked chicken. Simmer for 15 minutes until sauce thickens and the chicken is heated through.

Place chicken in a serving platter, garnish with chopped green onion and serve with rice.

GRILLED SHOYU CHICKEN:

Debone and cut chicken into chunks. Remove the skin if you wish.

Make a marinade with all the remaining ingredients; mix well to incorporate wet and dry ingredients. Add the chicken, covering completely with the marinade. Marinate for a minimum of 1 hour.

Remove the chicken from the marinade. Grill the chicken on a hot barbeque for about 10-15 minutes a side or until cooked through. Discard remaining marinade

Serve "plate lunch style" with steamed rice and Hawaiian macaroni salad.

REWENA PARAOA - MAORI BREAD (NEW ZEALAND)

When the Maori migrated to New Zealand, most of their staple plants did not survive the temperate climate. They struggled with ways to get enough *kai*, the starchy vegetables necessary for their diet. When Europeans arrived with cereal crops and plants like potato, suitable for growing in a temperate climate, the Maori started to adapt them to their cooking. *Rewena Paraoa* is leavened (rising) bread made without yeast; *rewa* (potato) serves that function. This rustic bread is the perfect accompaniment for a fish stew or steamed shellfish.

REWENA (the leavening):

- 2 cups **all-purpose flour**
- 1 teaspoon **sugar**
- 1 medium size **potato** (1 inch cubes)

Boil the potato in one cup of water until soft enough to mash. Do not remove from the water. Allow to cool and when lukewarm mash the potato in the water. Slowly add the other ingredients to make a firm batter, do not worry about any small lumps. Add lukewarm water if necessary. Transfer to a large (4+ cups) sterile container such as a glass jar, cover a cloth or cling film and leave in a warm place to "proof." By the next day, the starter will have to be fed to maintain fermentation: 1 teaspoon of sugar in half a cup of lukewarm potato water. Once it starts to rise and form bubbles, it is time to make the bread.

THE BREAD:

- 5 cups **all-purpose flour**
- 1 teaspoon **salt**
- 1 teaspoon **baking soda** (not baking powder)
- 4 cups **rewena**

Put the flour, salt and baking soda in a large mixing bowl. Create a well at its center into which you will pour four (4) warmed cups of the rewena. Mix all the ingredients into dough; add some lukewarm water if necessary. Turn dough out on a floured surface and knead for about 10 minutes. Place in a greased loaf pan(s) and leave to rise in a warm place for 1 ½ hours.

Bake in a preheated 400° F oven for 30—40 minutes, or until the crust is golden brown.

Saving Rewena "starter" for next time:

You can save several days of preparation by keeping "live" rewena to use whenever you want to make bread.

Take a tablespoon or two of the bread dough and place in sterile jar the same size as you started with. Feed the dough ½ cup of warm potato water one day and one teaspoon of sugar the next day. Continue alternate daily feedings.

MICRONESIA

Micronesia, *the Small Islands*, sprawling 3,000 miles across the Pacific from Palau to Kiribati, are barely specks on the map. Most Micronesians are atoll dwellers, whose far-flung communities share a similar environment. Perhaps, because the islands of Micronesia are small, without valuable resources, remote and vulnerable to catastrophe (being only a few feet above sea level), Westerners have never given them much thought; indeed, very few can name a single island—even those that were household names during and after World War II.

- The Republic of Kiribati, formerly the Gilbert Islands, 32 atolls and a single raised coral island, is the easternmost chain in Micronesia.

- The Marshall Islands, 29 atolls and 5 isolated coral islands, forming two chains, Ratak (Sunrise) and Ralik (Sunset).

- The Federated States of Micronesia (FSM) is a group of 607 small islands (part of the Caroline Islands chain) totaling 702 square kilometers of land and stretching 2,900 km. About 65 of the islands are inhabited. The FSM consists of four states: Pohnpei, Chuuk (formerly Truk), Kosrae and Yap, which are "high" islands among their constituent coral outer islands.

- Guam, an American territory, and the Northern Mariana Islands, a group of 4 limestone islands in the south and 11 volcanic islands in the north.

- The Republic of Palau, the main islands are Angaur, Babeldaob, Koror, and Peleliu with several populated outer islands to the north and the south.

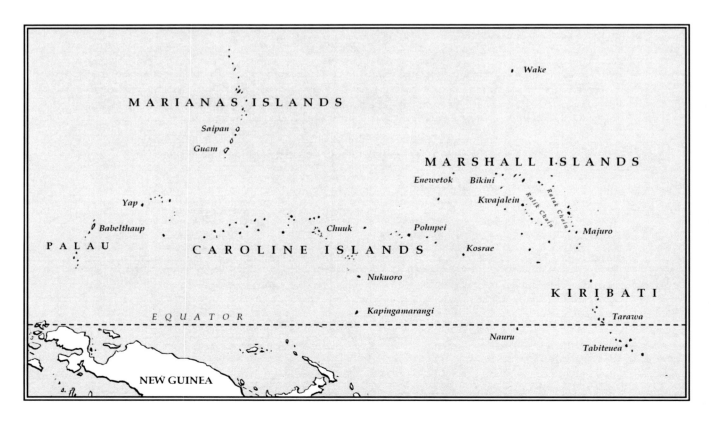

COCONUT TITIYAS (GUAM)

"Not TEE-TEE-YAHS," I was corrected, by my Chamorro acquaintance, "TIT-TEE-JAHS." Guam was one of the first Pacific Islands to be discovered by Europeans, namely the Spanish, whose influences can still be seen in the food. Titiyas are known in Mexico as *tortillas* or more properly, *tortillas harina*, flour tortillas. The difference being, Chamorro *titiyas* are made with coconut milk instead of water. This dense, flat bread substitutes for rice, taro, breadfruit, yams, etc.

- 4 cups **all-purpose flour**
- ½ cup **sugar**
- 4 oz **butter**
- 1 small can of **coconut milk**

Combine the flour and the sugar in a Mixing bowl. Melt the butter and drizzle into the flour. Mix the dry ingredients and the butter with your fingers until small crumbs form.

Add coconut milk a little bit at a time while mixing, until you get dough that separates from the side of the bowl and is not sticky. Flour your work surface and knead the dough for a couple of minutes, not too much.

Pinch off a piece of dough and form it into a ball about the size of a tennis ball. Flour your rolling pin and roll the dough into a flat round, about 7- 8 inches and a little less than ¼ inch thick. Don't worry if they don't look perfect, that's part of the process. Use a fork to prick the titiyas all over to release any internal steam while cooking.

Cook them on a medium heated pan for about two minutes each side or until the titiyas turn brown. Cut them into 6-8 pieces, squares or wedges. Serve warm.

Note: Hispanic markets sell wooden and cast aluminum tortilla presses. They can eliminate the rolling pin and speed up the process. And, they usually make rounder tortillas.

CHICKEN KELEGUEN (GUAM)

Here is your science lesson: heat changes the structure of proteins—we call that cooking. Then there is cold cooking, where mild acid does something similar. The acid we normally use for cold cooking is citric acid, i.e. lemons, limes. *Keleguen* uses both methods to cook chicken. Chamorro style *plate lunch* always includes chicken *keleguen*, AKA *Keleguen Mannok*.

- 1 whole **chicken**, cut into pieces (3 pounds)
- 1 cup **lemon** juice
- 1 medium **onion**, finely chopped
- ½ cup freshly grated **coconut**
- 1 small **serrano chili** or 3-4 Thai chilies, minced
- 3 **green onions**, chopped

Preheat oven to 350° F. Place chicken pieces in a roasting pan and roast for 30 minutes, no longer. Do not overcook. Take the chicken out of the oven and allow it to cool. When it is cool enough to handle, remove the skin and bones. Chop the meat to small pieces. **Aternately:** the chicken can be barbequed for that smokey flavor.

Grate coconut or use packaged grated coconut meat, the unsweetened kind.

Make a marinade of lemon juice, coconut, onions and chilies. Place the chopped chicken in the marinade, mix it all together and leave it for a minimum of one hour (stirring occasionally so everything marinates evenly) in the refrigerator. Stir again before serving.

Serve with *titiyas* or ordinary flour tortillas to scoop up the keleguen or make roll-ups using flour tortillas and perhaps a little finely chopped cabbage and *finadnne*, or a drizzle of sesame oil.

SHRIMP KELEGUEN *(KELEGUEN UHANG)*: Replace chicken with 2 lbs raw medium shrimp, parboil but do not overcook. Chop the shrimp and marinate for only 20 minutes before serving. Stir and pour off excess juice if any. If you wish, you may add finely chopped celery or sweet green pepper but not so much as to overwhelm the shrimp.

FISH KELEGUEN *(KELEGUEN GUIHAN)*: Same as Shrimp Keleguen, using firm white fish fillet or Ahi tuna cut into ½ inch dice. Do not cook the fish, the lemon marinade will do that just fine.

STEAK KELEGUEN *(KELEGUEN KATNE)*: Instead of chicken use 2 lbs flank steak, cut into thin strips, across the grain, cut into 1-inch pieces. Pat as dry as possible with paper towels. Add 1-teaspoon salt and several grinds of black pepper to the marinade, Marinate steak for a minimum of two hours (stirring occasionally so everything marinates evenly) in the refrigerator. Stir again before serving.

Because the flank steak is only cold cooked, the taste and texture may be unusual to non-Chamorros. If you wish, you can grill the flank steak briefly to remove some of the rawness, before marinating.

SPAM KELEGUEN: Chamorros eat a lot of Spam! Substitute Spam for chicken in the first recipe. Because Spam is already cooked, chop the spam and go right to the marinade step.

MANNOK KADON PIKA (GUAM)

Spicy stewed chicken. Chamorros love spicy food. *Pika* or *Peka* is derived from the Spanish *Pica* or spicy.

- 1 whole **chicken**, cut into pieces (2-3 pounds)
- ¾ cup **soy sauce**
- ¼ cup **vinegar**
- 1 tablespoon **red pepper flakes**
- ½ teaspoon ground **black pepper**
- 1 medium **onion**, sliced
- 1 small can **coconut milk**

Place cut up chicken in a large bowl and add all remaining ingredients, except the coconut milk. Marinate for 1 hour. Heat 1 tablespoon vegetable oil in a large pot and add the chicken (from the marinade). Brown the chicken pieces on all sides. Add the marinade and ¼ cup of water and bring to a boil. Reduce the heat and simmer for 40 minutes, stirring occasionally and skimming off any foam that comes to the surface. Season with salt and pepper to taste and add more pepper flakes if desired.

Add coconut milk and simmer another 10 minutes.

Substitutions:

Substitute chicken wings and drummets for whole chicken; it reduces prep time and makes a spicy finger food. Increase the cooking time by about 15-20 minutes.

Serve with *titiyas* or steamed rice.

GOLAI APPAN AGA (GUAM)

This dish tells you that the Chamorro really are Pacific Islanders. This is a slightly sweet compliment to savory foods. Serve as a side dish with any Island menu. It's not just a Chamorro recipe.

- 6 **bananas** (Cavendish or Red) just starting to ripen, but not soft
- 1 can (14 oz) **coconut milk** (or enough to cover bananas)
- 1 teaspoon of **salt**

Peel bananas; cut them in half, if necessary to fit the pot. Place in cooking pot with the coconut milk and salt.

Bring to a boil, reduce heat to simmer and cook for 15 minutes or until bananas are cooked, but still firm. Discard the cooking liquid. Place the bananas on a serving platter.

Serve when the bananas are cool.

MANGO CHICKEN (GUAM)

A simple chicken dish with a fragrant sauce. Search for ripe mangos with a strong flavor.

- 2 pounds boneless **chicken**, breast or thigh
- 2 tablespoon **cooking oil**
- ½ large **onion**, chopped
- 1 tablespoon **salt**
- 2 large **mangos**, peeled seeded and sliced
- ½ cup **coconut milk**
- 4 **mint leaves**, chopped and crushed, or 1 tablespoon dried mint
- 2 cups **water** or chicken stock
- 1 tablespoon of freshly squeezed **lemon juice**.

Cut chicken into small pieces. In a large pot, brown chicken pieces in one tablespoon of oil and set aside. Fry onions in remaining oil until soft and return the chicken pieces to the pot. Add salt, mint leaves and papaya slices to the pot. Add water or stock to just cover chicken pieces and simmer 45 minutes or until chicken is tender

Add lemon juice and coconut milk to the pot. Stir and return to simmer for 2 more minutes.

Serve with rice and/or *titiyas*.

FINADENE BIRENGHENAS (GUAM)

Guam has fallen in love with eggplant, specifically the small Asian variety that is cultivated locally. The smokey taste, imparted from charring the skin, is what I like. Some have called this recipe a salad. I call it a pâté. You can decide for yourselves.

- 6 small **Asian** eggplants with the stem
- 1 medium **onion**, finely chopped
- 1 teaspoon **salt**
- ½ cup freshly squeezed **lemon juice**
- 1 **serrano chili** or 3-4 Thai chilies, finely chopped
- ½ cup of **coconut milk**

Pierce the skin of each eggplant in 4-5 places to prevent them from bursting while on the grill. Lightly coat each eggplant with olive oil. Grill the eggplants on a barbeque or in a broiler to blacken the skin, keep turning to char all sides.

Cook the eggplant until completely soft. Allow them to cool enough to handle, hold by the stem and peel off the skin. Cut off the stem, cut into pieces and place in a food processor. Add onions, lemon juice, peppers and salt. Pulse to mash and combine. Add coconut milk and blend into a thick paste.

Transfer to a bowl and garnish with chopped scallions. Serve with warm, cut *titiyas*.

BREADFRUIT AND FISH CURRY (POHNPEI)

The high island of Pohnpei in Micronesia has some of the greenest landscapes in the Pacific, and home of one of the most amazing and mysterious stone structures in the Pacific, Nan Madol. Nan Madol was once a town complex, built between 500 and 1500 C.E. by the ruling Saudeleur chiefs on artificial islands. Nan Madol is an engineering marvel constructed out of prismatic basalt pillars weighing several tons each. No one is completely sure how it was accomplished, although there are several theories, some reasonable, some bizarre.

The women of Pohnpei developed this recipe to promote local breadfruit varieties, which they consider a National Treasure. Curry, mackerel and introduced Western and Asian vegetables are combined with breadfruit to make this home style stew.

- 1 tablespoon of **cooking oil**
- 1 large **onion**, chopped
- 1-2 cloves **garlic**
- 1-2 tablespoons **curry powder**
- 2 cups raw mature **breadfruit**, or substitute pale yam, ¾ inch cubes
- ¼ teaspoon of **black pepper**
- 1 cup **pumpkin**, chopped
- 2 cups **Chinese cabbage**, chopped, ¾ inch cubes
- 1 cup **eggplant**, peeled, cubed
- 1 can **mackerel** or tuna (in oil or brine)
- 2 teaspoons **lime juice**
- 2 cups of **water**

Heat cooking oil in a saucepan over medium heat. Stir in onion and garlic; fry lightly until soft. Stir in curry powder and cook for another minute (add a little liquid if necessary). Add the rest of the ingredients, except for the fish and lime juice. Add a little more water if necessary.

When the breadfruit and pumpkin are cooked, add the fish and cook until heated through. Salt to taste and add limejuice just before serving.

Breadfruit Forever!

Bread that grows on trees! Some people think the Pineapple symbolizes the Islands; to my mind, that honor can only be given to the Breadfruit. After all, Pineapple is a recent import from Central America; Breadfruit has been an Island staple for several thousands of years—brought by the earliest people to discover and settle Oceania.

Most Islanders like it roasted or boiled in coconut milk. In Tahiti, they also like to stuff partially cooked breadfruit with canned corned beef, and then return it to the fire to finish cooking—hearty comfort food indeed

There are hundreds of Breadfruit recipes; most are foreign recipes that have been modified to use breadfruit as a substitute for potatoes. Breadfruit can be made into biscuits and ice cream. There are recipes for Breadfruit Lasagna and Breadfruit Tempura! A particular Island favorite is roasted Breadfruit baked with butter and brown sugar. Breadfruit has even become a staple throughout the West Indies (see the sidebar on the next page).

CRAB & BREADFRUIT CAKES (MARSHALL ISLANDS)

Coconut crabs are ugly looking creatures, but amazing, nevertheless. They can climb 80-foot coconut trees and tear the husk off a mature coconut. Because they eat coconut, their flesh is rich in oil and coconut flavor. This recipe should use coconut crab, but that is hard enough to get in the Islands these days, so it would be just about impossible to get on the Mainland. This is a rather more complex recipe than I would expect for Islander fare; I would not be surprised if some version of it came out of a Peace Corps handbook.

- ½ pound **crabmeat** (any kind, fresh or canned)
- 1 medium **onion**, finely chopped
- 2 cloves **garlic**, minced
- 1 green **bell pepper**, cored, seeded, chopped
- ½ cup boiled **mature breadfruit**, mashed, or substitute cooked, pale yam
- 3 stalks **green onions**, chopped
- 2 teaspoons any prepared **mustard**
- ¼ cup **mayonnaise**
- 2 cups **bread crumbs**
- ½ cup grated **coconut**, unsweetened
- 4 **eggs**, beaten
- 1 cup **all-purpose flour**

Cook onion, garlic, and bell pepper in a sauce pan over medium heat until the vegetables are soft. Transfer the mixture to a large bowl. Let it cool slightly; add cooked breadfruit, green onions, crab, mustard, (salt, and pepper to taste). Mix well; stir in mayonnaise, ¼ cup of breadcrumbs, and ¼ cup of grated coconut (to simulate the flavor of coconut crab).

Chill for 1 hour or more.

Divide mixture into eight portions; shape into patties. Dip into the beaten eggs, then into flour, into the eggs again, and finally cover with the remaining breadcrumbs, mixed with remaining grated coconut.

Fry in medium-hot oil until golden brown on both sides. Drain on a wire rack or paper towels. Keep fried cakes hot in a medium oven (350° F).

Captain Bligh's Breadfruit

In 1787, William Bligh was commissioned, as the Captain of HMS Bounty, to bring Breadfruit plants from Tahiti to the Caribbean as food for slaves. On his return trip, his crew mutinied and set him adrift with eighteen crewmembers. The Mutineers took command of the Bounty, and dumped the breadfruit plants—the work of several months—overboard. Bligh and his men made a heroic open boat voyage of over 3600 nautical miles to a Dutch colony in Indonesia where he and the surviving crew were returned to England. Bligh was sent a second time to collect breadfruit from Tahiti and this time he returned successfully. Breadfruit is now cultivated in the Caribbean where it has become a staple in the Caribbean diet and eaten at all meals.

MELANESIA

Melanesia, *the Black Islands* are so named for to the dark skinned peoples who live there. The ancestors of Papuan peoples started to arrive in New Guinea 40,000 years ago while sea levels were low enough to walk most of the way from Asia. Papuans eventually occupied the whole of New Guinea, from the shores to the most remote mountain valleys. It took another 10,000 years for the Papuans to settle the nearby Bismarck Archipelago and the Solomon Islands.

Austonesians, seafaring peoples from the coast of Asia, came to New Guinea about 4,000 years ago. Perhaps finding the region populated with hostiles, they continued to search for more remote islands. They established colonies in the Bismarck Archipelago, the Solomons, and Santa Cruz Islands, and beyond to Vanuatu, New Caledonia and Fiji. Later, perhaps after the sea-routes had been discovered by Austronesian migrants, Papuan/Austronesian peoples followed and became the dominant populations on those islands. The islands of Fiji are the eastern outposts of Melanesia. Fiji is considered ethnically Melanesian but culturally Polynesian due to long and extensive contact with Western Polynesia.

Yams, sweet potatoes and cassava are the traditional staples. The sweet potato arrived around 1,200 to 2,000 years ago, yams and taro long before that. The cassava arrived in the 1950s, beans and peanuts arrived only in the last few generations. Domesticated pigs, chickens and wild game provide the protein. Of course, seafood is consumed by coastal dwellers and traded with inland dwellers for highland produce.

Native Fijian food is similar to that of Western Polynesia, but a permanent population of Indian immigrants arriving more than 100 years ago has had a profound effect on Fijian food. That will be covered in the section on "Curries and Stews."

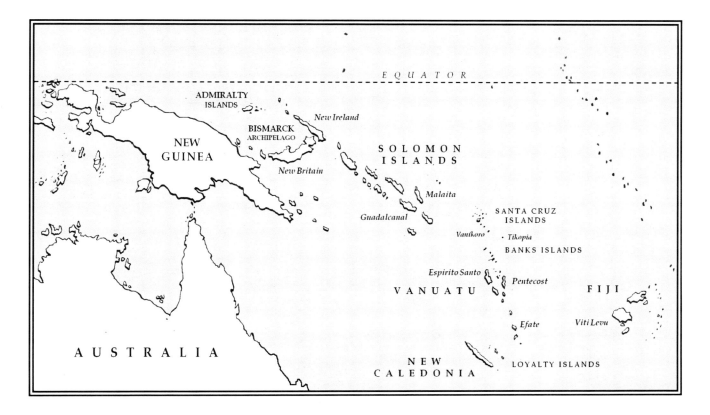

VAKALOLO, CASSAVA PUDDING (FIJI)

Cassava was only recently introduced to the Pacific but it has taken the place of some other starchy vegetables such as taro and breadfruit because it is easy to grow and it is not seasonal. Sugar growing and processing in Fiji make sugar cheap and widely used (overused) to sweeten a normally bland starchy diet. This is the Fijian version of *Po'e*. A variation on *Vakalolo* is *Vakalavalava*, which includes [mashed] banana (Hayden: 2009, 32)

- 4 cups grated **cassava**
- 1 cup grated **coconut**
- ½ inch fresh **ginger**, grated
- 1 cup **brown sugar**
- 1 cup **coconut milk** (cream)
- ½ teaspoon of **salt**

Use store-bought grated cassava, available in the frozen food section of Asian markets. Thaw it just before you are ready to use it and squeeze out any liquid. Or, you can peel and grate fresh cassava.

Mix the cassava, coconut, ginger and sugar together into a firm paste. Divide into 4 equal parts and wrap each in banana leaf or foil.

Place in a steamer to steam for 40 minutes. Unwrap and serve warm or cold in a simple coconut sauce.

Coconut sauce:

Heat the coconut milk and salt until it thickens slightly. Do not boil.

SOLOMON'S SUPSUP (SOLOMON ISLANDS)

A simple soup or stew from the Solomon Islands. There may be as many recipes for this dish as there are cooks to make it. Islanders use what is on hand, so it's a little different each time.

- 4 pounds **sweet potatoes** or yams, peeled and cut into bite-sized pieces
- 1 pound **long beans**, cut into pieces
- 2 bunches **green onions**, coarsely chopped
- 1 unripe **papaya**, peeled, seeded and chopped
- 2 cans **tuna** or 1 can mackerel (optional)
- 1 14 ounce can **coconut cream**
-   **salt** and **pepper** to taste

Wash all the vegetables and add all ingredients except coconut cream to a large pot. Add just enough water to cover and bring to a boil. Reduce to simmer and cook until the vegetables are fork tender. Add coconut cream and simmer another 5 minutes. Season to taste.

Note: Green papaya should be soaked in water for at least 30 minutes, rinsed and drained before consuming or used in recipes, to remove any bitterness.

LAP LAP (VANUATU)

The traditional dish of Vanuatu is a pudding called lap-lap. Lap-lap is made from grated starchy vegetables such as cassava, taro or yam mixed with coconut milk to form a paste—very much like Fijian vakalolo. On special occasions, pork, chicken or fish may be added, the traditional recipe calls for *bele* leaves, edible hibiscus, instead of spinach leaves

- 4 cups grated **cassava**
- 1 cup **coconut milk**
- 1 bunch *bele* or baby spinach, chopped
- 4 green **bananas**, peeled, grated
- 1 medium **onion**, finely chopped
- ½ teaspoon **salt** (or to taste)

If using spinach, remove stems and chop into small pieces

Mix all the ingredients together into a firm paste. Divide into 4 equal parts and wrap in banana leaf or foil.

Place in a steamer to steam for 40 minutes. Unwrap and serve warm or cold.

Variation:

Substitute 1 cup of cooked fish or cooked lean meat for the green bananas.

SAKSAK, PAPUAN DUMPLINGS (NEW GUINEA)

Saksak is made in the coastal regions of New Guinea. These dumplings are basic nutrition and very similar to vakalolo and lap lap, the difference being an additional cooking step. The traditional recipe calls for *sago*, a starchy flour made from the pith of the sago palm, a tree that is grown in my neighborhood as an ornamental palm. The starch is extracted by a very laborious process, however there is a side benefit for all their hard work; the sago palm is home to lots of very fat grubs, which are exposed when the palm is split open. The grubs are delicacies that are eaten on the spot. This recipe substitutes cassava for sago. Grated cassava is sold frozen in some Asian markets.

- 4 cups grated **cassava**
- 4 ripe **bananas**, peeled, mashed
- 2 cups of **coconut milk**

Mix the cassava and banana together into a paste. Divide into 4 portions and wrap each in banana leaves or foil. Steam the packages for 30 minutes.

Heat coconut milk to boiling in another pot and reduce to a simmer.

Remove the saksak from the steamer and unwrap. Put the saksak "dumplings" in the coconut milk and continue to cook for another 20 minutes.

Remove from the cooking pot and serve hot or cold with chicken or fish.

BOUGNA (NEW CALEDONIA)

Bougna is a communal feast dish made from whatever is available: chicken, fish, taro, sweet potato, banana, or yam. When preparing this dish, the cook lays out whole banana leaves (softened over a fire) to make a cooking package. She arranges chopped meats and vegetables on the leaves and pours on coconut cream. The leaves are folded into a bundle, 18-24 inches across, and cooked in a traditional earth oven. When it comes out of the oven, the bundle is unfolded and becomes the serving platter. The diners gather around to pick choice bits with their fingers. This is a veritable potluck dinner in a bundle.

"Proteins"	Starchy Vegetables	"Herbs"
• Chicken	• Taro	• Onions
• Pork	• Yams	• Tomatoes
• Fish	• Cassava	• Taro Leaf
• Corned Beef	• Green Bananas	• Spinach
• Beef	• Sweet Potatoes	• Chard
• Lobster	• Breadfruit	• Cabbage
• Shrimp	• Pumpkin	• Scallions
• Crab	• Potatoes, Turnips, Chayote, etc.	

There is no fixed recipe for *bougna*, but here are some general rules:

- The ratio vegetables to meats should be about 2:1 by weight.
- "Starchy Vegetables": choose 2 or 3 kinds from the list
- "Herbs": onions, tomatoes plus one other leafy green vegetable. Scallions are optional.
- "Proteins": the most typical choices are higher on the list. Choose one or two.

Wash all the "Herbs" thoroughly. If you are using fresh spinach, cut off and discard the stems. Slice onions and quarter tomatoes. Chop all leafy greens into pieces.

Wash, peel and chop the starchy vegetables. Cassava has a woody core that needs to be removed. Taro needs more cooking than the other vegetables and may be cut into pieces and parboiled or steamed for 10 minutes in advance.

Larger pieces of meat or meat with bones may take longer to cook than the vegetables, so you may want to use boneless, meat and poultry, cut into bite sized pieces. Fish should be firm. Cut fish into palm sized pieces that can stand a little longer cooking. Native cooks chop whole, cleaned fish into chunks. Use uncooked, unpeeled shrimp if you have it.

Continued...

BOUGNA, VERSION 1:

- 2 pounds **pork shoulder**, cut into bite size pieces
- 4 cups of **cassava** or breadfruit, 1 inch slices
- 3 chayote or **pumpkin**, 1 inch pieces
- 1 bunch of fresh **chard** (or spinach)
- 3 medium **onions**, sliced
- 3 large **tomatoes**, quartered
- 2 cups of **coconut milk**
- 1 teaspoon of **salt**

BOUGNA, VERSION 2:

- 2 pounds of boneless **chicken** pieces
- 2 **sweet potato**, peeled, cut into 1 inch slices
- 2 green **bananas**, peeled, cut into 1 inch slices
- 2 **chayote** or pumpkin, 1 inch pieces
- 2 medium **onions**, sliced
- 3 **tomatoes**, quartered
- 6 **scallions** (green onions) chopped
- 2 cups of **coconut milk**
- 1 teaspoon of **salt**

Line a 9x13x2 inch baking dish or casserole with heavy-duty foil. The foil should extend 1-2 inches beyond the lip of the dish. This will keep the juices from bubbling over the edge.

Layer the ingredients, starting with a starchy vegetable, the meat, greens, onion slices, the rest of the vegetables and tomato pieces. Continue as long as there are any ingredients left. This should more than fill the baking dish. Mix salt and coconut milk and pour it over the ingredients.

Fold the excess foil liner inwards. Cover the casserole tightly with aluminum foil. Poke 2 small holes in the cover with the tip of a sharp knife to let the steam escape. Place the casserole in a preheated oven to 375° F for one hour. When done remove the foil cover and serve.

PAPUAN CHICKEN AND TARO (PAPUA NEW GUINEA):

Versions of Bougna are made from New Guinea to Vanuatu. This slow cooker version is ideal for home kitchens.

- 2 pounds boneless **chicken** pieces
- 2 large **onions**, chopped
- 1 pound **taro**, ¼ inch slices
- 1 pound mixed "**herbs**" (bok choy, spinach, chard, tomatoes, etc)
- 1 cup **coconut milk**
- 1 teaspoon **salt**.

Place taro in the bottom of a slow cooker, followed by the "herbs." Place chicken on top and sprinkle on salt. Pour on coconut milk and a little water (to fill the pot half way). Cook for 8 hours. Add more coconut milk at the end of the cooking.

PORK AND PEANUTS (VANUATU)

Malnutrition is often a problem (in New Guinea, for instance) where sago starch or sweet potato provides basic sustenance. Peanuts are a recently introduced food, which, when added to such a diet, adds much needed proteins and fats. The protein content of peanuts is, in fact, higher than that of eggs, dairy products, meat and fish. Today, peanuts and peanut products are being exported from New Guinea to other countries in the South Pacific.

In the West, peanuts are normally roasted. The following recipe calls for white peanuts, that is, shelled raw or dried peanuts with the brown skins rubbed off. When these peanuts are boiled, they have a "beany" texture and flavor.

- 1 pound **pork loin**, cubed
- 2 tablespoons **vegetable oil**
- 3 cups **celery**, chopped
- 2 cups **onion**, chopped
- 2 cups **white peanuts**
- 1 cup **water**
- 3 tablespoons **soy sauce**
- ¼ teaspoon **black pepper**
- **salt** to taste

Heat vegetable oil in a heavy saucepan or wok. Add the cubed pork and cook until browned.

Add the rest of the ingredients, bring to a boil, and reduce to a simmer. Cook for 30 minutes.

PEANUT AND SWEET POTATO (NEW GUINEA)

This is just one of many ways that peanuts are used to fortify traditional root or cereal foods. Either white or roasted peanuts can be ground into "meal" with a spice grinder or blender.

- 2 cups **peanut meal**
- 2 cups cooked **sweet potato**, mashed
- 1 **egg**, beaten
- 3 tablespoons **coconut milk**
- 2 teaspoons **salt** (1 teaspoon if the peanut meal is salted)
- ½ cup **vegetable oil**
- ½ cup **all purpose flour**

Mix peanut meal, mashed sweet potatoes, salt and beaten egg. Use just enough coconut milk to make a stiff mash that holds together. Shape into small patties (2 inches) with your hands. Be sure to flour you hands and the patties so they will not stick.

Heat vegetable oil in a frying pan or wok and fry patties until golden brown. Don't over crowd the pan. Drain patties on a wire rack or paper towels.

SEAFOOD

Seafood was the main source of protein in Oceania. The lagoons and offshore fishing grounds were exploited for every imaginable source of food.

Fish and other seafood are a big part of all Islanders diet, so you may be surprised to learn there are not too many "recipes" for cooking fish, however there are cooking methods (see the section on Food Preparation and Cooking). Seafood was cooked without much fuss, extra ingredients or seasonings. Some recipes are most likely adaptations of foreign ideas, made in Island kitchens for local meals. See the "Soups" section for fish soups.

❧❧

In Oceania, fish is cooked simply; it is roasted in an underground oven, over an open flame or in glowing embers. One of finest fish dinners I ever had was a whole, cleaned *Aku* (bonito), purchased at the (Raietea) municipal market, wrapped in foil and placed in a campfire. It was broiled in its own juices and completely cooked without burning. The foil package was opened like a serving platter and we all ate with our fingers. On the Mainland, this means it's time to heat up the barbeque and grill your seafood. Fish, lobster or shrimp, cooked on a barbeque is just what our friends in the Islands are having for their get-together.

LAWALU (HAWAII)

Lawalu is technique to cook fish, rather than a recipe. In Hawaii, roasting whole fish could be done with or without leaf wrappers; cooking whole fish over hot embers did not require a wrapper but cooking small fish or pieces of fish requires a wrapper to hold everything together and protect exposed flesh from direct heat. It also made it possible to add herbs to flavor the fish. Snapper, halibut, or even tilapia will also work well.

- 2 pounds **red snapper fillet**, mahi-mahi, cod or salmon
- 1 cup **mayonnaise**
- 1 **lemon**, cut into thin slices
- ½ cup of thinly sliced **fresh ginger**.
- **sea salt**

Cut fish fillets into pieces into individual servings, about the size of the palm of your hand. Save any cut-offs to make another portion.

Place a piece of fish on a 12"x12" banana leaf (or foil) wrapper. Lightly salt the fish and top with dollop of mayonnaise and two or three thin slices of fresh ginger. Place two or three thin lemon slices to cover. Fold the banana leaf into a package and tie with a piece of string. "How to make banana leaf cooking packages" can be found on page 72, and aluminum foil is always an option.

Place the Lawalu packages on a shallow baking tray and cover with foil to seal in the moisture. Place the baking tray in a preheated oven to 350° F for 40 minutes

Serve the fish steaming in the package with boiled banana or steamed rice.

LOMI-LOMI SALMON (HAWAII)

Salmon is not a fish found in Hawaiian waters. Hawaiians first learned of it when American sailors arrived with barrels of salted salmon to barter for fresh food and (probably) the favors of Hawaiian *wahines*. There are no Hawaiian ingredients in this recipe, however its preparation is a typically Hawaiian; the preparer lightly massages (lomi-lomi) the raw fish with his fingers to soften the texture. I've tried making it with fresh salmon, but it's not the same. This is a bright, fresh side dish, served ice cold for "plate lunch" or *lu'au*.

- 1 pound salt cured **salmon**
- 1 medium Maui **onion** or any mild onion
- 2 fresh vine ripened **tomatoes**
- 3-4 **green onions**
- 2 teaspoons of **serrano chili**, minced or ¼ teaspoon of red pepper flakes (optional)

Place the salt salmon in a large bowl of fresh water to soak. Change the water after one hour and taste for saltiness. If it's too salty, continue to soak for another hour or overnight if necessary.

Rinse and dry the fillets and massage them lightly with your fingers. Tear or cut the salmon into small pieces (¼-inch dice).

Cut the onions into ¼-inch dice. Thinly slice the green onions. Cut the tomatoes into ¼-inch dice.

Mix the ingredients well. Chill for one hour and keep it cold; cover with ice cubes or crushed ice if it will be sitting out.

Salt Curing Salmon

IF YOU HAVE FRESH SALMON FILLETS, HERE IS A SIMPLE SALT CURING TECHNIQUE.

- Use a glass baking dish large enough to hold the salmon fillets. Find or make a board to fit inside that container. (You will need it later to press down on the fish.) Put a layer of Hawaiian sea salt or coarse kosher salt in the bottom of the dish. Do not use table (iodized) salt.
- Remove any skin and rinse the salmon fillets, dry them well, and place them on top of the salt in a single layer
- Cover the salmon with salt; make sure all sides of the fillets are salted too.
- Cover the salted salmon with plastic wrap. Place the "board," wrapped in foil on top of the fish and weigh it down with heavy food cans or a brick wrapped in foil.
- Refrigerate for 24 to 72 hours. The longer it is cured, the more water will be removed
- Rinse the salmon and dry it well before using it to make *lomi-lomi* salmon.

POISSON CRU (TAHITI)

To taste *Poisson Cru* is to taste Tahiti. The French call it *Poisson Cru* (raw fish) and *Salade Tahitienne*, but Tahitians call it *E'ia Ota*; in Samoa, it is called *Oka I'a*; in the Cook Islands, *Ika Mata*; and in Fiji, it is known as *Kokoda* (ko-cone-da). Raw fish is actually a misnomer, it's cooked without heat by marinating it in lemon or lime juice, turning the flesh opaque and firming up the texture, however the taste is milder and never dried out. *Maita'i roa!*

The Tahitians partially "cook" the fish in lime juice for as little as 3 minutes—they believe any more would toughen the fish—but Cook Islanders and Fijians marinate the fish much longer (overnight) and seem to prefer it that way. Tahitians make it with parrotfish, Fijians might use mahi-mahi or mackerel, Cook Islanders prefer flying fish. *'Ahi* tuna is my choice. Other versions call for red snapper, halibut or cod. Whatever you choose, try to get the freshest fish you can.

- 1 pound fresh **'ahi tuna** or mahi-mahi or both
- 1 cup of fresh **lime juice** (never use the bottled stuff—for anything)
- 1 medium **onion**, diced
- ½ cup diced **green** (bell) **pepper**
- ½ cup peeled and diced **cucumber**
- 2 large **tomatoes**, chopped
- 3-4 green **onions**, sliced
- 2 **serrano chili**, seeded and minced
- 1 can (14 oz) **coconut milk** (not coconut cream)
- **sea salt**, to taste

Use a very sharp knife to cut the 'ahi into ¼ inch thick "slabs" then into 1 x 1 ½ inch pieces. Place the pieces in a non-metallic bowl and add the limejuice; make sure all the pieces of fish are well covered. Thicker pieces will need more time in the marinade.

Allow the fish to marinate for one hour in the refrigerator stirring occasionally. It's possible that this will not "cook" all the way through and leave the fish a little raw in the middle. I don't mind raw fish (*'ahi* is very good that way), but you may wish to marinate for another 30 minutes.

Drain off the limejuice. Add green pepper, tomatoes, diced onions, green onions and chili peppers. Add the coconut milk and mix well. Add salt to taste. Chill in the refrigerator for 1 hour.

A Cook Islands recipe suggests that it be served with a "hard" vegetable, perhaps boiled taro, to compliment the "soft" fish. I suggest a crusty French baguette (long thin loaf of French bread).

POKE (HAWAII)

Fresh *poke* (po-kay) is an amazing taste treat. Fresh, clean textures, the crunch of seaweed or finely chopped vegetables, poke can transport you to the Islands from the first bite. The old Hawaiian method was to chop fresh fish into small pieces, lightly salt and mix it with chopped seaweed. Today making *poke* has evolved into fine dining and a competitive sport. No matter how many recipes there are, the basic recipes are still the favorites.

OLD STYLE POKE:

- 1 pound fresh raw **'*ahi* tuna steaks**, cut into ½ inch cube
- ½ cup ***limu kohu*** (seaweed), blanched, chopped
- ***'Inamona*** to taste (*'Alaea* salt and crushed, roasted *Kuku'i* nuts. See page 156)

BASIC RECIPE 1:

- 2 pounds fresh raw **'*ahi* tuna steaks**, cut into ½ inch cube
- 2 tablespoons **sesame oil**
- ½ cup ***limu manuea*** (*ogo* seaweed), blanched, chopped fine
- 1 tablespoon **red pepper flakes** (optional)
- ***Ala'ea***, Hawaiian red salt (crush large salt crystals) to taste

BASIC RECIPE 2:

- 2 pounds fresh raw **'*ahi* tuna steaks**, cut into ½ inch cube
- ½ cup **soy sauce**
- ¾ cup sliced **green onions**
- 2 tablespoons **sesame oil**
- 1 tablespoon **toasted sesame seeds**
- 1 tablespoon **red pepper flakes** (optional)

Note: Always use the freshest sashimi grade *'Ahi* (yellowfin tuna) you can. Look for a bright red color, not dull or dry. Avoid tuna with white lines (sinew) in the flesh.

Cut the tuna into ½-inch cubes. Combine all the ingredients in a non-metallic bowl and refrigerate for 1 hour before serving.

෴

Let's not stop with the basics, there are hundreds of recipes. Hawaiians love to invent new poke recipes. They may use various fish and/or different flavorings but somehow it remains poke. Here are a few more recipes:

Continued...

POKE WITH AVOCADO AND CUCUMBER:

- 2 pounds fresh *ahi* tuna steaks, cut into ½ inch cube
- ½ cup soy sauce
- ½ cup sliced green onions
- 1 ripe avocado cut into 1 inch cube
- 1 large cucumber, peeled, seeded, cut into ¼ inch dice
- 1 tablespoon sesame oil
- 1 teaspoon red pepper flakes (optional)

Combine all the ingredients in a non-metallic bowl and refrigerate for 1 hour before serving.

TAKO POKE (OCTOPUS):

- 1 pound cooked octopus tentacles, cut into ½ inch cubes
- ½ cup chopped onion
- ¼ cup soy sauce
- 1 large cucumber, peeled, seeded, cut into ¼ inch dice
- 2 tablespoons sesame oil
- 2 Thai chilies, chopped fine (optional)

Combine all the ingredients in a non-metallic bowl and refrigerate for 1 hour before serving.

CREAMY 'AHI MACADAMIA POKE:

- 1 pound fresh *ahi* tuna steaks, cut into ½ inch cube
- ½ cup *limu manuea* (*ogo* seaweed), blanched, chopped fine
- ½ cup macadamia butter (available at health food stores)
- ½ cup sliced green onions, green part only
- 2 tablespoons lime juice
- 2 tablespoons sesame oil
- 1 teaspoon *sambal olek* (hot chili paste)
- ¼ cup soy sauce
- ¼ cup chopped red onion

Dressing: Place macadamia butter, lime juice, sesame oil and soy sauce, onions, sambal olek and green onions in a food processor, puree until smooth. Add more lime juice to thin if necessary.

Combine the dressing and the ahi in a non-metallic bowl and refrigerate for 1 hour before serving. Dress individual servings with a pinch of *ogo*.

Suggestion: Poke can be made with other fish, cooked lobster or crab; *pipi kaula* or smoked salmon, even imitation crab. Experiment with these, and other ingredients.

Macadamia Butter can be made from dry roasted macadamia nuts (if unsalted, add a pinch) and a good strong blender. I don't want to endorse any particular brand, but we have a V*****X (Google "expensive blenders"). If yours will make peanut butter then you are all set, otherwise try to find Macadamia butter at the Health Food store.

FAFARU (TAHITI)

Fafaru stinks! It's made from fish left to rot in seawater. Fortunately, they throw the fish away; unfortunately, they keep the water. Tahitians love to marinate fresh fish in it. I have never been brave enough to have it while I was in Tahiti, but I believe there must be something good about it, so I have made a more palatable version. Asian cultures have perfected the art of making fermented fish sauce. It's called *Nam pla* in Thailand, *Patis* in the Philippines. It is used extensively in Thai recipes. *Nam pla*, fish sauce, is strong tasting but not too "fragrant." This is *Fafaru* for the rest of us.

- 1 pound firm fleshed **fish fillets**
- ½ cup *nam pla* **fish sauce**
- 1 cup of clean **seawater**,

Cut the fish into ½-inch wide strips, 1 inch long. Place the fish in a non-reactive bowl.

Add the fish sauce and seawater. Stir and cover with plastic film. Refrigerate for 6 hours, stirring occasionally. This is a form of cold cooking using seawater (alkaline) rather than citrus (acidic).

Serve as an appetizer, on a small plate or piece of banana leaf, with soy sauce or lime juice.

Making Your Own Seawater

SEAWATER IS A TRADITIONAL POLYNESIAN CONDIMENT. It is a complex brew of water (H_2O). Salt (NaCl) and other minerals. It can be collected with a calabash from the sea. The lagoon at Boro Bora has water that is clear as crystal; one can see fish swimming 80 feet below the surface. On the other hand, my (former) favorite surfing beach in California is under the lee of several offshore oil drilling platforms and near the runoff from a refinery; nice surfing with the faint aroma of petroleum. Where would you rather get a cup of seawater to season your food? If you need safe seawater, you can always make your own.

Salt-water aquariums—particularly inland—use synthetic seawater by mixing filtered tap water and dry salts. Here is a simple formula: one liter (1 quart) of whatever water you normally drink, (preferably filtered) and 35 grams (1 ¼ ounces) of natural sea salt. Allow the batch to sit for several hours. Agitate and aerate the mixture with a blender to assure complete dissolution of the salt (Tullock, 1997, 62).

ISLAND STYLE PAUA (NEW ZEALAND)

The New Zealand, *paua*, *Haliotis iris*, is a sweet tasting abalone with a marvelously iridescent shell. The Maori harvested *paua* along the shores for food and used their shells to inlay their woodcarvings. This recipe is from the New Zealand Abalone Farmers Association, and although it is a modern recipe, it uses a technique long employed in Polynesia—cold cooking with lemon and limejuice.

- 3 large **paua**, cleaned (or any fresh or farm raised abalone)
- 2 large **lemons** or 6 limes or a combination of the both
- 1 small hot **chili pepper**
- 1 clove of **garlic**

Slice the paua very thinly across the muscle (it probably wouldn't hurt to pound the slices a couple of times to tenderize). Layer the paua slices with finely chopped chili and garlic in a non-reactive bowl. Squeeze the lemon/lime juice and marinate for 1 hour in the refrigerator.

Serve on lettuce or banana leaves as an appetizer with freshly ground black pepper.

GINGER FISH (FIJI)

Namatakula Village is where guests are tutored in Fijian cooking, This is one fish recipe visitors are taught. Afterwards, visitors and villagers sit down to enjoy a home style meal together.

- 2-3 pounds of snapper, grouper or cod — or any **firm white fish**
- 1 **lemon**
- 2 tablespoon of **vegetable oil**
- ¼ cup **soy sauce**
- ¼ cup **corn oil**
- ¾ cups **white wine**
- 1 clove **garlic**, crushed
- 2 tsp fresh **ginger** root, grated
- 2 tsp **sugar**
- parsley, cilantro leaf or slivered ginger root for garnish

Rinse & dry fish well. Cut lemon in half and squeeze, rubbing juice into fish, inside & out. Refrigerate for about an hour then rub with vegetable oil and place in a shallow baking dish.

In a blender, mix thoroughly, soy sauce, corn oil, white wine, garlic, sugar and ginger. Pour over fish. Bake at 350° F for about 40 minutes until the fish flakes easily and juices are opaque. Baste frequently with sauce.

Garnish & serve.

WHOLE FRIED FISH (SAMOA)

I first had this dish in the Apia town market. It was sitting out at a food stall and I was not too sure if it was safe to eat, but being young and hungry, I tried it anyway; it was good and there were no ill effects. There is a Samoan deli nearby where they serve this. Whenever I visit, I always take an order home. Their recipe uses tilapia, but Samoans are only too glad to work their way through the bones for every morsel of tasty fish. I don't know how Samoans came to use onion gravy, but it works for me.

- 2 whole cleaned and scaled **tilapia** or red snapper fillets
- 2 cups **peanut oil**
- 2 large **onions** thinly sliced
- 1 large **lemon**, juice of
- 3 ounces **butter**
- 1 pint **beef stock**
- 2 tablespoons **oyster sauce**
- 1 cup **all-purpose flour**
- **salt and pepper**

Onion Gravy:

Cook onion in butter in a heavy skillet over medium high heat, stirring frequently, until onion is softened and browned, about 15 minutes.

Add 1 tablespoon of flour and stir for another minute. Stir in beef stock and oyster sauce and simmer, stirring and scraping up brown bits, until gravy is thickened, 8 to 10 minutes. Season with salt, pepper and additional oyster sauce, to taste.

Fish:

Use tilapia small enough to fry whole, or red snapper fillets cut into serving sized pieces. Wash the fish under running water and dry with paper towels.

Add enough peanut oil to a wok or deep pan to fill 1 ½--2 inches deep. Heat the oil to 375° F (use a frying thermometer).

Cut 3 or 4 diagonal slashes on each side if you are using a whole fish. Drizzle lemon juice and sprinkle salt on the inside and outside of the fish.

Season flour with salt and pepper. Dredge the fish in the flour and shake off the excess.

Gently place fish in the hot oil to avoid splashing. Don't crowd too many pieces of fish at once as it cools down the oil. Cook fish, turning occasionally, until lightly browned, about 2-3 minutes.

Remove fish and place on a wire rack or papper towels to drain. Spoon a little less than half the onion gravy on a serving platter. Carefully place the fish on the onion gravy and spoon the rest on top of the fish.

Serve with boiled taro or boiled green bananas.

DRIED AHI (HAWAII)

Hawaiians dried fish to preserve it, but they liked the taste and texture too. Cleaned and scaled fish were generously salted and strung up to dry in the sun or laid on sun-baked stones. There were two stages of drying fish: partly dried—*i'a maemae*, and well dried—*i'a malo'o*. (Titcomb, 1972, 22, 23). See page 67 for thoughts about Drying Fruit, Meat and Fish.

>Thinly sliced **ahi**, albacore or yellow fin tuna
>*Pa'akai*, Hawaiian sea salt (see page 49 for more information)

Cut the thinly sliced ahi into 1-2 inch pieces. Salt the *ahi* generously and set it aside for one hour. Alternately, you can marinate the fish in soy or teriyaki sauce for 1-2 hours instead of salting.

Lay the *ahi* pieces out to dry, on a clean wire-mesh tray in a sunny place for 1 to 2 days or in a warm oven for two hours @ 100°F or until flesh is completely dry. Turn strips over regularly. The fish is ready when the flesh is dry and has a tough and chewy texture.

Eat the dried fish as a snack or grill on the barbeque. If the fish seems too dry, try soaking it in a dish of water before grilling. Refrigerate leftovers.

DRIED AHI AND ONIONS:

>**Dried ahi**
>1 tablespoon of **cooking oil**
>1 **onion**, chopped
>**coconut cream**

Soak and rinse dried fish in water for a few minutes. Heat cooking oil in a pan, and add chopped onions. Sauté for a few minutes to soften the onions. Add fish and coconut cream to cover. Simmer to heat through. If you wish to thicken the coconut milk, add 1 tablespoon of flour or cornstarch mixed in ¼ cup of water. Season to taste, but the fish should already be salty, so taste first.

FAKAI IKA (NIUE)

>1   whole **snapper**, cleaned and scaled
>1   medium **onion**, chopped
>1   14 ounce can **coconut milk**
>½   cup **water**
>½   teaspoon **salt**

Wrap snapper in foil and bake @ 350°F for one hour. Remove from the foil, remove bones and break the cooked fish into 2-4 inch pieces.

Place the fish piece in a greased, 8 inch baking dish. Cover with chopped onions. Mix coconut milk, water and salt; Pour over the fish and onions. Cover the dish with foil and bake @ 350°F for one hour.

WHITEBAIT FRITTERS (NEW ZEALAND)

These fritters are a real New Zealand favorite. Whitebait are the juveniles, of various fish species and don't need to be cleaned before cooking. I found the tiny (1-inch) fish in an Asian market frozen in 1-pound packages. This is essentially a fish omelet or pancake.

- 1 pound **frozen whitebait**
- 1 tablespoon **all purpose flour**
- 3 **eggs**, beaten
- ¼ cup chopped **parsley** (optional)
- 1 **fresh lemon**
- **salt and pepper** to taste

Thaw the frozen fish, rinse in fresh water and drain well. Beat the eggs well, then sift in the flour and stir in the parsley. Add the whitebait and mix well. Let the batter rest for a few minutes before frying.

Melt butter in a frying pan, griddle or wok over moderate heat. Drop spoonfuls of fish batter into the hot pan to make 4-8 inch fritters. Check the bottoms of the fritters; turn them over when they become golden brown. When both sides are done, remove from the pan to a serving platter. Keep warm in a low oven until all the fritters have been cooked.

Serve hot. Season with salt, pepper and a squeeze of lemon. Eaten in NZ between slices of bread.

Note: There is Tahitian version made with a batter of eggs, flour and beer, minced onion, and whitebait. The result is more of a pancake than an omelet.

REEF CAVIAR (SAMOA)

A short walk from Apia, Samoa, there is a spot just off the beach called Palolo Deep, where you can spend the day swimming and lounging on a raised platform built over the coral. From there you can look down and see the deep blue hole from which the *palolo worms* rise (rather, their detached tails do) for a few nights every year. The locals scoop them up and eat them on the spot or save them in any containers they have. Some local restaurants might offer them for a few days afterwards, spread on toast like caviar – they have the same salty taste of the sea – they are usually lightly sautéed in butter and onions. The best we can do on the mainland is real caviar or maybe anchovies.

- 8 ounces **caviar** (your choice), anchovies or *palolo* if you can get it
- 2 tablespoons **butter**
- ½ small **onion** or 2 shallots, minced
- 12 thin slices of crusty **baguette**, toasted
- **white pepper** to taste

Sauté minced onions in butter and white pepper until soft. Add caviar just long enough to warm through. Season to taste. Serve a small dollop of the caviar and onion mixture on slices of toasted baguette.

QARI VAKASOSO (FIJI)

Fijians living near the sea often walk out onto the reefs and collect what they need for their dinners, be it octopus, mollusks or crabs. This is more typical fare than chicken, pork or even fish. Qari (ngari) is a Fijian marine crab; substitute cooked Dungeness crab, lobster or shrimp.

- 1 **crab**, per diner (Dungeness), cooked (1 cup crab meat or substitute)
- ½ cup **coconut milk** per crab
- 1 **tomato** per crab
- 1 cup chopped **onion**, per crab
- 1 small **red chili**, per crab (optional)
- ¼ cup **fresh lemon juice**, per crab
- 1 teaspoon **all purpose flour** per crab
- **salt and pepper** to taste

Break open claws and legs and pick out the cooked crabmeat. Remove any bits of shell or connective tissue.

Chop tomatoes, onions and chilies and place in a saucepan. Add lemon juice, flour and coconut milk. Mix well. Slowly bring to a simmer and cook for 10 minutes. Add the cooked crabmeat from all the crabs and remove from the heat. Season to taste.

Use individual coconut half-shells or Japanese soup bowls. Divide the coconut/crab mixture between the dishes. Serve with rice or boiled cassava.

FISH HEADS AND BELE (FIJI)

Bele is a plant related to okra and shares some of okra's reputation for sliminess. This quality is considered desirable in some cultures and used in the West to thicken stews. I have to thank artist Tevita Kunato for this recipe and the technique to keep it from getting "slippery."

- 2-3 pounds **whole fish**, cleaned and scaled (preferably parrot fish or ahi heads)
- 2 pounds **bele leaves**
- 2 **cups coconut** milk + 1 cup **coconut cream**
- 2 cloves **garlic**, minced
- 1 inch piece **fresh ginger**, grated
- 1 small **onion**, chopped
- **salt and pepper** to taste

Mix coconut milk, onions, ginger, garlic and salt. Layer the bottom of a 9x13 inch baking pan with bele leaves and pour in the coconut mixture, be sure to mix and coat all the bele leaves.

Cut whole fish in pieces and place on the bele leaves, including the head(s). Cover with foil and place in a preheated 350° F oven for 30 minutes or until the fish is cooked through. ***Do not stir the bele while cooking or it will get slimy.***

Serve with boiled cassava.

SOUPS

We have an unusual wooden bowl from Wuvulu, a coral island, off the north coast of New Guinea. The bowl sits on the top of a bookcase in my office. There is a description of the type in *Power and Prestige: The Arts of Melanesia and the Polynesian Outliers*, published by Hurst Gallery, Cambridge, Massachusetts:

> Narrow-waisted, shallow, rectangular bowls, *apia nie*, were cut from a solid block of calophyllum wood and are considered a marvel of the woodworker's art. The bowls come in many sizes they have thin sides, and are deepest in the middle with flat, upwards sloping ends. The deep centers collect broth and fat from cooked fish which is served in them (Hambruch, 1907: 102).

This is the only reference I have ever found that even remotely resembles soup being made in the Pacific Islands of old, however, it sounds very much like something I had in Yap, Micronesia. Fish had been wrapped in foil and broiled over an open fire. One package was opened and offered to me with the words "try some soup"; the juices in the foil were delicious.

GREEN PAPAYA AND FISH SOUP (NEW CALEDONIA)

Captain Cook discovered and named New Caledonia in 1774 but it is currently a French colony. The *Kanaks*, as the people refer to themselves, were fierce warriors always in conflict with their neighbors and the white settlers. The main island itself is called *Grande Terre* by the French and *Kanaky* by the *kanaks*. It's a beautiful place, surrounded by the world's second largest barrier reef, after the Great Barrier Reef of Australia. The territory of New Caledonia includes the Loyalty Islands to the north. With such a magnificent lagoon, this is wonderful place for seafood, cooked with French culinary sensibility. This recipe, however, is a little more home style.

- 2 pounds **whole fish**, scaled, cleaned and chopped into large pieces.
- 4 cups of **water**
- 2 cups of **green papaya**, coarsely grated
- 1 tablespoon of **soy sauce**
- 1 cup of **coconut milk**
- **salt and pepper**

Bring water and fish to a boil in a soup pot. Reduce heat and simmer for 20 minutes.

Many Asian supermarkets sell pre-shredded green papaya, or cut green papaya in half lengthwise, de-seed, remove the peel and grate. Green papaya should be soaked in water for at least 30 minutes, rinsed and drained before eating or cooking, to remove any bitterness.

Add the grated green papaya and soy sauce to the pot; simmer for another 10 minutes.

Add the coconut milk and return to a simmer.

Because New Caledonia is a French colony, serve with crusty French bread (baguette). Because it is New Caledonia, mind the fish bones.

SUA I'A (SAMOA)

This recipe from Samoa uses a simple poaching technique to cook fish gently in coconut milk. Islanders are not too bothered by fish bones; heads and tails are their favorite part of the fish. Mainlanders may wish to forgo those pleasures and opt for boneless fillets.

- 1 small **onion**, chopped
- 1 small **green pepper**, chopped (optional)
- 1 ½ cups of **coconut milk**
- 4 **mahi-mahi fillets** or any white fish, or whole fish cut up, with bones
- 1 inch of **ginger**, matchstick chop
- 2 green **onions**, chopped
- 1 tablespoon **all-purpose flour**
- **salt and pepper**

Use a pan deep enough to poach the fish you are using.

Chop the onion and green pepper into ¼ - ½-inch dice.

Pour the coconut milk into a poaching pan; add the onions, green pepper and, ginger. Bring the sauce to a boil and reduce to a slow simmer. Add salt and pepper to taste.

Add the fish and add a little water, if needed, to cover the fish. Bring back to barely simmering. Continue to poach for about 10 minutes or until the fish is done (opaque and flakey).

Serve as a soup (*sua*) or plate the fish and thicken* the sauce to pour over the fish. Garnish with chopped onions in either case.

Serve with taro, breadfruit, boiled green bananas, or yam.

*For a thicker sauce, add 1 Tbsp of flour, mixed well in ½-cup cool water, to the simmering sauce. Continue to simmer and stir until the sauce thickens.

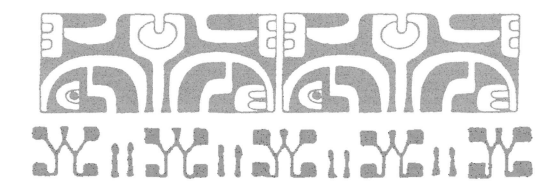

RAMEN AND SAIMIN (HAWAII)

Ramen is that dry package of noodles and flavorings that you can buy 10 for a dollar. I've had Ramen for breakfast in Pohnpei (or Ponape as we used to call it) that was a full meal. I've packed it along when traveling. I've shared it and given it as a gift. It's delicious and easy to make, but if you make it to the instructions on the package you are not making the best soup you can. The secret: do not to make the broth with the water you used to boil the noodles.

RAMEN:

- 1 package of **Ramen**, any flavor
- 2 **green onion** chopped, separate white from green
- 1 tablespoon of toasted **sesame oil**
- 1 hardboiled **egg**, sliced
- 2 ¼ inch slices of **Spam**
- ½ cup of finely sliced **cabbage**
- Tabasco sauce

Boil 2 cups of water. Add the contents of the flavoring package and the white part of the chopped onions. Reduce heat to simmer.

In a separate pot, boil the noodles according to the recipe on the package. Break the noodle "block" in half or quarters if you cannot handle long noodles.

Fry slices of Spam in a non-stick pan until heated through and just starting to turn brown.

Drain the noodles but do not rinse; divide among 2 serving bowls (although in Micronesia this is a single serving).

Pour the "broth" over the noodles. Place a portion of the finely sliced cabbage on top. Place a 3 or 4 egg slices (fanned) on one side of the bowl. Pour some sesame oil over the soup and place a slice of fried Spam in each bowl.

This ramen has a clear broth and the savory fragrance of sesame oil. It may be a shame to add Tabasco sauce, although everyone I ate with used it quite librally, including myself. It's cheap enough to try both ways.

❧

ROSE'S SPECIAL RAMEN (YAP): Boil noodles per the recipe above. Cook cabbage and shredded carrot in broth. Cut spam slices into ½ inch strips and add to the broth to heat. Combine noodles and broth in serving bowls and top with a fried egg. Garnish the fried egg with a few freshly sliced (i.e., raw) onion rings, cut into quarters and a tablespoon of diced cucumber.

Continued...

SAIMIN:

This is fast food for Hawaiian locals. The name is Chinese, the noodles are Japanese; both deny inventing it. It evolved in the communal kitchens of the old plantations, where every ethnic group contributed something to the pot. A basic bowl of broth and noodles, garnished with leftovers or garden produce.

Soba translates to "noodles" There are several types of soba; it is important that you get Chuka soba, a wheat noodle, <u>not</u> the buckwheat soba. (Use ramen noodles only if you can't find the other)

- 2 quarts **water**
- 1 (8-ounce) package dried **Chuka soba noodles** (not buckwheat soba)
- 2 **eggs**
- 4 cups **chicken broth, dashi-no-moto** or **oden-no-moto**
- 1 tablespoon fresh grated **ginger**
- 2 tablespoons **soy sauce**
- ½ **kamaboko fish cake**, sliced (available at Asian markets)
- 3 **green onions**
  toasted sesame oil
  various garnishes

Boil 2 quarts of water to a large pot. Cook noodles according to directions on the package (usually 3-4 minutes). Remove from heat, drain, and rinse under warm, running water.

Beat 2 eggs in a bowl. Add a little vegetable oil to a non-stick pan and pour in the eggs, stir and spread out in a thin layer in the pan until it sets and carefully flip. Cut the thin egg "pancake" into ½-inch strips.

Cut green onions into 2-inch lengths and then in half, lengthwise.

Garnishes: your choice of Char Siu (Roast Pork), Spam Slices, Bok Choy (Cabbage), Bean Sprouts, Sliced Mushrooms, Green Peas, Cooked Shrimp, Sliced Tofu, Scrambled Egg Slices, Sliced Kamaboko Fish Cake. Select what you like to eat; use your artistic sensibilities to arrange them over the noodles.

Add broth (or dashi) and ginger to a large pot; bring to a boil. Reduce heat to simmer. Add soy sauce and the garnishes you've chosen; simmer for 5 minutes longer or until everything is heated through. Remove from the heat.

Divide the cooked noodles into 2 large Japanese soup bowls. Arrange the garnishes in each bowl and ladle hot broth over the noodles and garnishes. Drizzle a teaspoon of sesame oil in each bowl for a hearty aroma. Top with egg strips and green onions.

Eat Saimin with chopsticks and a spoon. Slurp your noodles and drink the broth from the bowl. Just a suggestion, if you tell anyone that I said to do that, I'll deny it. Hey, do what makes you happy!

COCONUT CRAB SOUP (MARIANAS ISLANDS)

Coconut crab *(ayuyu)* is rich, delicious and tastes slightly of coconut, its principal food. Unfortunately, you and I are not likely to find coconut crab on the Mainland, so substitute any fresh or frozen crab legs you can find for this simple soup. The Chamorro name is *Kadun Ayuyu*.

- 2 pound **crab legs**, fresh or frozen (snow or king crab)
- 2 tablespoons of **butter**
- 1 medium **onion**, sliced
- 2 cloves **garlic**, peeled and sliced thin (optional)
- 4 cups of **fish stock** or water with 2 fish bouillon cubes or 4 tsp lobster base
- 1 cup of **coconut cream**
- 1 teaspoon **tumeric**
- **salt** and **pepper** to taste

Cut crab legs into manageable pieces; separate at the joints and use a cleaver to cut into 2 ½-3-inch lengths, but don't pick out the meat. Crack the shells and check the crabmeat; pick out any pieces of shell or connective tissues. The crab meat stewed in the shell imparts more flavor to the broth.

Melt ½ the butter in a saucepan on medium heat and add the sliced onions. Sauté until the onions are soft. Add crab pieces, salt, garlic, coconut cream, tumeric and stock. Simmer for about 20 minutes, add the remainder of the butter and stir. Season with salt and pepper to taste.

Serve with *titiyas* or steamed rice.

FISH AND COCONUT SOUP (FIJI)

This is a recipe from Namatakula Village recipe, where guests are taught to prepare and cook Fijian food.

- 2 pound **fish heads & carcasses** (cod, snapper or similar)
- 7 cups **water**
- 2 tsp **salt**
- 1 large **onion**, sliced
- 1 dash **chili pepper sauce**
- 1 small whole **chili**, chopped
- 1 tablespoon **lemon juice**
- 2 cups thick **coconut cream**
- **lemon slices & chopped green onions** for garnish

Bring first six ingredients to a simmer and maintain until fish is soft. Skim periodically. Strain the stock and adjust seasoning if necessary. Stir in lemon juice & coconut cream and heat thoroughly, but do not boil.

Garnish with lemon slices & chopped green onions.

MUSSELS IN BROTH (NEW ZEALAND)

When the Maori discovered New Zealand, many of their traditional food plants could not survive the temperate climate. On the other hand, seafood was abundant, particularly mussels and clams.

- 2-3 quarts of live **mussels**
- 1 tablespoon **butter**
- 1 medium **onion**, chopped
- 1 stalk **celery**, diced
- 1 clove **garlic**, minced
- 1 inch of **ginger**, minced
- 1 cup **coconut milk**
- 1 cup **fish or chicken stock**
- 2 **green onions**, green part only, chopped
- **salt and pepper**

Clean mussels: scrape off any foreign matter; scrub clean with a brush under running water. Mussels should be closed, discard any that are open and won't close with a tap. Pull off the byssus (beard) just before cooking.

Melt butter in a large pot; add onion, garlic, ginger and celery, sauté until onion is soft but not brown. Add fish stock and green onion. Bring to a boil and reduce to a simmer. Add coconut milk and salt and pepper to taste.

Add mussels and simmer for about 6-8 minutes or until the shells open. Shake the pot occasionally to keep the weight of the mussels on top from preventing the mussels on the bottom from opening. Discard any shells that have not opened.

Serve family style, from a common bowl, but pour equal portions of the cooking broth into individual bowls.

Samoan Plate Lunch, Pacific Islander Festival – Huntington Beach, California

Tongan Plate Lunch, Pacific Islander Festival – Huntington Beach, California

Errata

Page 147 should read:

This is called *Hineksa' Aga'ga'*, Red Rice. You will find Red Rice at all Chamorro fiestas." The red coloring comes from Achiote seeds, also known as Annatto, a slightly sweet, peppery natural pigment, used to color some processed foods.

- 2 cups **Calrose rice**
- 1 tablespoon cooking oil
- 6 slices **bacon**, chopped
- ½ **onion**, chopped
- 2 level tablespoons **achiote powder**
- ½ teaspoon **salt**
- 2 ½ cups **water**

Rinse the rice in cold water, at least twice and drain in a strainer.

Heat the cooking oil in a large pot. Add the bacon and stir until the fat renders then add onions and cook until they soften. Drain off any excess fat.

Add the rice, then achiote powder and salt. Stir the rice to mix the achiote and the other ingredients until the mix is uniformly colored. Add the water and bring to a boil. Stir the rice one more time and reduce to a simmer then cover the pot and cook on low for 15 minutes.

Fluff rice with a fork and serve with Chicken Keleguen, barbeque ribs or fish, Titiyas.

CURRIES AND STEWS

When the *Lapita*, the ancient ancestors of many Oceanians, embarked on their colonization of the Pacific, they manufactured and traded ceramic pots. Pots lend themselves to cooking stews. Somewhere, along the way pottery was abandoned and so were the ancient recipes that must have existed. Our loss, but the Europeans and Asians who arrived 4000 years later reintroduced pots, stews, and curries.

Indian curry has become as much a part of the Fijians' diet as their native food. The aroma of curry is everywhere. Sadly, Fiji, in recent days, has been troubled by ethnic strife; the Fijians wish to maintain political control of the islands of their ancestors, the Indians (Indo-Fijians), whose ancestors were transported to these islands more than a century ago, wish to attain equal rights as citizens.

Island Food transcends ethnic and political differences. Eating and sharing food is one way to unify the new and old. Unfortunately that, alone, will not be enough to unite Fiji, yet, not even the most militant Fijian politician would ever propose a senseless boycott against Indian food to politically taunt or punish his Indian rivals; you can bet your "Freedom Fries" on that.

Curries have become popular all around the Pacific. Fiji's neighbors Tonga and Samoa have integrated it into their own cooking referring to it as *Kale* or *Kare*.

CHAPATI (FIJI)

Chapati is a flat bread eaten with curries; tear off a piece and use it to scoop up the "bits" and sop up the "gravy." You might expect Fijians to only eat chapatis in the urban centers such as Nadi and Suva, but I have watched it being made and eaten on the outer islands where there is no Indian population. Since it is made for eating curries, we will start with that. Here is the simple recipe.

- 1 cup **white all-purpose flour**
- 1 cup **whole wheat flour**
- 1 cup hot **water**, as needed
- 2 tablespoons **olive oil**
- 1 teaspoon **salt**

Place the white and wheat flour and the salt in a mixing bowl and stir together. Stir in the olive oil and enough hot water to make soft dough that is elastic but not sticky. Knead the dough on a floured surface until it is smooth. Divide into 8-10 balls and allow to rest for 5-10 minutes.

Roll a ball of dough out (flour hands and work surface) to about 7-8 inches (or use a tortilla press). Cook on a Hot, lightly oiled skillet for about 30 seconds, flip and cook for another 30 seconds., If they puff up, you're doing it right. Stack them, covering with a cloth to keep warm.

Hispanic markets sell wooden and cast aluminum tortilla presses. They can eliminate the rolling pin and speed up the process. And, they usually make rounder chapatis.

EGG CURRY (FIJI)

Years ago, in Suva, the cheapest, most filling meals were served at the little Curry shops, found around town. At the time, money was scarce and I had to make the most of every meal. This is a curry I had several times. The whole meal cost one dollar, and included *dal* (lentils), rice and *chapati*. This was a very popular place for all ethnicities and classes of people.

- 6 **eggs**, hard boiled and peeled
- 2 tablespoons **vegetable oil**
- 1 large **onion**, chopped
- 2 large **potatoes**
- 2 cloves **garlic**, chopped
- 1 inch piece fresh **ginger**
- 1 **hot chili pepper** (serrano or jalapeño), seeded and chopped
- 1 medium **tomato**, peeled and chopped
- ½ bunch **cilantro** (coriander) leaves, chopped
- 2 teaspoons **curry powder** (imported indo-Fijian if possible)
- 1 teaspoon **cumin powder**
- 2 cups **coconut milk**
- **salt** to taste

Boil potatoes in their skins for 20 minutes or until fork tender. Peel and cut into ½ inch dice.

Heat oil in a heavy bottomed pan. Add onion and fry until they turn light brown. Add ginger, garlic, curry powder, cumin powder and sauté well.

Stir in tomatoes. Add the green chilies, coconut milk, and salt to taste. Simmer for another ten minutes, stirring frequently. Add the potatoes and whole boiled eggs in the last two minutes.

Garnish with chopped coriander (cilantro) leaves. Serve with white rice and chapati.

COCONUT CHUTNEY (FIJI)

This fresh chutney is a condiment usually eaten with curries and rice. It can be added to recipes and eaten with fish dishes.

- 1 cup of **freshly grated coc**onut
- ½ cup fresh **cilantro** (coriander) leaves, chopped
- ¼ cup **lemon juice** or a little more if too dry
- 1 **green chili** (serrano or jalapeno), minced
- **salt** to taste

Mix all ingredients together and serve as a side dish. Can be refrigerated for up to 2 weeks.

- A similar recipe from New Caledonia, is made with grated coconut, chopped parsley, salt, pepper and a little olive or peanut oil.

CHICKEN-BACKS AND DALO (FIJI)

Chicken-backs and necks are not something you normally find in U.S. markets, In the U.S. they are sold in bulk as cheap raw dog food. These cuts, of mostly bone and fat, are being exported to the Pacific, where they are eaten with much pleasure.

- 1 ½ pounds of **chicken wings and drumettes** (or chicken backs if you must)
- 1 pound **taro** (dalo), cooked and cut into 1 inch pieces (See page 62)
- 1 medium **onion**, chopped
- 1 large **carrot**, thick slices
- 1 pound **green beans**, canned or frozen
- 2 cloves **garlic**, chopped
- 1 **hot chili pepper** (Serrano or jalapeño), chopped
- 2 teaspoons **curry powder** (imported Indo-Fijian if possible)
- 2 cups **chicken stock** or water
- 1 tablespoon **all purpose flour** or cornstarch
- **salt** to taste

Heat olive oil in a large saucepan over a medium heat. Add the onions, garlic, curry powder and chili. Sauté until the onions are soft. Add the chicken and brown.

Pour in stock to just cover the chicken, bring to a boil and reduce to a simmer. Simmer for about 30-40 minutes.

Add the taro, green beans, and carrot, adding a bit more water if needed. Simmer until the carrots are cooked, about 5 minutes. Add 1 Tbsp of flour, mixed well in ½-cup cool water, to the simmering sauce. Continue to simmer and stir until the sauce thickens.

Serve with rice and chapati.

Chicken Backs

SUVA WAS A GOOD PLACE FOR NIGHTCLUBS AND DANCING. Many years ago, before I was married, my favorite club was *Lucky Eddies*, on the second floor of a building near the harbor. That's where I met a pretty Fijian girl and made a lunch date for the next day. Surprisingly, (1) she showed up, and (2) on time.

Her favorite spot was a Fijian-run food shop hidden down a back alley. They served cheap country-style Fijian meals. That was lucky for me because my cash had to last until the end of the month. We ordered through a tiny window in the back wall and waited for the food to be served, or rather, passed back through that same tiny window. Her meal of choice was *Chicken-Backs and Dalo*.

I knew Dalo was Fijian for Taro, but I was unfamiliar with "chicken-backs." It turns out, they were, indeed, the backbones of chickens—the discards after all the parts I was familiar with, had been trimmed away. This was poverty food but she ate as if it were *filet mignon*. She could hardly believe I had never eaten chicken-backs—"Doesn't your mother make it for you?"

CHICKEN CURRY WITH FEI AND 'UMARA (TAHITI)

Curry has been spreading across the Pacific. (*Curry de Poulet au Fei (Banane) et Patates Douces*). I believe this was a traditional Tahitian dish that was updated after the introduction of curry. Like most Islanders, Tahitians like spice when they can get it.

- 1 pound **boneless chicken**, 1-inch pieces
- 2 tablepoons **soy sauce**
- 1 **sweet potato** ('umara) or white yams ('ufi)
- 2 tablespoons **cooking oil**
- 1 medium **onion**, chopped
- 2 **garlic** cloves, chopped
- 1 **hot chili pepper** (Serrano or 3 Thai), seeded and chopped (optional)
- 2 teaspoons **curry powder** (or Thai yellow curry paste)
- 1 tablespoon **fish sauce** (nam pla)
- 14 oz **coconut milk** (one 14 oz can)
- 2 **fei** (or ripe bananas, firm—not over-ripe)
- 1 **green onion**, sliced for garnish

Place chicken pieces and soy sauce in a bowl and mix well. Allow to marinate for 10 minutes

Boil the sweet potatoes, skin on, in saltwater until fork tender. Remove from the water, peel and cut into 1-inch slices, cut in half.

Heat oil in a large saucepan. Cook the onions, garlic, chili, currypowder and chicken pieces until the chicken is cooked through. Add coconut milk and fish sauce. Stir well and bring to a simmer.

Peel and cut bananas into 1-inch slices. Add banana and sweet potato. Continue to simmer, stirring occasionally, for 5 minutes or until bananas begin to soften. Add a little water to thin if necessary.

Garnish with chopped green onions and serve with rice or sliced baguette.

Pork Option: Substitute pork, cut into 1-inch pieces, for the chicken. Marinate in soy sauce.

Vegetarian Option: This curry can be made without chicken and soy sauce. Increase the amount of sweet potato and/or bananas or add ripe (but firm) papaya, peeled, seeded and cut into bite-sized pieces.

PORK CURRY WITH TARO (TAHITI)

Islander households cook their meals in pots these days, it's more practical; one no longer has time to prepare an *ahima'a*. The fact is, almost everyone works for wages now and families purchase cuts of meat and vegetables each day at the markets and prepare meals after work. This is the sort of Island stew you might find cooking in a village cookhouse or in a restaurant kitchen. Now that curries have become popular in Tahiti, this island stew is now a curry.

- 1 pound **taro** corm
- 2 teaspoons **cooking oil**
- 1 medium **onion**, chopped
- 2 cloves **garlic**. chopped
- 1 ½ pound **pork loin**
- 1 teaspoons **all-purpose flour**
- 3 teaspoons **curry powder**
- 3 teaspoons **paprika**
- 1 cup of **coconut milk**
- **salt and pepper** to taste

Wash and peel the taro, cut into 1-inch cubes and boil for 15 minutes in salted water.

Peel and chop the onion and the garlic. Cut the pork into 1-inch cubes. Dredge the pork cubes in flour. Sauté the onions, paprika and curry in a little cooking oil. Add the meat and sear it brown on all sides

Add water to cover, add the garlic and the taro. Simmer for 30 minutes stirring regularly.

Add the coconut milk; simmer while stirring for another minute or two. Salt to taste.

Serve with rice or sliced baguette.

KALE KAPA IKA (TONGA)

Kale Kapaika is Canned Fish, Curry and Cucumbers! This is a real down-home Island invention. I never would think to combine these ingredients but that just reinforces my theory that Islanders have a different way of thinking about food and taste combinations.

    15 oz of **canned mackerel**, salmon or tuna (*kapa ika*)
    2   **cucumbers**
    2   large **tomatoes**
    1   tablespoon **vegetable oil**
    1   tablespoon **curry powder** (*kale*)
    1   medium **onion, chopped**
    1   clove **garlic**, minced
    1   cup **water**
        salt and pepper to taste

Place the canned fish in a bowl (do not drain) and mash it to pieces with a fork. Peel the cucumbers and cut into four (4) quarters lengthwise, then into 1-inch chunks. Chop tomatoes into small chunks.

Heat vegetable oil in pan and add onions, garlic and curry powder; cook until the onions are soft. Add water and bring to a simmer. Add the mashed fish and mix and continue to cook about 3 minutes. Add cucumbers and tomatoes and stir. Stir to mix all ingredients. Continue cooking until heated through. Season to taste, salt, pepper, hot sauce or whatever.

Serve with taro, boiled green bananas or rice.

SALADS

The definitions of a salad seem to split into two extremes: (1) a dish, usually cold, consisting of leafy vegetables, such as lettuce, spinach or cabbages, with tomatoes, cucumbers, etc., covered with a dressing. (2) various dishes consisting of meat, starchy vegetables, seafood, eggs, pasta, or fruit usually cut up, mixed with a dressing, and served cold, e.g. chicken salad; potato salad. Neither type of salad is native to Oceania.

Taro greens and most other vegetables found in Oceania required cooking to remove irritants and toxic components. The only "vegetable" that was eaten raw was seaweed, and then usually as a garnish in another dish. The introduction of salads, particularly the starchy salads, has been enthusiastically embraced by Pacific Island peoples, but Islanders have their own way of doing things, so expect a few twists.

SESAME CABBAGE SALAD (HAWAII)

This is a fresh, crunchy salad that goes well with, kalua pork, and laulau, in fact most Hawaiian lu'au foods. The sweetness and acidity is the perfect foil for salty and starchy foods too. Make this at the last minute for maximum crunch and freshness.

- 1 head shredded **cabbage** or one package of coleslaw mix
- 2 bunches **green onions**, chopped
- ½ cup **vegetable oil**
- 2 tablespoons **toasted sesame oil**
- ½ cup **cider vinegar**
- ¼ cup **sugar**
- 2 oz **sliced toasted almonds** (optional)
- 1 teaspoon **sesame seeds**, white or black (optional)

Put cabbage and green onions in a large mixing bowl.

In a separate bowl, combine vinegar, vegetable oil, sesame oil and sugar; whisk until the sugar is dissolved. Toss cabbage with the oil and vinegar dressing.

Garnish with sliced toasted almonds and/or sesame seeds and serve.

HAWAIIAN MACARONI SALAD (HAWAII)

"Mac" salad is present at every lu'au and on every plate lunch. This is contemporary Hawaii's substitute for traditional starchy vegetables. This carbohydrate extravaganza is called an *opu* (stomach) popper. No one will go home hungry. Having a big lu'au? Double the recipe.

- 1 pound package "small" **elbow macaroni**
- 2 pounds **new potatoes**
- ½ cup sliced **black olives**
- ½ cup **carrots**, shredded (optional)
- 3 hard **boiled eggs**
- ½ bunch **green onions**, sliced, white and green parts
- 4 stalks **celery**, fine dice
- 1 cup **mayonnaise**, more or less to suit (preferably Best Foods, Hellman's)
- 1 tablespoon **vinegar**
- 1 teaspoon sweet **paprika**
- **salt and pepper** to taste.

Cook the macaroni per the instructions on the package, rinse in cool water. Don't allow to clump.

Cover potatoes with cold water, bring to a boil, reduce to simmer, cook for 15 minutes for small potatoes, 20-25 minutes for large or until a toothpick goes in easily. Drain, cool, peel. cut into ¾ inch cubes. For this recipe, the potatoes should be soft enough to mash while mixing.

Chop the hard-boiled eggs, fine dice. Shred carrots with a box grater, large holes. .

When the hot ingredients are room temperature, place macaroni, potatoes, black olives, carrots, celery, eggs, green onions, vinegar and mayonnaise in a large mixing bowl and mix until all ingredients are coated and evenly mixed.

Transfer the Mac salad to a serving bowl (if you are not serving from the mixing bowl) and sprinkle sweet paprika over the top to decorate.

PAPAYA SALAD (COOK ISLANDS)

This fresh, crisp salad is appropriate for any Island or Mainland feast. Papaya plays two roles: as an ingredient and a dressing. See page 69 for instructions about using green papaya.

- 1 small **green papaya**, peeled, seeded and cut into julienne strips
- 1 head **red lettuce**, torn or cut into bite sized pieces
- 1 medium **red onion**, thinly sliced
- ¼ cup **cilantro leaves** or basil, chopped (optional)
- **Papaya Dressing/Marinade**, see page 155

Place all ingredients in a salad bowl, dress with Papaya Dressing and toss.

MAINUS - POTATO SALAD (COOK ISLANDS)

Mainus - Cook Island Potato Salad. *Mainus* is the Cook Islander pronunciation of *mayonnaise*. It is also known as Pink Potato Salad, from the color it takes when beetroot is used.

- 5 pounds **new potatoes**
- 1 (15 ounce jar) **pickled beets**, or more to suit your taste
- 1 **red onion**, small dice
- 1 **green pepper**, small dice
- 2 stalks **celery**, small dice
- 6 **eggs**, boiled and chopped
- 1 cup **mayonnaise**, more or less – to taste
- 1 tablespoon **vinegar**
- **salt and pepper**

Cover potatoes with cold water, bring to a boil, reduce to simmer, cook for 15 minutes for small, 20-25 minutes for large or until a toothpick goes in easily. Drain, cool, peel. cut into ¾ inch cubes.

Drain the liquid from the jar of pickled beets and reserve. Rinse the beets in water and dice.

Combine all ingredients in a large bowl and mix well. The salad should appear pink, but if you want more color add a tablespoon or more of the reserved beet juice. Salt and pepper to taste.

Chill for 1 hour. Serve with boiled cassava root and barbecued chicken.

OGO SEAWEED SALAD (HAWAII)

This is a crunchy salad with the taste of the sea. *Limu manauea* or *ogo* can be purchased dried or fresh on the Mainland. Dried ogo must be rehydrated by placing it in a large bowl of water to soak for 1 hour. Ogo swells when rehydrated so, be sure the bowl is big enough and there is enough water to cover. Squeeze out the excess water and chop into, roughly, 1-inch pieces. One ounce of dry ogo makes 1 cup of rehydrated. "*Mo betta wen fresh.*"

- 2 tablespoons **vegetable oil**
- 1 tablespoon **lemon juice**
- 1 tablespoon **fish sauce** (*nam pla*)
- 2 tablespoons **sugar**
- 2 cups **ogo**, chopped into one inch pieces
- 1 cup **napa cabbage**, thinly sliced
- 3 **green onions**, thinly sliced
- ¼ cup **cilantro**, chopped

Make a dressing by combining vegetable oil, lemon juice, fish sauce, sugar and pepper flakes. Mix until the sugar is dissolved. Taste for seasoning; add salt and pepper to taste.

Place ogo, sliced onions, cilantro and cabbage in a serving bowl, add dressing and toss.

RARO TARATI (COOK ISLANDS)

Remeniscent of *Salade Niçoise*, *Raro Tarati* is normally made with corned beef, dressed with coconut cream. This version suggests a creamy dressing made with coconut cream for western palates.

- ½ pound **mixed salad greens** or lettuce, torn
- 8 ounces NZ canned **corned beef** (not So. American!) or Povi Masima, shredded
- 1 **cucumber**, chopped
- 1 **red onion**, thinly sliced
- 3-4 **tomatoes**, cut into wedges, or 12 cherry tomatoes
- 1 sweet **green pepper**, sliced

Immerse the unopened can of corned beef in boiling water for 5 minutes to melt any fat. Open the can and drain off the fat. Empty onto paper towels to cool. *If you wish, substitute shredded Povi Masima, chunk style albacore tuna, cooked crabmeat, lobster or shimp for the canned corned beef (no heating required).*

Wash and prepare all the vegetables. Arrange the lettuce leaves in a shallow salad bowl. Place mounds of corned beef (or tuna, etc) on the lettuce and distribute the other vegetables around and over. Dress with *Sam Choy's Creamy Oriental Dressing* (see sidebar below), thinned with coconut cream or your choice of dressing.

Sam Choy's Secret

SAM CHOY IS ARGUABLY THE MOST FAMOUS CHEF IN HAWAII TODAY. I've watched him cook (on TV) and read several of his books. Sam has been doing something that caught my attention and I don't think anyone else has noticed, or at least commented on it. Sam uses mayonnaise in, what otherwise would be, traditional Hawaiian dishes!

Here is my theory: Traditional Polynesian cookery has a fat component, which carries the flavors. The use of butterfish in *Laulau*, for instance, renders while cooking, providing a hint of oil and salt. Coconut cream and seawater provide the same salty/oily tastes. Sam mixes mayonnaise with soy sauce to obtain a similar effect using ingredients that are easy to obtain in western markets.

Here is Sam Choy's Creamy Oriental Dressing for salads:

- 3 cups mayonnaise
- ½ cup soy sauce
- ¾ cup granulated sugar
- 1 ½ tablespoons black sesame seeds
- 1 tablespoon sesame oil

Place all ingredients in a bowl and whisk until blended. Mix with a little water for thinner consistency. ***Try substituting one-cup coconut cream for one cup of mayonnaise!***

HO'I'O FERN SALAD (HAWAII)

"Fiddlehead" or Ostrich ferns may be used. Avoid *Warabi, Pteridium aquilinum*, or fernbracken, which may be sold at Asian markets (possibly carcinogenic). Asparagus or long beans could substitute.

- ½ pound of **fern shoots**, or asparagus or long beans
- 1 teaspoon **Dijon mustard**
- ¼ cup **vegetable oil**
- 2 tablespoons **lemon juice**
- 1 teaspoon **sugar**
- 2 **tomatoes**, diced
- 1 **mild onion**, sliced
- ¼ pound **small shrimp**, cooked and peeled (optional)
- **salt and pepper**

Blanch the fern shoots (asparagus or long beans) until softened, not cooked through, a little crunchy. Immerse in cold water to stop the cooking and drain.

Make a vinaigrette by combining Dijon mustard, vegetable oil, lemon juice, and sugar. Whisk until sugar dissolves, add more lemon juice if necessary. Season with salt and pepper to taste.

Arrange the fern shoots (or substitutes) in a serving bowl, layer chopped tomatoes, sliced onions and shrimp. Dress with the vinaigrette.

DAIGO KIMCHEE (GUAM)

This sweet and spicy appetizer combines cucumber and daikon radish (daigo). The kimchee part comes from a Korean condiment made of garlic, salt, chili, sugar, ginger, and vinegar – kimchee base

- 8 ounce whole **pickled *daikon* radish** (*daigo*) sliced in half lengthwise
- 1 **cucumber**, peeled and cut in half lengthwise
- 1 tablespoon coarse **sea salt** or Kosher salt
- 1 tablespoon **kimchee base** (or *sambal olek*) use more if you like it hotter
- ¼ cup **vinegar**

Cut *daigo* and cucumbers into thin slices. Put cucumber slices in a bowl and cover with kosher salt, let set for 1 hour in a colander/strainer. Rinse off salt and pat dry.

Place *daigo* and cucumber slices in a mixing bowl with kimchee base and vinegar. Mix thoroughly and refrigerate for at least an hour before serving.

SWEET POTATO TOPS (POHNPEI)

Sweet potato tops are the tender new leaves and shoots of the sweet potato. They are prolific growers in Micronesia. The tops must be cooked before eating and can be used as a cooked green vegetable. In salads, the leaves are dressed with the juice of the calamondin also known as *kalamansi* in the Philippines and *gingang* in Yap. Calamondin have a remarkable flavor but very astringent.

- 2 pounds of **sweet potato tops** or substitute fresh young spinach
- ¼ cup of **calamondin juice** or substitute fresh lemon juice
- ¼ cup of **mayonnaise**
- **salt** to taste

Rinse greens well to remove all dirt and grit. (Using spinach? Remove the stems) Blanch for three minutes. Drop into cool water to stop the cooking. Drain in a colander and pat dry with a towel.

Dress the greens with mayonnaise and calamondin juice (or lemon or lime juice). Salt to taste.

Refrigerate, and serve cold.

Sweet Potato Tops

RICE

Relatively cheap, filling and easy to prepare, rice has been replacing the traditional staples, taro, breadfruit and yams, across the Pacific. Islanders don't eat just any rice, it must be the short-grained variety preferred in Japan. On the Mainland, that goes by the name, Calrose. The object is for the rice to clump together so that it can be eaten with chopsticks or fingers.

One morning, I ordered rice with breakfast at a restaurant in Waikiki. "Oh," the waitress asked, "are you from here?" Apparently, she thought only *locals* eat rice for breakfast.

STEAMED RICE (HAWAII)

Making steamed rice looked so simple the first time I tried, what a mess. It was my turn to cook and I ruined it. My Hawaiian roommate good-naturedly gave me a lesson, but no one trusted me until I got it right for the third time. It's not hard, once you know how.

- This is the most important step: Use Japanese or Calrose rice, not Thai sticky rice, not brown rice, not long grain rice, not instant rice from a box.

- Rinse the rice with cold water and drain, at least twice. It has rice "dust" from the grains rubbing together, possibly chaff and sometimes stones! Drain rice in a colander and allow it to sit for 30 minutes.

- Place the rinsed rice into a clean pot with a tight-fitting lid. Rice expands when cooked, so the pot must be large enough to accommodate the amount you are preparing.

- Because this is Japanese style rice, use about 1-¼ cups of water for every 1 cup of Calrose rice*.

- Bring the rice and water to a boil over high heat with the pot uncovered.

- Stir the rice and cover the pot. Reduce the heat to a slow simmer. Let the rice cook for 15-20 minutes.

- Remove the rice from the heat. Allow the rice to sit covered for 10 minutes. Fluff with a fork just before serving. Serve with a bamboo rice paddle.

If you find scorched rice sticking to the bottom of the pan, you may need a reduce the heat a little more or use a flame diffuser for your stove or try adding a little more water next time.

Of course, you could buy a rice cooker, as I did. Use the same rice to water ratio and let the rice soak in the water for 15-30 minutes before turning on the rice cooker. After the cooking is done, do not uncover, allow another 10 minutes for the rice to steam. I get perfect rice, with no scorching, every time.

---

* This ratio works for me, but if your rice is too dry try 1-½ cups of water. I know other recipes call for 2 cups of water to 1 cup rice, but I find it makes soggy rice. Do what works for you.

FRIED RICE (HAWAII)

Fried rice is something one does with yesterday's leftover rice. It cannot be done with today's steamed rice. Don't even try. Furthermore, this is a recipe for all your leftovers. Most people who make fried rice at home end up with a greasy plate of rice and wonder why their fried rice does not turn out as it does at the Chinese restaurant. The key is to use a large enough wok and a burner that delivers really high heat, that, and the proper technique. The cooking technique is called <u>Chǎo, stirring and tossing quickly.</u> Perhaps you have seen Chinese cooks at their woks, using those long handled ladles and turners to chǎo the food.

Basic recipe

- 3 cups cooked **rice** (cold, leftover from the previous day is best)
- 1 tablespoon **vegetable oil**
- ½ medium **onion**, chopped small dice
- ¼ cup small dice **celery**
- ¼ cup small dice **carrot**
- ½ cup **cooked pork** or cooked chicken, chopped into small pieces
- 2 **eggs**, beaten
- 1 tablespoons **soy sauce**
- 2 stalks **green onion**, sliced thin

Put the (cold) cooked rice in a mixing bowl and use your hands to break up the clumps.

The stoves in most home kitchens cannot put out the BTUs to do a proper job of wok cooking, so I cheat. I place the cold rice in the microwave for 60+ seconds to get it hot.

Heat a wok on maximum heat. Add the oil and the onions, carrots and celery and <u>chǎo</u> for one minute. Add the eggs, scramble with the vegetables until it starts to firm, and add the meat. <u>Chǎo</u> for another minute then add the (re-heated) rice and continue to <u>chǎo</u> for yet another minute, until all the meat, vegetables and bits of fried egg are distributed throughout.

Drizzle soy sauce on the rice and <u>chǎo</u> until well mixed. The taste of the soy sauce should be subtle; some people omit it altogether. It's up to you.

The whole process should not take longer than 3½ to 5 minutes.

Transfer to a serving dish and garnish with sliced green onions.

&ear;&ear;

Use your imagination to make endless fried rice combinations. Try Chinese sausage, shrimp, lobster, duck, ham or bacon. Try adding water chestnuts, peas, chilies, pineapple, nuts or green peppers. Season with oyster sauce, ginger or garlic. Search your icebox for leftovers to use.

RED RICE (MARIANAS ISLANDS)

This is called *Eneksa Agaga*, Red Rice. You will find Red Rice at all Chamorro (Guam and the Northern Marianas) "fiestas." The red coloring comes from Achiote seeds, also known as Annatto, a slightly sweet, peppery natural pigment, used to color some processed foods.

- 4 ounces **achiote Seeds**
- 1 ½ cups **water**
- 2 slices **bacon**, chopped
- ½ **onion**, chopped
- 2 cups **Calrose rice**

Place achiote seeds in 2 cups of hot water for 30 minutes. The water should become dark red. Strain out the seeds and reserve the water.

Fry the onions and chopped bacon until cooked but still soft. Drain off excess oil.

Put rice, onion and bacon into a pot. Add achiote water and stir to combine all the ingredients. Bring pot to a boil and reduce to a simmer. Cover and cook on low for 15 minutes.

Fluff rice with a fork and serve with Chicken Keleguen, barbeque ribs or fish, Titiyas

Plate Lunch, Chamorro Cultural Festival, San Diego

MUSUBI (HAWAII)

Musubi is a way to eat rice with your hands. Because it is wrapped in nori, a sheet of seaweed, you may think is is a type of sushi; it is not. Sushi uses specially prepared, vinegared rice; musubi uses plain steamed rice. When you find musubi at food shops and festivals, it will usually be "spam musubi," but you can make it with egg, chicken or salmon. Plastic musubi molds are available in 4 and 8-inch lengths. (This recipe assumes 4-inch musubi.) They are cheap and make nice looking musubi.

- 2 cups **steamed Calrose rice**
- 1 package **nori** (seaweed sheets)
- 2 tablespoons **soy sauce**
- 2 tablespoons **sugar**, or honey
- 1 can of **spam** (or fried egg, or chicken, or salmon)
- **furikake** (your choice)

SPAM MUSUBI

Make 2 cups of steamed rice. See page 145.

Cut 8x8 inch nori sheets in half.

Mix soy sauce and sugar in a bowl. (Add sugar to the soy sauce to balance sweet/salty to your liking.)

Cut Spam in ¼-inch slices (approx 2x4 inches); you should get 8-10 slices.

Spam is already cooked, so the idea is to heat through and add a little flavor—don't burn it. Fry spam slices in a non-stick pan on medium-hot heat for 1 minute, then add the soy/sugar mixture. Fry for another minute and fry the other side for a minute. Adjust the heat if it gets too hot. Remove the Spam slices to a plate.

Lay down a 4x8 inch nori sheet. Dip the musubi mold in water and place in the middle of the sheet.

Wet your hands in water and put about a tablespoon of rice in the bottom of the mold press down evenly. The mold should be slightly less than half-full. Sprinkle furikake on the rice.

Place a slice of spam on the rice and (wet your hands) put more rice on the spam to fill the mold.

Use the part that fits in the mold to press down the rice while you lift the mold. You should have a block of rice and Spam sitting on the nori sheet.

Fold the nori up the sides and wet the outside edge of one side and fold down; fold the other flap over on top of the other.

Congratulations, you've made one. Remember to rinse the mold and your hands before the next one.

Serve musubi warm.

Continued...

Using the previous recipe; substitute chicken, egg or salmon in place of Spam.

CHICKEN MUSUBI

Slice thin slices of chicken breast trimmed to strips 2 x 4 inches (or combine smaller pieces to fit 2 x 4 inch mold), Sauté in soy/sugar mixture and layer chicken strips in the mold, in place of Spam.

EGG MUSUBI

Combine 1 large egg with ½ teaspoon of water in a bowl and beat with a whisk until frothy. Heat a non-stick skillet to medium and add a little oil or butter. Pour the beaten egg into the skillet and allow them to flow out into an "egg pancake," you may have to tilt the pan to help. Fry until the eggs set and carefully flip over and cook the other side for a few more seconds.

Lay the "pancake" out on a plate or cutting board and cut into 2-inch strips, 4-inches long. Layer egg strips on top of a slice Spam in the mold. Also, try layering: egg, Spam, egg.

SALMON MUSUBI

Slice salmon trimmed to strips 2 x 4 inches, Lightly fry in soy/sugar mixture and layer salmon in the mold, in place of Spam.

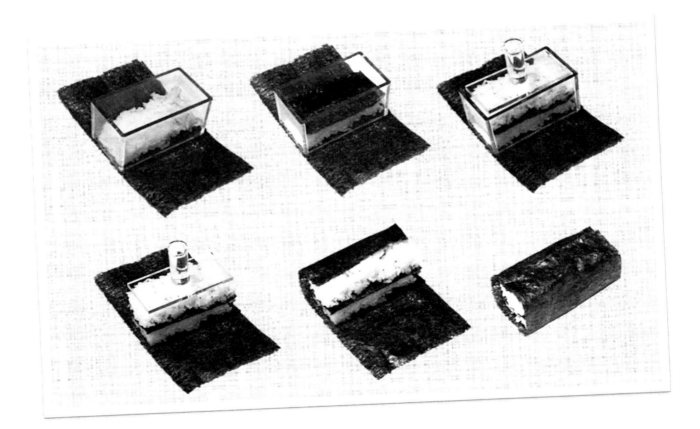

BROILED SUSHI (HAWAII)

Hawaii produces more cookbooks than anywhere else in the world; every political candidate, women's club, PTA and high school swim team publishes a cookbook to raise funds or advertise. That means Hawaiians are always trying to come up with new recipes. I chose this one because it represents new local food without resorting to the old cliché of adding pineapple to any type of recipe and calling it Hawaiian.

This recipe definitely falls under the topic of Contemporary Island Favorites—food created by "locals" for "locals." I cannot find the origin of Broiled Sushi, but it is undoubtedly Hawaiian. I have searched for variations but every recipe is the same, which tells me that it cannot be a very old recipe. This is the sort of recipe that will spawn a dozen more versions in the years to come.

- 4 cups of **cooked Calrose rice**
- 1 cup **sour cream**
- 1 cup **mayonnaise**
- 1 pound **imitation crab meat**, chopped
- 10 **shiitake mushrooms**, chopped (fresh or dried)
- **furikake nori**
- **nori sheets**

Soak mushrooms in water until soft, squeeze out excess water, then chop the caps, discard the stems. Mix chopped mushrooms, chopped/shredded crabmeat, sour cream and mayonnaise.

Spread an even layer of cooked rice into a 9x13 baking pan. Sprinkle furikake nori, generously, over rice. Top with crabmeat mixture, spread evenly across the rice.

Broil for approx. 8-10 minutes until browned. Keep checking after 4 minutes if your broiler is as hot as mine. If your broiler doesn't brown evenly you might want to consider baking in a preheated 350° F oven for 15 minutes.

Cut sheets of nori into quarters. Spoon a portion into a quarter sheet of nori and fold like a taco, so it can be picked up and eaten (like a taco).

Spicy Broiled Sushi: Mix 1 tablespoon of Sriracha hot sauce in the mayonnaise and sour cream.

CANNED MEATS AND FISH

Canned meats and fish are relatively cheap, portable and keep well in the Tropics. They make good emergency meals when you spend the night on a remote beach and make the perfect gift when dining with village families. In my student days in Hawaii, my friends and I lived on boiled rice and locally canned tuna ("hot" from the cannery at 10¢ a can). Flying from Samoa to Fiji, the in-flight meals feature *Pisupo* "tinned" corned beef. When camping in the Society Islands, I always tried to pack some canned salmon, when I could find it and mackerel when I couldn't. In Micronesia, I ate Spam at least once every day.

Canned meats may seem cheap to Western travelers, but not to the locals. One night while talking to an islander of our acquaintance, the topic of food came up and he told my wife and me that he couldn't afford to eat canned meat. Kathy and I looked at each other and decided not to mention that we had been feeding the village dogs corned beef and cocktail wieners!

SPAM

Next time you are in the Islands go to the local market and have a look at the "Spam Aisle," self upon shelf of Spam (and corned beef, beef stew and cocktail wieners) Spam now comes in the following flavors: *Classic Spam, Spam Lite, Spam Hot & Spicy, Spam Hickory Smoke Flavor, Spam with Garlic, Spam with Bacon* and *Spam with Cheese*. Some of these are only available in Guam.

SPAM AND EGGS are a good Island breakfast: two scoops of white rice, two fried eggs and two slices of fried Spam.

SPAM RAMEN is another Islander breakfast or lunch. A large bowl of noodles and broth, topped with slices of Spam. See page 128.

CORNED BEEF

In the Islands, corned beef is usually imported from Australia or New Zealand and is different from what is found in the U.S., which comes from South America. Make the effort to buy *Aussie* or *Kiwi* Corned beef at an Asian Market. Some brands are more fatty than others, but the only way to find out is to buy it and open the can. However if you suspect the corned beef is too fatty, immerse the unopened can in boiling water for 5 minutes to melt the fat. Open the can and drain off the fat.

CORNED BEEF "STEW" (KIRIBATI)

- 1 can **corned beef**
- 1 tablespoon **tomato ketchup**
- 1 tablespoon **cooking oil**
- **soy sauce** to taste

Fry corned beef in a pan with cooking oil. Add ketchup and soy sauce to taste. Serve over rice.

Continued...

CORNED BEEF AND BREADFRUIT HASH (HAWAII)

- 1 cup cooked **mature breadfruit**, or white or yellow yam
- 1 can **corned beef**
- 1 tablespoon **cooking oil**

Mash or mince cooked breadfruit.

Heat oil in a frying pan. Add corned beef, stir to breakup chunks and cook evenly for a minute

Add cooked breadfruit. Stir to combine with the corned beef. Alternate pressing and mixing until slightly browned and heated through.

Serve with eggs for breakfast or as a side dish with lunch or dinner.

CORNED BEEF MANAPUA (HAWAII)

- 1 can **corned beef** (preferably a New Zealand brand)
- 2 tablespoons **Hoisin sauce**
- 3 tablespoon **brown sugar**
- 8 ounces **water chestnut**, minced
- 2 stalks **green onion**, finely chopped
- 2 **eggs**
- 2 cans refrigerated **crescent rolls**

Beat one egg in a mixing bowl. Add corned beef, Hoisin sauce, soy sauce, sugar, water chestnuts and green onions in a bowl and mix thoroughly.

Open the crescent rolls and lay each piece of dough flat on your work surface. Place a teaspoon of the corned beef mixture and roll it up, pinching the ends to seal in the filling. Place on a cookie sheet or pan and brush each "bun" with beaten egg. Place it in a preheated 350°F oven for 20-25 minutes.

SALMON, SARDINE, TUNA AND MACKEREL

Canned fish is a fact-of-life in Oceania; it is often emptied onto a plate to be shared family style, accompanied by taro, cassava or rice. Islanders use it as a replacement for, even more expensive, fresh fish.

CANNED FISH LOMI-LOMI (HAWAII)

See page 116 for Lomi-lomi Salmon recipe. Substitute canned salmon, tuna or mackerel (packed in water) for fresh salmon. Drain the liquid from the canned fish and lomi-lomi as you normally would with salmon.

SARDINES AND ONIONS (HAWAII)

- 1 medium **onion**, sliced
- 2 tablespoons **sugar**
- 1 tablespoon **soy sauce**
- 1 can **sardines**
- ¼ cup chopped **tomatoes** (optional)

Heat oil in a frying pan and add sliced onions. Sauté until softened and just turning brown. Add sugar and soy sauce and a little water to dissolve the sugar. Continue to cook until most liquid has boiled off and the onions are caramelized. Add chopped tomatoes if you choose to use them.

Drain the sardines (If they break, they break…). Add to the pan, mixing with the caramelized onions. Cook just long enough to heat through.

Serve with rice.

In Fiji, this dish omits the sugar and soy sauce, but adds chopped *bele* or spinach leaves.

VEGETABLE CURRY WITH MACKEREL (CHUUK)

This was shared with me as a recipe from Chuuk, formerly known as Truk, the capital of Chuuk State in the Federated States of Micronesia (FSM). Locally grown eggplant and green beans with store bought mackerel make this a fancy home-style meal. It also looks like something the local Peace Corps Volunteer (PCV) might toss together, but this is just what I would expect from Micronesian kitchens.

- 2 tablespoons **vegetable oil**
- 1 **onion**, chopped
- 2 tablespoons **curry powder**
- 2 cups **water**
- 1 can **mackerel** (in oil or brine)
- 3 cups **eggplant**, peeled, cubed
- 1 **red chili pepper**, cored, seeded, and minced (optional)
- 3 cups **long beans** or frozen sliced green beans, defrosted

Heat oil in a saucepan over medium heat and stir in onion and curry powder. Sauté until onions become soft. Add water and mackerel; bring to a boil.

Stir in eggplant, cut up long beans and chili pepper. Cook for 5 minutes; add green beans. Cook for 3 minutes more, or until beans are done but still green. Season with salt and pepper to taste.

Serve with steamed rice, taro, boiled bananas or yams.

CONDIMENTS, DRESSINGS, MARINADES

A little salt or seawater, some coconut milk, condiments were very simple in ancient Oceania. Islanders developed more combinations of local and foreign ingredients to add flavors to a bland diet.

FINADENE (GUAM)

The Chamorro love Finadene on almost everything. Salty, sour and spicy, this dipping sauce has evolved from the simple briny and fishy condiments of their ancestors into what you see here; the following recipes should be a good introduction.

SOY AND VINEGAR FINADENE (recommended for pork and poultry)

- ½ cup **white vinegar** or **lemon juice***
- ¼ cup **soy sauce**
- 1 small **onion**, finely chopped or 3 stalks green onion finely sliced.
- 1 tablespoon, finely chopped **chili peppers**, (serranos, jalapenos or Thai chilies)

COCONUT FINADENE (recommended for fish and poultry)

- 1 cup **coconut milk**
- 4 **garlic** cloves, minced
- 1 tablespoon fresh **ginger**, peeled and grated
- 1 small **onion**, finely chopped or 3 stalks green onion finely sliced
- ¼ cup fresh **lemon juice**
- 1 tablespoon **chili peppers**, finely chopped, (serranos, jalapenos or Thai chilies)
- salt and pepper to taste

LEMON FINADENE (recommended for seafood)

- 1 cup fresh **lemon juice**
- 2 tablespoons **fish sauce** (nam pla), or more to taste
- ½ cup **cold water**
- 1 small **onion**, finely chopped or 3 stalks green onion finely sliced
- 4 **garlic** cloves, minced
- 1 tablespoon, finely chopped **chili peppers**, (serranos, jalapenos or Thai chilies)

Bruise the onions, garlic and chili peppers in a bowl to release the volatile oils before adding the liquid ingredients. Stir and serve with your meals.

---

* Calamondin is used sometimes in place of lemon, which changes the taste entirely.

PAPAYA DRESSING/MARINADE

This is not a recipe from the Island tradition, but it would be a shame to cut open a papaya and throw away the seeds. Papaya seeds have the spicy flavor that, with a little help, can become a delicious salad dressing or a marinade for meats, poultry or fish. Papaya and its seeds have enzymes that can tenderize meats.

- 1 tablespoon **papaya seeds** (more or less to taste)
- 1 **shallot**, chopped
- 1 cup **cider vinegar**
- ¼ cup **sugar**
- 1 teaspoon **Dijon mustard**
- 1 teaspoon **salt**
- 1 cup **vegetable oil**

Cut open a fully ripe papaya and scrape out the seeds. Soak the seeds in water to remove the soft covering, drain and dry them in the sun. Try to use them as soon as possible for the most flavor.

Place shallot and papaya seeds in a food processor and pulse until finely chopped. Add cider vinegar, sugar, mustard and salt; process until the mixture is smooth.

While the food processor is running, slowly add vegetable oil, forming a thick emulsion. The papaya seeds should be tiny dark flecks in the emulsion.

Use as a salad dressing or marinade.

CHILI PEPPER WATER (HAWAII)

Hawaiian home made chili pepper water. You need really hot peppers for this to work.

- 10 **red chili peppers** (Asian red pepper or Thai Chilies), roughly chopped
- ¼ cup **white vinegar**
- 2 cloves **garlic**, thinly sliced
- 2 teaspoons grated fresh **ginger**
- 2 teaspoons **sea or kosher salt**
- 2 cups **hot water**

Bring water to a boil. Take off the heat and add the remaining ingredients. Run the mixture through a blender and pour into a sterilized jar. When the mix cools to room temperature, cover with tight lid. Refrigerate. Allow time for the flavors to infuse for at least 8 hours.

Option: Kick up the heat with ½ Habanero pepper seeds removed.

Caution: Use care when working with chilies, see page 35 for more information.

`INAMONA (HAWAII)

Salt is the universal condiment. A traditional Hawaiian meal wouldn't be complete without it. Hawaiians couldn't leave it at that, they had to flavor their salt too. *'Alaea* salt is red because it is mixed with a bit of the local red clay. The next step was to add crushed, oily kukui nut. *Ahi poke* is better with *'inamona*. Like most Islander condiments, this is really simple to make.

- ¼ cup roasted **kukui** nuts, or **unsalted cashews** or **macadamia nuts**
- 2 tablespoons **'alaea**, Hawaiian red sea salt (or un-refined sea salt)

Crush the roasted nuts with a mortar and pestle to the consistency of roughly ground black pepper. Add 'alaea to taste. Use as you would table salt.

TAI OPORO (COOK ISLANDS)

The soluble oils in coconut milk make a good base for chilies: red Asian, jalapeno or habanero. I was skeptical, myself, until I tried it.

Fill a bottle or a glass jar with coconut milk and chilies, cap the bottle and allow the chilies to infuse for a few hours. Ferment at room temperature. Within a few days, this will become a tangy chili sauce. Keep refrigerated after that. Shake before using.

Every time you use *tai oporo*, fill the bottle back up with more coconut milk and chilies.

Caution: Use care when working with chilies, see page 35 for more information.

MITI HUE (TAHITI)

This is a fermented flavoring for fish and starchy vegetables. It uses the soft "meat" of green coconuts. The original recipe calls for 2 cups of freshly caught prawns, crushed and the liquid squeezed into the bowl. You could do that too, but this recipe calls for fish sauce instead.

- 5 green **coconuts**
- 1 tablespoon **fish sauce** (nam pla)
- 2 cups **fresh water**

Open green coconuts and reserve the liquid if you wish. Cut the nuts in half and scrape out the "jelly-like" meat with a spoon, into a bowl.

.Add water and place the bowl in the hot sun for 24 hours. Add fish sauce.

MITI VITI (FIJI)

Fijians know how to cook! Even plain boiled cassava tastes better when it's served in a Fijian home. If you are around when they have fish, you are in for a treat. Fijian cooks have their own version of a coconut sauce for fish that is good enough to eat like a cold soup—if that were polite to do.

- 2 cups **coconut cream** (heaver than coconut milk)
- 1 **lemon**, juice of
- ½ medium **onion**, chopped
- ½ bunch **green onions**, chopped
- ¼ cup **cilantro** (coriander), chopped
- 2 **chili peppers**, seeded, chopped
- **salt and pepper** to taste

Combine all ingredients in a bowl, mix and let mixture steep for 1 hour.

Serve with baked, grilled or fried fish.

Caution: Use care when working with chilies, see page 35 for more information.

MITIORE (COOK ISLANDS)

This recipe from the Cook Islands is a kind of a fermented relish, a variation of *miti hue* from Tahiti. Live prawns or small crabs are supposed to be collected and mashed for their liquids; here we use fish sauce instead. Feel free to use either method.

- 2 cups fresh grated **coconut**
- 1 tablespoon **fish sauce** (nam pla)
- 1 tablespoon **rice wine vinegar**
- 2 tablespoons finely diced **onion** or similar amount of finely sliced green onion
- 1 small can chopped **clams**, drained, or crab pickings (optional)

Mix the coconut, and a little fresh water in a bowl, and set in the sun to ferment for 6-12 hours. Unless it is a long, hot, sunny summer day this may not work. The result should be like a crumbly cottage cheese.

Add diced onions, fish sauce, rice wine vinegar and mix.

Serve as a relish with shellfish, or alone as an appetizer.

SWEET AND REFRESHING

You won't find any *Mai-Tais*, *Typhoons* or *Blue Hawaiis* here. Islanders will indulge in beer, wine or coconut toddy on occasion, but the traditional beverages of the Islands are plain water or the refreshing juice from a green coconut. Kava is consumed socially and ceremonially in Fiji, Tonga and Samoa. Here are recipes for a couple of non-alcoholic Island drinks and a sweet icy sherbet.

'OTAI (TONGA)

This is a Tongan fruit drink made from the pulp of the fruit as well as the juice. Watermelon is the fruit of choice in Tonga and it makes a refreshing summer drink. Use whatever fruit is plentiful (and cheap). I think 'otai recipes are merely suggestions, Tongans make it up "by instinct" to the taste and texture they like. If you follow this general recipe, you can modify as you go, making it to your own taste, perhaps substituting pineapple juice for some of the sugar.

'OTAI MELENI

- 1 **watermelon**, seedless if possible
- 1 can of **crushed pineapple**
- 1 pint cold **water**
- 1 cup **sugar** (more or less to taste)
- 1 14 oz can of **coconut milk**
- ½ cup of coarsely **grated coconut** or slivered coconut meat

Cut watermelon in half and scrape out the black seeds, the light colored ones can stay. Shred the melon into a mixing bowl using a fork. To make it easier to handle, cut the melon into quarters or eights.

Add the crushed pineapple (with juice. The *'otai* should be diluted enough to drink, but pulpy (slushy?). Add water to thin; add more grated watermelon to thicken. Add sugar to taste.

Add coconut milk and grated coconut. Mix well and chill for an hour. Stir before serving

Serve in tall glasses with ice cubes (not crushed ice). Tongans will sometimes put vanilla ice cream in the glass and fill it with '*otai* (otai float).

'OTAI MANGO

Substitute mango for watermelon in the recipe above. Peel ripe mangos and coarsely grate the fruit with a box grater, collect the pulp and juice. Start with 10-12 cups of grated mango and adjust the quantities of the other ingredients according to the taste and quantity of mango.

Make 'otai from whatever fruit is in season, Apples, Pears, Peaches, Nectarines or Guava.

GURI GURI (HAWAII)

I think everyone knows about Shave-Ice, it's a well-known treat in Hawaii, but do you know about Guri Guri? It's a kind of ice cream or a sherbet. It's a Maui tradition (i.e. addiction) dating back to the 1920s, when it was thought-up by Jokichi Tasaka and sold from his shop. Originally called *Goody Goody*, Japanese plantation workers pronounced it Guri Guri and the name stuck. The Mecca for Guri Guri is still Tasaka's, who has kept their recipe secret. In spite of that, families in Hawaii have come up with their own recipes and variations. I have to thank my friend Joe Kaloi for letting me in on this secret. This simple recipe has only three ingredients, two of which could be changed but the remaining ingredient is mandatory: sweetened condensed milk.

- 2   12 ounce cans **strawberry-guava juice** (or orange soda)
- 1   12 ounce can **7-Up** brand lemon-lime soda
- 1   14 ounce can **sweetened condensed milk**.

Combine all the ingredients in a bowl and mix well. Place the bowl in the freezer, for one or two hours, or until partially frozen.

Take the bowl from the freezer and stir the contents, breaking up the ice crystals into a kind of "Shave-Ice" texture. You may have to refreeze and stir, one more time, to get the proper texture.

Transfer the guri guri to individual serving containers, such as paper or plastic ice-cream cups, and freeze for another 8 hours or more before serving.

Variations

The 7-Up and condensed milk make a frothy base to carry the flavor from the other fruity ingredient(s). Orange juice, pineapple juice and POG (passion fruit, orange, and guava) are possible flavor substitutions. Fresh or frozen fruit (e.g., mango, peach, strawberry or persimmon) can be pureed in a blender; use them alone or in combination with other flavors.

Experimentation is good, but you will probably like the basic recipe so well, it will be a while before you want to go changing things.

... or you could have coconut water...

KAVA COLADA

Your non-islander friends may find the taste of kava more of a challenge than a treat. Nevertheless, kava has redeeming qualities they might appreciate if they could get past the muddy taste (see page 54). Obligingly, kava producers have developed kava extracts that can be combined with other, more palatable, drinks.

This recipe comes from the book "Psyche Delicacies" by Chris Kilham. The drink is based on *Piña Colada*, with kava in place of rum. "*The fat in the coconut would help absorb the kavalactones in the kava extract. The pineapple, coconut milk, honey, and vanilla would all blunt the bitterness of the kava ... The drink was impressively delicious, and we all felt the effects of the kava immediately.*"

Kava is normally consumed at the end of the workday and before supper. After drinking kava, people tend to eat less food. If you have a big lu'au planned, maybe you should limit your guests to only two drinks. If they will be driving home soon, definitely limit the kava.

- 14 **pineapple juice ice cubes**
- 1 can (14 oz) **coconut milk**
- 1 oz **kava extract**
- 1 teaspoon **vanilla extract**
- **honey** to taste

Freeze pineapple juice in ice trays the day before making this recipe

Put all ingredients in a blender and blend until smooth and creamy.

Sharing Kava

Sharing *kava* is a particularly effective method to promote solidarity between kin, friends, and acquaintances. Kava drinking is a ritual activity, even when consumed informally. There is a ritual to prepare the drink, to serve and to accept it. Observing the ritual is a mark of belonging to the group; for outsiders, learning the ritual is a sign of good faith. Such affirmations can promote solidarity by themselves; but sharing under the influence of kava strengthens the bonds between kava partners.

Recipe: Use 3 to 6 rounded teaspoons of ground kava powder to one quart of water (depending on the potency you desire). Place the kava powder in a cotton or silk bag. Immerse the bag in the water and massage thoroughly for about 1 to 2 minutes. The idea is to infuse the water with the kava while keeping the solid particles out.

You need to really squeeze and work the kava in the strainer bag! At the end of this process, wring the remaining liquid from the bag and discard the grounds. The kava is now ready to drink.

For larger quantities, use 4 to 5 ounces of ground kava powder to one gallon of water.

IMAGINARY SOUTH SEAS RECIPES

Some Island hosts fear that foreign guests won't like their humble food, so they may serve what they imagine to be Western food. On one occasion, Fijian friends asked me to eat with them; they told me there would be special "Western food" just for me: a watery orange drink made from a dry mix, and canned cocktail wieners! Of course, I was properly appreciative but convinced them that we should all share it and that I would share what they were having: boiled octopus and cassava root. I mention this because Islanders are not the only ones with peculiar ideas about foreign foods.

South Sea restaurants on the Mainland sell the illusion of Romance in the Tropics by serving concocted island food and exotic cocktails in an imaginary setting of carved tikis and bamboo. For an hour or two, we can indulge ourselves in rum-fueled fantasies of being castaways on a tropical island while dining on Chinese food, served by pretty girls in sarongs and listening to a three-piece combo play sweet Hawaiian music—*an Imaginary South Seas for daydreamers.*

I love that sort of thing but I know it's only a fantasy, however my Mainland friends and relatives still believe it's a perfectly reasonable vision of the South Seas. There is no point explaining; it would only ruin the fun, so serve a "watery orange drink," or rather a pseudo-Polynesian dish once in a while; keep the Romance of the Tropics alive; keep it fun.

RUMAKI

One story about the invention of this dish has Donn Beach, *Don the Beachcomber,* buying whole chickens to get the best prices from his poultry dealer. When he saw his cooks throwing away the livers because they didn't need them, it was like throwing away money. His chef came up with this recipe and it became one of the most popular mock-Polynesian appetizers, ever. It was my favorite when I was a kid; I didn't realize it was made from chicken livers, back then.

- 6 **chicken livers**, halved
- ¼ cup **soy sauce**
- 2 tablespoons **ketchup**
- 1 tablespoon **vinegar**
- ¼ teaspoon **pepper**
- 2 cloves **garlic**, crushed.
- 1 can sliced **water chestnuts**
- 6 slices **bacon**, cut in half
- ½ cup **brown sugar**

Combine soy sauce, ketchup, vinegar, pepper and garlic in a bowl. Add chicken livers and coat well in the marinade. Cover the bowl with plastic wrap. Refrigerate one hour.

Drain chicken livers and discard the marinade. Wrap 1 liver piece and 1 water chestnut slice in ½ slice of bacon, secure with toothpick. Roll in brown sugar, Bake on a wire rack placed over a shallow baking pan (to catch the drippings) in a preheated 400° F oven for 20 to 30 minutes, or until the bacon is crisp.

CRAB RANGOON

Rangoon . . . just the word makes me think of a Joseph Conrad* setting, a steamy tropical port with native boats and rusting tramp steamers, piers and wharves loaded with bundles of cargo ready to be transported "up-river," tough old sea captains and dissolute "white men" sweating in linen suits, drinking gin and tonic in waterfront dives, ceiling fans turning so slowly they barely disturb the smoky air. Imagine an idealistic young sailor jumping-ship, running off with a pretty girl with almond eyes, never to see his home again. I think you get the idea, romantic fiction, just like this dish. Crab Rangoon is exotic and delicious. You can almost taste the romance and the adventure.

- 8 ounces canned **crab meat chunks**, drained and flaked
- 8 ounces **cream cheese**
- 2 teaspoons **Worcestershire sauce**
- 1 teaspoon light **soy sauce**
- ½ teaspoon **white pepper**
- 1 **green onion**, finely sliced
- 1 clove garlic, minced
- 1 package **wonton wrappers**

Pick through the crabmeat, removing any bits of shell.

Combine all ingredients except wonton wrappers in a bowl and mix well.

Place 1 teaspoon filling into the center of each wonton wrapper.

Fold the wrapper in half to form a triangle. Work out any air between wrapper and filling. Moisten edges with water. Press the edges together to seal. Place each wonton package on a sheet of wax paper, covered with a moist towel until all are ready to cook.

Put 2 cups of peanut oil in a wok and heat to 375°; use a thermometer. Deep-fry 6-10 of the wonton packages at a time until they turn golden brown. Use a slotted spoon or a spider to remove the packages and place on paper towels or a wire rack. If you have a lot to fry, keep the cooked ones in a heated oven until all have been deep-fried.

Serve hot with plum sauce or Chinese mustard and ketchup.

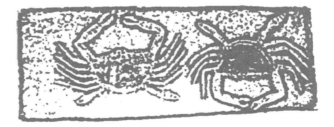

---

* Cultural icons come and go, so for those who are not familiar with Joseph Conrad and his novels about flawed men in tropical settings may substitute the name, Indiana Jones—a more contemporary icon of adventure in exotic places.

SHRIMP AND PAPAYA CURRY

When my mother was moved to cook "exotic food," she would make "curried shrimp." The recipe was dead simple: heat Cream of Mushroom soup, mix in curry powder, add small cooked shrimp. Serve over Minute Rice. Obviously, this recipe owes more to Betty Crocker than the South Seas. However, while researching "Imaginary South Seas Recipes" I ran across several recipes for "Hawaiian Shrimp Curry"—essentially, my mom's recipe. This was the sort of thing you could find at South Seas restaurants; it fulfills a mainlander's desire for exotic food without going too far out of his comfort zone, and I'm all for that, besides, curried shrimp is one of my favorite *faux* island foods.

Here is another version; it's based on a French-Tahitian recipe, *Crevette au Curry et à la Papaye*.

Papaya Nectar:

- ½ medium **papaya**, ripe
- ¼ cup **honey** or agave nectar
- ¼ cup **water**

Slice A papaya in half and remove the seeds. Scoop out the fruit with a spoon and sprinkle with lemon juice. Set half aside for later. Place the other half in a blender with honey and water. Blend until smooth. Yields about 1 cup of papaya nectar.

Shrimp Curry:

- 2 tablespoons **butter**
- 1 medium **onion**, finely chopped
- 2 cloves **garlic**, finely chopped
- 2 tablespoon fresh **ginger**, chopped
- 2 tablespoons **curry powder**, or yellow Thai curry paste.
- 1 cup (8 oz) **coconut milk**
- ½ teaspoon **sea salt**
- 1 tablespoon **all-purpose flour** (optional)
- ½ cup **papaya nectar** + ½ cup **fresh papaya pieces**
- ½ pound large **cooked, peeled shrimp** (31/35 shrimp per pound)
- 2 tablespoons **fresh cilantro leaves**, rough chop

Using a heavy saucepan, sauté chopped onion and garlic in butter (cook until onions are soft). Add curry powder, cumin, garlic and ginger. Stir until well mixed and starting to make a paste. Add a tablespoon of water if it gets too dry. Continue until fragrant (about a minute).

Add the coconut milk and salt. Bring to a simmer but do not allow to boil. Stir until the ingredients are well mixed. For a thicker curry, add 1 Tbsp of flour, mixed well in ½-cup cool water, to the simmering sauce. Continue a low simmer for about 2 minutes.

Add papaya nectar and papaya pieces, Simmer for one minute. Add cooked shrimp; remove from the heat and season to taste. Allow time for the shrimp to heat through before serving.

Serve hot over steamed rice. Garnish with chopped cilantro leaves.

KONA KRAB SALAD

The inspiration for this dish was Tahitian *Poisson Cru* crossed with Hawaiian *Macaroni Salad*. I know that sounds strange and it would be if those two things were actually combined, but there's a long road between *inspiration* and *execution*. Krab is a term for imitation crab; it is nothing like real crab[*], but it is much cheaper. It's a cooked product that has a subtle flavor made for this kind of salad. The lemon juice, green onions, celery and cilantro give it a fresher taste and texture than macaroni or potato salads. I kept re-working this recipe for over a year, until I came up with this version. This is what we take to potluck dinners and serve at barbeques.

- ½ pound uncooked "small" elbow macaroni
- 3 – 4 stalks of **celery**
- 2 bunches of **green onion** (3 bunches if they are thin)
- 1 cup of fresh squeezed **lemon juice**
- ½ teaspoon fresh **ground black pepper**
- 1 - 1 ½ pounds **imitation crab**
- 1 cup **mayonnaise**
- ½ cup **cilantro leaves**, rough chop, no stems
- **salt and pepper** to taste

Cook macaroni according to the package instructions. Drain, <u>rinse well</u> and allow it to cool.

Chop celery into small dice. Slice the green onions—all of the white part and half the green. Add onion, celery, black pepper and lemon juice to a large mixing bowl.

Tear or cut the imitation crab into small pieces and add to the mixing bowl. Mix well in the lemon juice and other ingredients.

Add the cooled (or slightly warm) macaroni to the mixing bowl. Mix well with the other ingredients. Allow this to marinate in the refrigerator for at least one hour, mixing occasionally.

Just before serving add the mayonnaise and chopped cilantro, Mix well and adjust seasoning.

LOW KARB KONA KRAB SALAD

For those of us who are trying to reduce our carbohydrate consumption, this version is made like the one above with the following changes:

- Omit the elbow macaroni

- Add ½ pound of small peeled and cooked shimp (51/60 shrimp per pound)

- Reduce the mayonnaise by half.

---

[*] There is a crustacean called the "Kona crab," not to be confused with Kona Krab.

KOREAN BARBEQUE

Whenever I go to a Pacific Islander event on the Mainland, I head straight for the food booths. It seems that no matter what ethnic specialties are served, there is always barbequed chicken. This marinade is one of my favorites and goes well with Island or mainland dishes. Marinated meats taste best grilled on the barbeque. If you don't have a barbeque, add a few drops of liquid smoke to the marinade.

THE MARINADE:

- ½ cup **soy sauce**
- 1 tablespoon **sesame oil**
- 1 tablespoon **brown sugar**
- 2-3 cloves **minced garlic**
- 2-3 chopped **scallions**

Add all ingredients to a bowl. Add your choice of chicken or beef slices and marinate for at least one hour, preferably overnight, in the refrigerator.

CHICKEN:

- 2 pounds **boneless, skinless chicken thighs**

Lay the chicken in a single layer on a cutting board. Cover with plastic wrap and, using a meat mallet or rolling pin, evenly pound to a ½ -inch thick. Marinate chicken pieces in the marinade.

Remove the chicken from the marinade; let any excess drip off and let it sit at room temperature while the grill heats up to a medium high heat, at least 20 minutes.

Place the chicken on the grill and cook, turning rarely, until it starts to char and the juices are running clear, about 10 minutes total.

BEEF:

- 2 pounds **sirloin,**

Slice the beef into very thin strips across the grain. This works best if the beef is partially frozen (firm not solid). Marinate beef strips in the marinade.

Remove the beef from the marinade; let any excess drip off and let it sit at room temperature while the grill heats up, at least 20 minutes.

Place the slices on the grill and cook, turning rarely, until it's seared, about 5 minutes total.

Outside Uturoa Municipal Market, Raiatea, French Polynesia

GLOSSARY

Pronunciation

The languages of Oceania are, many and varied. There are over 800 languages spoken in Papua New Guinea and over 20 Micronesian languages. Every Polynesian group and outlier speaks a language descended from a common ancestor; however, pronunciation differs among Polynesian languages.

With the exception of Fiji, I will not attempt to describe the pronunciation of Melanesian or Micronesian languages; for those words, simple English pronunciation will suffice.

Most of the vowels are pronounced as they are in Italian or Spanish, and are easy to master.

Vowels

a	'a' as in 'father'
e	as 'ay' in 'hay'
i	'i' as in 'ski'
o	'o' as in 'hope'
u	as 'oo' in 'zoo'

Long Vowels

There is an additional way to pronounce vowels that can change the meaning of a word. They are pronounced slightly longer and indicated in writing by a *macron* (a line) over the vowel. (ā, ē, ī, ō, ū).

Consonants

All consonants are similar to English with some exceptions. The character (') is called an *'okina* and represents a glottal stop, like the stop in "uh-oh."

*See Page 28 for **Island codes**, e.g., (HA) (FJ) plus China (CH), Japan (JA), Philippines (PH), Thailand (TH), Indonesia (IN)*

Hawaiian (h, k, l. m, n, p, w)

    w   sometimes pronounced 'v', for example: *Haleiwa* (Ha-lay-ee-va)

Tahitian (f, h, m, n, p, r, t, v)

    r   short rolled 'r', as in Spanish

Maori (h, k, m, n, p, r, t) plus the following:

ng	like 'ng' as in 'sing'
wh	Sounds like a soft 'f' in most cases

Samoan (f, g, h, k, l, m, n, p, r, s, t, v)

    g   like 'ng' as in 'sing'

Fijian (b, c, d, g, k, l, m, n, q, r, s, t, v, w, y)

b	like 'mb' as in 'member'
c	like 'th' as in 'then'
d	like 'nd' as in 'candy'
g	like 'ng' as in 'sing'
r	short rolled 'r', as in Spanish
q	like 'ng' as in 'younger'

Macron and 'Okina Examples

Ahimā'a	Earth oven (TA)
Ātia Fai'ai	A Samoan recipe (SA)
Autī	Ti (TA)
Fāfaru	Marinade for fish (TA)
Hāhā	Taro stalks (HA)
Hākari	Feast (NZ)
Ī'ītā Po'e	A Samoan pudding (SA)
Kāmano	Salmon (HA)
Kō	Sugarcane (HA)
Lū'au	Taro leaf or Feast (HA)
Māpē	Tahitian Chestnut (TA)
Ō'io	Bone fish (HA)
Sāmoa	Samoa, (SA)
Sī	Ti (TO)
Tāmā'ara'ā	Feast (TA)
Tō	Sugarcane (TA)
Wāwae'iole	Limu species (HA

Ahi — Tuna sp. (TA)
Aga — Banana-ripe, see chota (GU)
Ahi — Yellowfin tuna (HA)
Ahimā'a — An earth oven (TA)
'Āiga — Family (SA)
Aku — Skipjack tuna or bonito (HA)
Alaea — Sea salt containing reddish clay (HA)
Autī — Ti, *Cordyline fruticosa* (leaf) (TA)
Ayuyu — Coconut crab (GU)

Babui — Pig or pork (GU)
Bele — Edible hibiscus leaves (FJ)
Bin — Beans (NG)
Birenghenas — Eggplant (GU)
Bu — Green coconut, for drinking (FJ)
Bula makau — Beef (FJ)
Butterfish — Black cod, Sable fish HA)

Calamansi — Calamondin (PH)
Chapati — Indian Flat Bread (FJ)
Chota — Banana-green, see aga (GU)
Chicken luau — Chicken & taro leaves (HA)
Chili water — Mild all-purpose condiment (HA)

Daigo — Pickled radish (GU)
Dalo — Taro, the corm, stalks and leaves (FJ)

Esi — Papaya (SA)

Fafa — Taro leaves (TA)
Fāfaru — A marinade for fish (TA)
Fafine — Woman (SA)
Fanihi — Fruit bat (GU)
Fara — Pandanus (TA)
Fei — Mountain Banana (TA)
Feke — Octopus (TO)
Fiafia — Feast (SA)
Fiesta — Feast see Lu'au (GU)
Furikake — Seaweed seasoning (JA)

Guihan — Fish (GU)
Gamson — Octopus (GU)
Gingang — Calamondin (YP)

Ha'ari — Coconut, tree and nut (TA)
Hāhā — Taro stalks (HA)
Hākari — Feast (NZ)
Hala — Pandanus (HA)
Haole — A foreigner. Caucasian (HA, GU)
Hangi — See imu (NZ)
Haupia — Coconut pudding (HA)
Haura — Sword-fish (TA)
He'e — Octopus (HA)
Heiva — Festival (TA)

Ho'i'o — Fern (HA)
Hoisin — Chinese spice or sauce (CH)
Honu — Turtle (TA, HA)

I'a — Fish (TA, HA)
Ītā — Pawpaw (tree) (SA,TA)
Ika — Fish (FJ)
Imu — An earth oven (HA)
Ivi — Fijian chestnut (FJ)

Jaina — Banana (FJ)

Kadon — Soup, stew (GU)
Kai — "Food," starchy vegetables (NZ)
Kai — Water (HA)
Kale, Kare — Curry (FJ,TO,SA)
Kalo — Taro, the corm, stalks and leaves (HA)
Kalua pig — Pork, cooked whole in an imu (HA)
Kāmano — Salmon (HA)
Kamaboko — Fish cake (JA)
Kamuti — Sweet potato (GU)
Kane — Man (HA)
Katne — Beef (GU)
Katoanga — Feast (TO)
Kaukau — Food, Hawaiian pidgin (HA)
Kaveu — Coconut-crab (TA)
Kawawar — Ginger (NG)
Keke — Child (HA)
Kelaguen — Salad (GU)
Ki — Ti, *Cordyline fruticosa* (HA)
Kiawe — Algaroba tree (HA)
Kinaki — "Relish," fish, meats, etc. (NZ)
Kō — Sugarcane (HA)
Kokoda — Raw fish cooked in lime juice (FJ)
Kuku — Mussels (NZ)
Kulolo — Taro pudding (HA)
Kumala — Sweet potato (FJ)
Kumu — Edible greens (NG)
Kuwawa — Guava (FJ)

Lana — Coconut grater (TA)
Laulau — Leaf wrapping (HA)
Lauti — Ti, *Cordyline fruticosa* (leaf) (SA)
Lemmai — Breadfruit (GU)
Lialia — Bean thread noodles (SA)
Lilikoi — Passion fruit (HA)
Limu — Seaweed (HA)
Locals — Non-Hawaiians born in Hawaii (HA)
Locals — In general, island born people, native or otherwise (Pacific)
Loco moco — Fried egg, burger, rice, gravy (HA)
Lolo — Coconut milk (FJ)
Lomi-lomi — Massage (HA)
Long rice — Noodles of mungbean flour (HA)

Lovo — See imu (FJ)
Lu — Talo leaf (TO)
Lū'au — 1. Feast, food cooked in an imu (HA)
Lū'au — 2. Kalo leaves (HA)

Magiti — Feast (FJ)
Mahi — Fermented fruit of breadfruit-tree (TA)
Mahi-mahi — Dolphin fish (HA, TA)
Mai'a — Banana (HA)
Maiore — Breadfruit tree (TA)
Manapua — Chinese-style pork filled buns (HA)
Mannok — Chicken (GU)
Manu — Bird (TA)
Mā'ohi — Tahitian or Cook Islander (TA)
Maori — Native Polynesian New Zealander (NZ)
Māpē — Tahitian Chestnut (TA)
Maqo — Mango (FJ)
Marara — Flying fish (TA)
Maui onion — Mild white onion (HA)
Maururu — Thank you (TA)
Meia — Banana (TA)
Mendioka — Cassava (GU)
Meleni — Watermelon (TO)
Moa — Chicken (TA, HA)
Moi — Threadfish (HA)

Naau — Stewed beef intestines (HA)
Nam pla — Fish sauce (TH)
Niyok — Coconut (GU)
Niu — Brown coconut (FJ)
Nori — Seaweed (JA)

Ogo — Limu manauea (JA)
Ohelo — Plant with edible berries (HA)
Ohelo berry — Similar to a huckleberry (HA)
Ō'io — Bone fish (HA)
Onaga — Red snapper (HA)
Ono — Similar to mackerel or tuna (HA)
Opakapaka — Pink snapper (HA)
Opihi — Limpets (HA)
Ota — Young fern, boiled with lolo (FJ)

Pa'akai — Sea salt (HA)
Pakeha — New Zealander of European descent. See Tauiwi (NZ)
Popo — Papaya, pawpaw (NG)
Pahua — Giant clam (TA)
Paina — The ancient name for feast, lu'au (HA)
Palagi — A foreigner (SA)
Palusami — Taro leaves in coconut cream (SA)
Paniolo — Hawaiian cowboy (HA)
Papa'a — A foreigner, Caucasian (CK)
Papālagi — A foreigner (TO)
Patis — Fish sauce (FI)

Pe'epe'e — Coconut cream (SA)
Pele — Edible hibiscus leaves (TO)
Pipi kaula — Hawaiian beef jerky (HA)
Pisupo — Canned corned beef (SA)
Plate lunch — Hawaiian fast food (HA)
Po'e — Pudding of starch and fruit (TA)
Pohaku 'eho — Red hot stones for boiling (HA)
Poi — Boiled taro pounded into a paste (HA)
Poi olu — Boiled breadfruit poi (SA)
Poke — See Poe (CK)
Poke — Diced raw fish, seaweed and soy (HA)
Popa'a — A foreigner, Caucasian (TA)
Popoi — Fermented uru or banana (TA)
Povi masima — Salted beef brisket (SA)
Pua'a — Pig or pork (TA, HA)
Puaka — Pig or pork (FJ)
Pūhā — Wild sow thistles (NZ)
Pūpū — Seashell, also appetizer or snack (TA, HA)

Qari — Marine crab (FJ)

Rourou — Boiled taro leaves (FJ)
Rukau — Boiled taro leaves (CK)

Sago — Palm (with a starchy pith) (NG)
Saifun — Beanthread noodles (CH)
Saimin — Noodle soup of Hawaii (HA)
Saka — Boiled, as in boiled vegetables (SA)
Sakau — Kava (Pohnpei)
Sambal olek — Chili sauce (IN)
Sī — Ti, *Cordyline fruticosa* (TO)
Siaine — Banana (TO)
Sriracha — Chili sauce (CH)
Sua — Soup, liquid, coconut milk (SA)
Suni — Taro (GU)

Tāmā'ara'ā — Feast (TA)
Tama'a — To eat, to have a meal (TA)
Tamāloa — Man (SA)
Tane — Man (TA)
Taporo — Lime (TA)
Tapu — Forbidden, taboo (TA)
Taro — Vegetable corm, stalks and leaves (TA)
Taufolo — Mashed breadfruit, coconut milk (SA)
Tauiwi — A foreigner, not Maori or Pakeha (NZ)
Tavioka — Cassava root, like a potato (FJ)
Ti — Ti, *Cordyline fruticosa* (TA)
Tinito — Chinese (TA)
Titiyas — Chamorro flat bread (GU)
Tō — Sugarcane (TA)
Toa — Chicken AKA Moa (FJ)
Toddy — Palm wine (PH)
Tupa — Land crab (TA)

Yaqona — Kava (FJ)

'Uala — Sweet Potato (HA)
Uhang — Shrimp (GU)
Uhi — Yam, genus Discorea (HA)
Uku — Grey snapper (HA)
Umara — Sweet potato (TA)
Umete — Wooden dish (TA)
Umu — See imu (SA)
Umukai — Feast (CK)
Ulu — Breadfruit (HA)
Uru — Breadfruit (TA)
Uto — Breadfruit, fruit not the tree (FJ)
Uto — Meat from a sprouting coconut (MQ)
Uvi — Yam (FJ)

Vahine — Woman (TA)
Vi — Mango (TA)
Vivili — Shellfish (FJ)
Vono — Turtle (FJ)
Vudi — Plantain (FJ)

Wahine — Woman (HA)
Wai — Water (NZ)
Wana — Sea urchin (HA)
Wāwae'iole — A type of limu, seaweed (HA)
Wheke — Octopus (NZ)

Greetings and Goodbyes

Cook Islands
Hello — Kia orana
Goodbye (to person going) — Aere ra
Goodbye (to person staying) — Noo ake ra
Thank you — Meitaki

Fiji
Hello — Bula
Goodbye — Au se gole mada
Thank you (very much) — Vinaka (vakalevu)
Thank you for the meal — Vinaka vakalevu na kākana

Samoa
Hello — Tālofa
Goodbye — Tofa soifua
How are you? — 'O ā mai oe?
Thank you (very much) — Fa'afetai (tele)

Tahiti
Hello — Ia ora na
Goodbye — Pārahi
Welcome — Maeva
Thank you (very much) — Māuruuru (roa)

Tonga
Hello — Mālō e lelei
Goodbye (to person going) — 'Alu ā
Goodbye (to person staying) — Nofo ā
Thank you (very much) — Mālō ('aupito)

Yap
Hello — Mogethin
Goodbye — Kefel
Excuse me — Sirow
Thank you — Kammagar

SELECTED BIBLIOGRAPHY

Beaglehole, Ernest and Pearl Beaglehole (1962) - The Endevour Journal of Joseph Banks 1768-1771, 2 vols Sydney Angus and Robertson

Beaglehole, J.C. (ed) 1967. The Voyage of the Resolution and Discovery 1776–1780. London:The Hakluyt Society.

Best, Elsdon (1929) - Fishing Methods and Devices of the Maori, Wellington, NZ, V. R. Ward Government Printer

Bligh, William (1789) - *A Voyage to the South Sea, Undertaken by Command of His Majesty for the Purpose of Conveying the Breadfruit Tree to the West Indies, in His Majesty's Ship the Bounty, Including an Account of the Mutiny on Board the Said Ship,* 2 vols. London, G. Nicol

Ferdon, Edwin N. (1987) - Early Tonga: As the Explorers Saw It 1616-1810 Tucson University of Arizona Press

Firth, Raymond (1966) - *We the Tikopia: Kinship in Primitive Polynesia,* Boston, Beacon Press

Frisbie, Robert Dean (1929) - *The Book of Puka-Puka ,* New York, The Century Co.

Grimble, Sir Arthur (1952) - *We Chose the Islands: A Six-Year Adventure in the Gilbert Islands,* New York, William Morrow & Company

Haden, Roger (2009) - *Food Culture in the Pacific Islands,* Santa Barbara, ABC CLIO

Handy, Willowdean Chatterson (1965) - *Forever the Land of Men: An Account of a Visit to the Marquesas Islands,* New York, Dodd Mead & Company

Hiroa, Te Rangi [Sir Peter Buck], (1930) - *Samoan Material Culture,* Honolulu, Bernice P. Bishop Museum

Kirch, Patrick Vinton and Roger C. Green (2001) - *Hawaiki,Ancestral Polynesia: An Essay in Historical Anthropology,* Cambridge, UK Cambridge

Leach, Helen (2010) - From *Kai to Kiwi Kitchen: New Zealand Culinary Traditions and Cookbooks,* Dunedin, NZ, Otago University Press.

Levy, Neil M (2003) - *Micronesia: Moon Handbooks,* Emeryville, CA, Avalon Travel

Manderson, Lenore, (2001) - *Shared Wealth and Symbol: Food, Culture and Society in Oceania and Southeast Asia,* Cambridge, Cambridge University Press

Murai, Mary, Florence Pen and Carey D Miller (1958) - *Some Tropical South Pacific Island Foods: Description, History, Use, Composition and Nutritve Value,* Honolulu, University of Hawaii Press

Tcherkezoff, Serge, ed (2008) - *The Changing South Pacific: Identities and Transformations.* Canberra, ANU E Press

Titcomb, Margaret (1972) - *Native Use of Fish in Hawai,* Honolulu, University of Hawaii Press

Titcomb, Margaret (1978) - *Native Use of Marine Invertebrates in Old Hawaii,* Honolulu, Pacific Science vol. 32 no. 4, The University Press of Hawaii

Tullock, John H., (1997) - *Natural Reef Aquariums,* Shelburne, Vt., Microcosm Ltd.

Kalua Pork Plate Lunch, - The Loft, Cerritos, California

Laulau and Lomi-lomi Salmon Plate Lunch – The Loft, Cerritos, California

APPENDIX A:
THE ETIQUETTE OF SHARING IN OCEANIA

The people of Oceania are hospitable and generous, and it seems like the more humble the circumstances, the greater the hospitality. This is most often expressed by sharing food.

When an island family invites us to share food they treat us as part of their extended family; the act of partaking shows that we agree to that. Afterwards, most visitors will move on with only a word of thanks, but sharing should work both ways. Islanders are not selling a service and they would be offended if we offered to pay for their hospitality, but a gift from a friend is fine. Gifts of food are always welcomed (present them on arrival), as well as kava or tobacco (if they use it), but use discretion about beer or wine. Other small gifts should be of a personal nature, a scarf, t-shirts, a music CD or pocketknife, but not worn-out castoffs.

Gifts should be practical and heartfelt. Island people will see condescending behavior for what it is. Treat them as you would your friends at home. Research what things the locals may need, before visiting. Village families are usually cash poor but are as sophisticated as their city cousins. Trinkets and beads went out 200 years ago; today they carry iPods rather than spears. Education is valued and many Islanders (even in villages) have gone to college and have traveled abroad.

If we intend to stay in a village with our new host family, a gift of kava should be presented to the chief of the village (This is the custom in Fiji). Depending on how long we stay with the family (days, weeks, months), we may be asked for "favors" from time to time, maybe help with the expenses or perhaps the loan of a shirt, or a dive mask. A loan will be of indefinite duration, during which time it may be re-loaned to someone else. If we can't afford to lose the article, politely decline, explaining why we cannot loan it, but try to be flexible; maybe bring some extra "things" for these occasions. At the same time, we should lock our luggage to avoid misunderstandings. Exercise good judgment, observe local laws and stay clear of dicey situations.

At the end of our stay, parting gifts are in order. Guitar strings, t-shirts, school supplies for children, fishing gear, and dive knives are all good. Gifts of money will be accepted if you make it clear it is not payment for hospitality ("this is to help with the xyz repairs," "for fuel for the boat," etc.). You may be asked to donate something to the local school, village fund or church. Be kind because this will demonstrate our generosity to the village and our host family will gain status.

Local customs, particularly about food, may seem arbitrary and perplexing; our most polite Western table manners may be viewed as inappropriate or rude! So, how can we promote goodwill between host and guest and avoid offending someone? Most Islanders will tolerate some ignorance about their customs from travelers; learning a few words of the local language and a few of the local customs, helps to increase that tolerance. Just follow your host's lead and enjoy yourself; everything will work out fine even if we make mistakes.

Hawaii and Guam, which appear to be totally westernized, modern societies, have some distinctive local customs, but Island hospitality is integrated with Western etiquette, so we are not as likely to make any major social blunders. On some islands, socializing can appear to be as unrestrained as a Spring Break in Fort Lauderdale. However, just like home, drunkenness can lead to unpleasant consequences, so use discretion about what you do and with whom you socialize. That being said, you should find most Islanders generally sober and friendly.

A simple meal with a family is usually informal, but we should be aware of the following customs. (Usually found in Fiji or Samoa, but similar customs exist across the Pacific.) As we walk through villages, it is customary for the locals to ask passers-by "Have you eaten?" This can sometimes be just a polite greeting. Stop and talk, if it is a genuine request to have food with them, they will persist. If you wish to decline, say you have just eaten. It is impolite to ask what they are having before you decide to accept or not. If you accept, eat what is offered. It's all part of the adventure.

If some customs seem sexist or unfair, do not argue or comment about them, these rules are accepted by the people you are dining with. Some of the rules may be relaxed for visitors, but not for the locals. Rest assured that everyone will be fairly treated by their own standards.

- Visitors should not enter a dwelling until asked. Remove shoes or sandals before entering and leave them at the door. Sit where the host indicates. Sit before chatting.

- If there are no chairs, sit with your legs crossed or underneath you; do not stick them out straight in front of you. It is considered rude to point the soles of your feet towards anyone. If you need to stretch your legs, cover your feet with a mat or a cloth of some sort.

- Eat what is offered. If you are not hungry, eat what you can, to show appreciation for the hospitality. If you have a medical reason not to eat something, explain it, otherwise to refuse food implies that you find some fault with the food or the host. If others are eating with their hands, eat with yours. Water and a cloth to wash your hands are normally provided at the end of the meal.

- Guests in Samoa, who are being honored formally, will be served first with the best food and lots of it. We may find ourselves eating alone or with one or two people of high rank. Eat what you want and push the "eating mat" away when you are done. The uneaten food will be given to others, who eat later. Male family members will eat next; women and children eat last. Do not invite others to eat with you or offer food to children who may be there to serve.

- In Fiji, as in Samoa, honored guests are offered the largest share of the best food. But, keep in mind that no food is held back for others. Guests should be sensitive to leave enough food for those who will eat afterwards.

- Samoans do not engage in conversation while eating. Samoans love to talk, but not during meal time. Also, do not eat while standing, unless the meal is truly informal.

- A Fijian host wants us to enjoy our meal and looks for signs that show we do. Sip your soup loudly and nod your head to show how much you enjoy your food. Use both hands to eat, if you just pick at food with two fingers, it will mark you as a finicky eater. Unlike Samoa, the host will notice if we are eating quietly and encourage us to talk, to give feedback about the food. At the end of the meal, when we say, *"Thank you for the meal,"* it will seem like empty words without these displays.

- We should not immediately move away from the "mat" after finishing a meal. We should wait for the head of the house to finish and move away first. Usually a sign or a word is given to signal the end of the meal, or ask permission to be excused.

Customs vary from place to place but this should give you an idea of what you may encounter. Again, most "rules" are relaxed for visitors and most situations will be more informal. Have fun and get to know the local people.

APPENDIX B: SUGGESTED READING

THE ISLANDS AND THEIR PEOPLE AREN'T PERFECT, but we don't love something because it's perfect. To love something is to love it in spite of its flaws. These books reveal the little flaws lurking in Paradise.. This may be a strange list to find in a food book; however, they should put you in an Island frame of mind, ready to appreciate Island food, although it's more likely to put you in the mood to daydream. Most of these books are dated and long out of print but still available if you search.

The Book of Puka Puka, Robert Dean Frisbie. After WWI, an American is sent to operate a trading station in the Cook Islands and falls in love; not as syrupy as it sounds. An autobiographical sketch of a beachcomber. Frisbie is considered one of the best writers in the South Seas genre.

Forever the Land of Men, Willowdean Handy. Accompanying her archaeologist husband in the 1920s, Mrs. Handy finds the once proud and fierce Marquesans decimated, but not altogether broken by colonization. The descendents of great artists and cannibal warriors sat, staring blankly, as they arrived. Handy sets out to learn the language and searches for the humanity behind the stoic faces, and finds it. Compare Handy to Hyerdahl.

Fatu Hiva: Back to Nature, Thor Heyerdahl. In the 1930s, a young university graduate and his bride leave Norway to live a back-to-nature fantasy in the Marquesas Islands. They are warmly received by the Marquesans, who build them a house and share what they have, but after a short while the jungle reclaims their home and things go downhill from there. Eventually they flee the Marquesas, fearing for their lives. Heyerdahl formed his theories about Polynesian migrations here.

An Island to Oneself, Tom Neale. New Zealander, "Old Pacific Hand" and friend of Robert Dean Frisbie, just wants to live a solitary life on a remote atoll in the 1950s. Neale realizes his dream only to contend with wild pigs, hermit crabs, sharks, hurricanes and illness. My boyhood fantasy.

Changes in Latitude, Joan McIntyre Varawa. Varawa (McIntyre) wrote a popular book about whales and dolphins in the 1970s, *Mind in the Waters*. Now, middle-aged, divorced with a grown son, she travels to Fiji to find romance in the South Seas. Meeting and marrying a much younger man, she goes to live in his village and gets a good dose of Culture Shock. This is the poignant inverse of a male fantasy, a cautionary tale for both sexes.

White Savages in the South Seas, Mel Kernahan. Ms. Kernahan searches for Paradise in the Pacific but finds some lesser angels instead. She wanders the Pacific meeting the wise, the brave, the arrogant and the clueless, and shows us who the savages are. Compelling tales of mis-understanding, treachery, triumph and humor. Over two dozen short stories set in Tahiti, the Cook Islands and a few places back on the mainland.

We Chose the Islands, Sir Arthur Grimble. Grimble was the Resident Commissioner of the British Protectorate of the Gilbert and Ellis Islands—now called Kiribati and Tuvalu. Grimble spoke the language of the *i Kiribati* and earned their trust. This is his account of the people and challenges of colonial administration. Never the arrogant bureaucrat, his affection for the people and their well-being is evident. A movie was made in 1956 (Pacific Destiny) based on his experiences.

More Suggested Reading:

SOUTH SEAS FICTION IS A LITERARY GENRE in its own right. Authors such as Herman Melville, Mark Twain and Robert Louis Stevenson; William Somerset Maugham and Joseph Conrad elevate it above mere adventure fiction. The works of some authors were almost entirely set in the Pacific, Becke, Frisbie, Nordhoff and Hall, to name a few.

Return to Paradise, James Michener. After serving in the Pacific in WWII, Michener wrote *Tales of the South Pacific*, which was the inspiration for the musical, *South Pacific. Return to Paradise* was his next book, which alternates short stories with essays about the islands where the stories were set. Next, go on to read **Hawaii**, the first of his multi-generational epics.

By Reef and Palm, Louis Becke. Becke, an Australian, started as an island trader, whaler, beachcomber, castaway, pearler, "blackbirder" and supercargo, before turning to writing. He stood trial as an accomplice of the American buccaneer and all-around villain, Bully Hayes, but was acquitted. Becke wrote some thoughtful stories about the white and brown peoples of the Islands. This anthology will keep you daydreaming, shaking your head and mesmerized all the way through. If it ends too soon, these next two books will keep you going a little longer, **South Seas Supercargo** and **Pacific Tales.**

The Hurricane, Nordhoff and Hall. A well-done tale of injustice and redemption. Only N&H could have built a compelling novel out of a few South Seas clichés, a brutal drunken white man, a noble savage, a pretty island girl and an unbending colonial bureaucrat, a tale told on a voyage through the Tuamotu Archipelago. Follow this with **No More Gas**, the tale of carefree Tahitian family who come into a fortune.

Best South Seas Stories, A. Grove Day (editor). An anthology of selected stories by some of the best writers about the South Seas, Stevenson, Melville, Hall, Michener, Becke, Frisbee and more. Day was an educator, prolific author and Hawaii historian who wrote or edited more than 50 books, mostly about the Islands.

Pouliuli, Albert Wendt. Wendt is a Samoan, raised and educated largely in New Zealand. It is one thing to know a subject intimately and another to tell the tale successfully; Wendt qualifies on both counts. Samoa is hardly a paradise; Samoans experience hope, fear, love and conflict just like anyone else, but things <u>are</u> different in Samoa. This is a story worthy of Shakespeare or Sophocles; it contrasts moral weakness with courage, and wisdom with folly. The truth beneath the fiction is, Samoan society can be wound as tight as a coiled spring.

Thunder from the Sea, Willowdean Handy. Mrs. Handy brings the ghosts of the vanished Marquesan people back to life in this novel, set in the days just before colonization. Written by a speaker of the Marquesan language, the words and idioms read as if spoken by the native peoples. These people were elaborately tattooed warriors, cannibals and artists, but that's all gone now. You can still see the steep valleys where they lived, but the culture that was once there, now lives between the covers of this book.

APPENDIX C:
THE CANOE PLANTS

Survival in the Pacific would not have been possible if the people of Oceania had not been expert gardeners, although you may have your doubts when viewing the apparent chaos of a native garden, seemingly random and overgrown. The food plants that are growing so casually on the hillsides and along the streams were intentionally brought from South Asia, Indonesia and Papua New Guinea. With a thousand years of accumulated knowledge and a sharpened stick (the only agricultural tool they had) they cultivated these plants throughout the Pacific.

The following is a list of the plants that came to Hawaii by way of Tahiti or the Marquesas. However, that was only the last stop on their way from Asia, a journey that took thousands of years, moving from island to island, across the Pacific.

`Ape	*Alocasia macrorrhiza* (giant taro or elephant ear)
`Awa	*Piper methysticum* (kava)
`Awapuhi	*Zingiber zerumbet* (shampoo ginger)
Hau	*Hibiscus tiliaceus* (Hibiscus)
Ipu	*Lageneria siceraria* (calabash or gourd)
Kalo	*Colocasia esculenta* (taro or kalo)
Kamani	*Calophyllum inophyllum* (Alexandrian laurel)
Ki	*Cordyline fruticosa* (ti or kī)
Ko	*Saccharum officinarum* (sugar cane)
Kou	*Cordia subcordata* (kou tree)
Kukui	*Aleurites moluccana* (candlenut)
Mai`a	*Musa spp.* (banana)
Milo	*Thespesia populnea* (portia tree)
Niu	*Cocos nucifera* (coconut)
Noni	*Morinda citrifolia* (Indian mulberry)
`Ohe	*Schizostachyum glaucifolium* (bamboo)
`Ohi`a	*Syzygium malaccense* (mountain apple)
`Olena	*Curcuma domestica* (turmeric)
Olona	*Touchardia latifolia* (olona fiber)
Pia	*Tacca leontopetaloides* (Polynesian arrowroot)
`Uala	*Ipomoea batatas* (sweet potato)
Uhi	*Dioscorea alata* (`olena or turmeric)
`Ulu	*Artocarpus altilis* (breadfruit)
Wauke	*Broussonetia papyrifera* (paper mulberry)

Hala, *Pandanus tectorius* (screw pine); some varieties may have been indigenous and others brought by canoe. There is evidence to support both cases.

Giant Swamp Taro (Cyrtosperma chamissonis)

The "Giant Swamp Taro" is popular in Micronesia, but not so much in the rest of Oceania. The enormous corm it produces is awe-inspiring. This freshly dug specimen is almost 30 inches. There are two kinds, white and yellow. I don't think it's available (for eating) on the mainland, so none of the recipes in this book will call for it.

APPENDIX D: PACIFIC ISLAND RESOURCES

Resources printed in a book can become obsolete, even before the book reaches the stores. In order to see the most current Pacific Island Resources, check out our Resources webpage. We encourage you to contribute as well. Share your finds with us and help keep us up-to-date.

www.BOTM.OceanikaPress.com

AN ON-LINE DIRECTORY FOR YOUR ISLAND SHOPPING NEEDS:

- *Asian Markets*
- *Latin American Markets*
- *Island Specialty Shops*
- *Internet Resources*
- *Island Restaurants*
- *Islander Events*

INDEX

A
achiote, 147
ahi, 42, 67, 104, 117, 118, 119, 123, 125, 156

B
baguette, 10, 117, 124, 126, 136, 137
Banks, Joseph, 15
barbeque, 1, 26, 57, 96, 100, 106, 115, 123, 147, 165
beans
    green, 38, 95, 135, 153
    kidney, 95
    long, 38, 110, 143, 153
bele, 38, 111, 125, 153
Blanding, Don, 77, 98
Bligh, William, 13, 93, 108
Bougainville, Louis Antoine de, 21
breadfruit, 11, 12, 13, 14, 16, 18, 19, 20, 26, 27, 32, 57, 65, 80, 83, 86, 87, 88, 92, 103, 107, 108, 110, 113, 127, 145, 152

C
calamondin, 37, 144, 154
cassava, 27, 33, 41, 64, 66, 67, 85, 109, 110, 111, 113, 125, 141, 152, 157, 161
Chamorro, 21, 22, 23, 26, 84, 103, 104, 105, 130, 147, 154
chǎo, 57, 146
chili, 18, 35, 50, 51, 104, 106, 116, 117, 119, 121, 125, 130, 134, 135, 136, 143, 153, 154, 155, 156, 157
Choy, Sam, 142
citrus, 37, 120
coconut extract, 59, 61
cold cooking, 18, 37, 104, 120, 121
Cook, James, 15, 21, 39, 40, 92, 93, 126
cooking packages
    aluminum foil, 39, 65, 71, 72, 76, 80, 83, 84, 85, 87, 90, 96, 97, 98, 110, 111, 113, 115, 123, 125, 126, 139
    banana leaf, 52, 80, 93, 98, 115
    taro leaf, 30, 71, 83, 98
    ti leaf, 18, 74, 75, 98
corned beef, 41, 81, 82, 85, 87, 142, 151, 152
crab, 7, 16, 44, 77, 108, 119, 125, 130, 157, 162, 164
    imiitation crab, 119, 150, 164

D
dried
    ahi, 123
    beef, 96
    fish, 18, 67, 96, 123
    pork, 96

E
earth oven, 2, 17, 19, 57, 58, 97, 112
eggplant, 106, 107, 153
enzymes, 33, 36, 155

F
feast, 10, 24, 25, 26, 30, 77, 94, 112, 140
Firth, Raymond, 14
fish and poi, 15
fish heads, 125, 130
food classification
    kai, 13, 15, 16, 101
    kinaki, 13, 15
food preservation
    drying, 17, 18, 20, 49, 67, 96, 123
    fermentation, 16, 31, 101
    salting, curing, 17, 18, 40, 116, 123
fruit bat, 89

G
ginger, 19, 82, 94, 95, 99, 100, 110, 115, 121, 125, 127, 129, 131, 134, 143, 146, 154, 155, 163
green papaya, 69, 126, 140
Grimble, Sir Arthur, 46

H
haupia, 80
Heyerdahl, Thor, 34
hibiscus, 26, 38, 54, 111
Hiroa, Te Rangi (Sir Peter Buck), 13, 14, 57

I
imaginary south seas, 2, 77, 161, 163
inamona, 52, 53, 156
island inspired, 23, 26

J
juice extractor, 59, 61

K

Kamehmeha, 35, 40
Kilham, Chris, 160
krab, 25, 164

L

laulau, 10, 18, 22, 24, 42, 71, 72, 73, 74, 75, 77, 98, 139
lemon, 18, 31, 37, 51, 84, 96, 104, 106, 115, 117, 121, 122, 124, 125, 130, 134, 141, 143, 144, 154, 157, 159, 163, 164
lime, 37, 51, 107, 117, 119, 120, 121, 144, 159
limu, 48, 80, 118, 119

M

mackerel, 27, 41, 107, 110, 117, 138, 151, 152, 153
Magellan, Ferdinand, 21
mahi-mahi, 15, 42, 98, 115, 117, 127
mango, 17, 36, 68, 69, 158, 159
moa, 16, 39
mushroom, 49, 99, 129, 150, 163
mussels, 16, 45, 131
mutton flaps, 24, 87

N

nam pla, 50, 120, 136, 141, 154, 156, 157
noni, 37

O

oceanic eden, 11, 14, 16
octopus, 16, 17, 46, 47, 86, 119, 125, 161
onion gravy, 122
opihi, 1, 16, 45
oxalate crystals, 30, 62, 63

P

palolo, 16, 47, 124
patis, 50
paua, 16, 18, 25, 45, 121
pineapple, 2, 6, 7, 26, 36, 70, 71, 146, 150, 158, 159, 160
pipi, 40, 67, 96, 119
pisupo, 81, 85
plate lunch, 97, 98, 100, 104, 116, 140
po'e, 13, 19, 24, 25, 35, 76, 88, 92, 93, 110, 145
poi, 2, 7, 8, 15, 16, 19, 23, 26, 30, 33, 58, 62, 63, 64, 93, 97, 98
popoi, 14, 16
potluck, 25, 112, 164
pudding, 5, 13, 16, 24, 25, 30, 32, 33, 57, 63, 76, 80, 92, 93, 110, 111

R

rourou, 84
rukau, 84

S

saifun, 82, 95, 99
salmon, 18, 41, 42, 77, 98, 115, 116, 119, 138, 148, 149, 151, 152
sea salt, 18, 49, 96, 97, 115, 117, 123, 143, 156, 163
seawater, 11, 20, 49, 79, 120, 154
seaweed, 7, 18, 48, 51, 80, 118, 119, 139, 148
snapper, 98, 115, 117, 121, 122, 123, 130
spam, 42, 50, 104, 128, 148
squid, 16, 46, 47, 86
Stewart William, 21
sugar, 20, 29, 34, 37, 49, 50, 51, 52, 80, 88, 89, 90, 92, 93, 100, 101, 103, 110, 121, 139, 141, 143, 148, 149, 152, 153, 155, 158, 161, 165
sweet potato, 16, 19, 33, 34, 64, 66, 93, 109, 110, 112, 113, 114, 136, 144

T

taro corm, 30, 31, 62, 63, 64, 84, 137
Titcomb, Margaret, 15, 16, 19, 73, 123
tuna, 41, 42, 51, 76, 77, 104, 107, 110, 117, 118, 119, 123, 138, 142, 151, 152

V

Vancouver, George, 40

W

Wallis, Samuel, 21, 28, 78
wana, 16
watermelon, 25, 37, 158

Y

yam, 13, 33, 34, 35, 66, 79, 80, 107, 108, 109, 111, 112, 127, 152